Praise

"I am delighted that Jacqui and Johnny have written a golf book guiding the parent and junior player and its impact on them. Through golf, I learned at an early age the discipline that this game requires, the sportsmanship expected of players, and the manner in which you should conduct yourself on and off the golf course. Golf is a game that has at its foundation fundamentally positive values - we keep our own score, we call our own fouls - and these are values we can take into the rest of our lives. Golf is also a game for a lifetime. Whether you are 10 or 66, you can enjoy the game. It's a rare sport that allows you to play the same game with your spouse, your parent, your child, or as in my case these days, your grandchildren. And I think that's pretty special."

JACK NICKLAUS
Golf Legend and Winner of the Most Golf Majors in History

"The gift of golf is a gift for a life time."

DALE WALKER
Director of Golf, San Diego State University

"This book will get young players off to a great start. There is something for everyone including instructors, parents and players."

RENEE M. BAUMGARTNER Ph.D
Former collegiate golfer and coach, Senior Associate
Athletic Director-University of Oregon

"Golf lessons can become life lessons. I realized from my father, and I hope I am teaching my children the same, that golf can demonstrate to a young boy or girl the positive values they should want to incorporate in their daily lives."

JACK NICKLAUS II
Pro-Golfer and Golf Course Designer

"Invaluable head start for any parent or coach guiding the development of a young golfer."

ANDREA GASTON
Women's Head Golf Coach, University of Southern California

An Important Message to Our Readers

Golf

Guide for Parents and Players

Secrets of Success
for Junior & College Golf,
Professional Tour and Beyond

Jacqui Nicoletti McSorley
&
Johnny Gonzales

A Big Smiling Series Book
Mansion Grove House

Golf Guide for Parents and Players
Secrets of Success for Junior and College Golf, Professional Tour and Beyond

By Jacqui McSorley & Johnny Gonzales
Published by Mansion Grove House
Based Upon The Big Smiling Series Original By Keith Kattan
ISBN-13: 978-1-932421-14-9
ISBN-10: 1-932421-14-9

Original Content: Copyright © 2007 Jacqui McSorley & Johnny Gonzales
Series Content including Adaptations: Copyright © 2007 Mansion Grove House

Mansion Grove House. PO Box 201734, Austin, TX 78720 USA.
Website: mansiongrovehouse.com
For information on bulk purchases, custom editions and serial rights:
E-mail sales@mansiongrovehouse.com or write us, Attention: Special Sales.
For permission license including reprints, excerpts and quotes: E-mail
permissions@mansiongrovehouse.com or write us, Attention: Permissions.

Printed in the United States of America

Library of Congress Cataloging-in-Publication Data
McSorley, Jacqui.
   Golf guide for parents and players : secrets of success for junior
and college golf, professional tour and beyond / Jacqui McSorley and
Johnny Gonzales.
      p. cm.
   Includes bibliographical references and index.
   ISBN-13: 978-1-932421-14-9 (pbk. : alk. paper)
   ISBN-10: 1-932421-14-9 (pbk. : alk. paper)
   1. Golf--Miscellanea. I. Gonzales, Johnny. II. Title.
GV967.M383 2007
796.352--dc22

                                    2007002808

Big Smiling Golf Team!
Permissions & Reviews: **Maureen Malliaras**
Cover Designer: **Bill Carson**
Content Design: **Eileen Llorente**
Copy Editor: **Greg Ball**
Illustrator: **Richard Catron**
Marketing Development: **Kelly Handel**

Credits: See Appendix "Credits"

About Jacqui & Johnny

Jacqui Nicoletti-McSorley brings to this book a wealth of golf experience. As an avid and highly successful junior golfer, collegiate player at the University of Southern California, as a playing professional on the Japan LPGA Tour, and now a sought-after LPGA Teacher, she offers amazing insights for parents. A prolific contributing writer for golf magazines, she has also shared her know-how on radio and television. Jacqui actively supports the growth of golf in her community and started an LPGA-USGA Girls Golf site in San Diego's north county.

Johnny Gonzales played professional golf in the United States, Canada & Mexico. A Golf Digest Top 50 teacher in California, San Diego PGA Teacher of the Year and PGA. Junior Golf Leader of the Year, he is now The Director of Golf at Sycuan Resort and President of the California Junior Tour. Johnny is recognized for his Outstanding Service to juniors and contributes his unique breadth of golfing experience for the benefit of the parent and player.

Introduction

"Before I got married I had six theories about bringing up children; now I have six children and no theories."

John Wilmot, Earl of Rochester

Golf offers your children unparalleled benefits. Non-golfers say golf is a game. Golfers know that it is much more than that. To us it is so much more. For many of us, it's a major part of our lives; a part of us so ingrained in our lifestyle. Who we are and who we've become have evolved out of our golf experiences. The game has given us opportunities and blessings beyond belief – travel around the world, college scholarships and eventually great career choices. Beyond that, the game has given us life lessons, character development, cherished friendships and a myriad of memories. Whether you love the game or are just getting started, whether you are a parent of an adventurous toddler or of a surly teenager, this book spells out the amazing opportunities available for children involved in the game. You'll find advice ranging from when and how to get started to the nuts and bolts of managing a promising protégé.

A wise man once said, "Personal experience is the worst teacher." He also advised, "Someone else's experiences – their successes and their failures – are most valuable." Parenting is a lot like walking through a minefield; you don't want to experience blowing up to know that the mine is there. If your friends have brats for children, are you going to ask them for parenting tips on behavior? Probably not. Find someone to emulate. Follow someone who has done what you want to do. If you want the same results, you must do the same things. While no two lives can share the exact experiences and, even if they are similar, people will interpret them differently, there are things you can do to assure a higher chance of success. It is essential to learn what works and what does not when parenting children in sports.

Our experiences as juniors, college players, tour players and teachers, combined with countless hours of working with young golfers pursuing their own dreams – as well as tons of study, research and interviews of the best in the field – have given us a roadmap for parents and coaches alike. Unabashedly, we recognize there is not one way to achieve success, but there are some methods that will almost certainly lead to failure. Let us help you wade through the information available and show you how to discern it so you don't hit overload once you start to devour all that is available.

Before we get started, let us introduce you to our families, especially our parents. They most definitely raised Big Smiling Golf Kids. While this book is not intended to be a Chicken Soup for the Golfer-type book, it is a privilege to share a couple of memories that really make us smile:

"Look at all of those happy people!" Robert Nicoletti would exclaim every time his family drove by a golf course. Because Dad had the tendency to toss a club or two, often times us kids would tease back, "You mean the guy who just threw his putter into the tree?" He would smile and laugh, "Yeah, him too!" Nicoletti, who grew up in Los Angeles, had caddied at Griffith Park Golf Course as a kid. Raised in a large poor family, golf wasn't a privilege he was able to enjoy. However, he loved the game and the people around golf and knew he wanted to expose his kids to the sport. My husband and kids can attest that to this day, I (Jacqui) can't pass a golf course without saying, "Look at all those happy people!"

Juan Gonzales wanted his kids to love the game, too. Yet, never in his wildest dreams did he think that one selfless act of parenting would have such an impact on his son. Ten-year old Johnny really wanted to make some extra money – he wanted to caddy at the local golf course. However, all of the other caddies were much older, stronger and more experienced, so he wasn't about to be hired. Juan talked with a young military man and wondered if he might hire his son. The man said he would love to, but couldn't afford the caddy fee. Juan said he would pay the fee as long as little Johnny never found out about it. I (Johnny) was mesmerized by the game that day, totally falling in love with everything about the sport. Dad kept his "little secret" for over 20 years, finally fessing up when I was 33 years old and well into a golf career.

Why do we share this with you? Because our fathers gave us a legacy – a love of the greatest game ever played. Both of our fathers were hairdressers – yes, they were career barbers. Both of our mothers were career homemakers, which included being taxi drivers, cheerleaders, short-order cooks, tutors, scorekeepers and part-time psychologists. While neither were golfers, Linda Nicoletti-Ogaard says she could probably be a good golf teacher since she sat through endless hours of golf instruction. We were raised in middle-class homes. Similarly, our dads played golf, but both were self taught. They loved the game and did an amazing job raising Big Smiling Golf Kids. Needless to say, they were thrilled when we took to the game and grew to love it!

I (Johnny) played junior golf, but never had a formal lesson until college. I have always been small in stature, but the more someone told me I couldn't achieve something, the more determined I became to prove him wrong. Often, I was told by high school teachers and counselors to never consider college because I wouldn't make it. These humble begin-

nings inspired me to go on to play golf in junior college, at the New Mexico Military Institute and then eventually on the team at USIU (United States International University) in San Diego, California. It was at USIU that my dreams of becoming a professional golfer were ignited. After playing tournament golf for three years, I realized my true love was teaching. Currently, I have the privilege of being the PGA Professional, the Golf Operations Manager and Academy Director for the Singing Hills Country Club at Sycuan Resort (formerly Singing Hills Country Club) near San Diego. I am also a partner in two other exciting golf ventures. When my kids were younger, partners and I acquired Sun Valley Golf Course, a really fun par-3 golf course for beginner golfers and families. When Seve was in his teen years and looking for more competitive golf, partners and I founded the California Junior Tour. My plate is full, but I thoroughly enjoy all of the different aspects of the game with which I get to be involved.

I (Jacqui) can remember being 10 and walking down the fairway of a local course with an elderly gentleman when he politely asked me, "What do you want to be when you grow up?" My response was quick and to the point – a professional golfer. As a kid, I loved to practice and go to professional events, and once I experienced my first success as a player, I was hooked. I loved the accolades, but more importantly I knew this was my ticket to college. If I practiced hard and proved myself, I could earn a golf scholarship. Title IX was in the works.

My dad provided for lessons, but my favorite thing to do was go to PGA Tour tournaments. I would watch the players for hours and study their swings on the driving range, and walk at least 18 holes with the likes of my idol, Jack Nicklaus, and Tom Watson. When my friends were headed for the beach, I was off to the golf course. The practice and dedication paid off, and I was blessed with a good junior career, and a full scholarship to the University of Southern California. After graduation, I went out to pursue a playing career. Eventually, I ended up in Japan, where I enjoyed playing on the JLPGA Tour for seven years.

I played in my last professional tour event seven months pregnant with our daughter. Since my playing days, I have owned a golf school with and taught with Golf Digest Top 100 Instructor Dean Reinmuth. Also, I have become a member of the LPGA Club and Teaching Division. It has been exciting coaching girls' and boys' high school golf, and I have been thrilled to start the USGA*LPGA Girls Golf San Diego program. Participating in charitable golf events and teaching people of all ages how to play golf at Encinitas Ranch Golf Course is the best way I can give back to a game that has given me so much.

All of our siblings have played golf – however; some enjoy it more than others. Michael Gonzales never did take much interest in the game after being over-zealously reprimanded by an adult on the course. Jennifer Gonzales was not interested in the game as a kid, but has taken it up as an adult and enjoys it a lot more.

Bob Nicoletti played every sport he could, and played them all well. He is a natural athlete and enjoyed lots of junior golf success. He dabbled with a career as a professional before deciding against it in order to go into the business world. Bob continues to play with family, business associates and friends – many of those same friends who often teased him for playing "an old man's sport" as a kid.

Karen Nicoletti started to play golf at age 5 and was a phenom player of her day – winning almost everything she played in during her early junior career. She is a two-time Junior World Champion, but by the time she was a teenager, she had had enough. Exploring other interests and sports, she didn't play a lot of golf in her teen years. At age 20, she was drawn back to the sport she had enjoyed so much as a kid. For years, she traveled through Europe as an equipment representative for many of golf's top companies. Karen has enjoyed teaching golf in Europe, Florida, Louisiana, Massachusetts, and California; and is currently a LPGA teaching professional at the Reynolds Plantation in Georgia.

Married to wonderful and supportive spouses, there was no doubt we would introduce our kids to the sport we loved with all of our hearts. When they were little, it was easy; we just kept exposing them to the game. However, there comes a time when the love of the game has to be theirs – not ours. Like you, as parents we asked the same questions of ourselves. What sports do we expose them to? Will they like sports, or are they more into the arts? Is it their choice, or are we forcing them to play? Are they having fun? Do they like golf? Do they feel pressure to perform? What if they show talent? Should they compete or not compete? What do we do when they fail, or when they succeed?

All of our children have had golf clubs in their hands from the time they could walk. At this point in our lives, we can proudly say all four of our children like golf – and one truly loves it! They all enjoy playing the game.

Elizabeth Gonzales played a lot of local junior golf and four years of high school golf. She was the proud captain of her high school team, but isn't sure if she is going to play golf in college. She is studying at Point Loma Nazarene University and is concentrating on classes that will either lead her to medical school or a career as a chemistry teacher.

Seve Gonzales (who do you think he was named after?) loves the game. He is a scratch golfer and has had an outstanding junior career. Seve will play golf at Yale University. He is also an accomplished wrestler, and both he and Elizabeth are members of The Red Robe Choir that has traveled to and performed all over Europe.

Annie McSorley is our "social golfer." She played in her first tournament at age 8, but we soon realized competitive golf was stealing her joy of the game. She loves to play – just to play! At this point (she's almost 14), she has more fun playing with mom, friends and her Papa Nic. She continues to improve and prides herself on knowing the rules – she is our little rules official. The USGA would be proud!

Justin McSorley, from the time he was able to speak clearly, has emphatically said, "I don't want to play junior golf, mom. I want to play baseball – I am going to be in the Hall of Fame!" Lofty goals, I would think, and at his remarks I would stab my hand into my heart and say, "You are killing me-e-e-e." And he would giggle! At age 11, he is a decent golfer but a darn good ballplayer. He has enjoyed a lot of success in his sport. His dad and I support his dream, yet, my heart sings when he asks to go to the golf course with me.

It has been our honor and privilege to coach hundreds of kids over the years. However, many of our students have gone on to achieve national rankings, earn full scholarships and play professional golf. Between us, we have thousands of hours coaching kids and counseling parents. In the end, it is like being in the grocery store. You have many options before you. Some you might like to have; others you may want to leave behind. Other things you may not like but know that they are best for you and your child and will be more difficult to buy into. Choose wisely; at some point, allow your golf child to choose his own path and lead in the direction he wants to go. We have always maintained that, in order to have a better chance of success, juniors need three things when they start their journey down the path of competitive golf:

1. **Internal desire** – They must dream to be the best they can be.
2. **Parental support** – Parents need to encourage and support their desires and fuel their dreams. Also, parents must always demonstrate unconditional love.
3. **Coach support** – Good coaching and a knowledge base are keys at each phase of development.

> "Golf is life.
> If you can't
> take golf, you
> can't take life"
>
> *Author Unknown*

To be successful, the parent, coach and kid have to be in sync. Kids have to do their part. It has been said that, "When the student is ready, the teacher will appear." Fortunately, as coaches, we have seen our share of talented youngsters and enthusiastic parents; but, unfortunately, we have also seen them destroy their relationships, give up on the process or burn out from too much golf (more accurately, too much pressure associated with golf). Professionally, we can recognize the pitfalls that commonly swallow up even the most unsuspecting families.

This book presents safe, practical steps to help you decide how to address your junior's level of interest. It will explain when it's best to push and when it's best to back off. Several chapters have been devoted to sharing the business side of golf. Knowing how the system works gives your kid an advantage. The more knowledge you have, the more you will be able to fuel your child's dreams.

"More info:" This phrase, used throughout the book, will connect you to important websites and references. Linking this way makes the book an easy read while allowing access to thousands of pages of up-to-date and in-depth information and contacts.

The overriding emphasis of the book is to offer a complete and practical roadmap for the golf parent and coach. If your kids are currently pursuing other sports, we hope this work inspires you to introduce them to the game of golf. Obviously, we believe golf lessons are important because golf is something they can play their entire lives. Golf is easier to learn as a child, and the game adds so much to their being.

We invite your thoughts on the usefulness of the book. We also welcome suggestions and stories of methods that have worked well for your child – we would love to hear your success stories! We pray our book will empower you to raise kids who love golf and who will enjoy swinging down the fairways with big smiles for years to come. It is our desire that God's blessings be given to you and your kids both on and of the golf courses of the world.

Jacqui Nicoletti McSorley
Email: jngolf@san.rr.com

Johnny Gonzales
Email: jgonzales@sycuanresort.com

1
Getting Kids Interested

••

**"Golf gave me the chance to teach my sons good values –
without boring them with lectures. There's nothing
like a game of golf to show honesty in action."**

Dave Stockton, Senior PGA Tour Professional, FamilyGolf.org

••

Young Michael and Susie have a wide variety of sporting options next
season – basketball, baseball, soccer, hockey, gymnastics, tennis,
swimming and golf, to name a few. Mom and Dad encourage them to
focus on two organized sports each season. So what will it be for
Michael and Susie next season? How do Mom and Dad help them
choose what to play? Mom and Dad have an interest in golf, but will
their kids? There are many good reasons to pick golf as one of their
extra-curricular activities.

Why Golf? The Right and Wrong Reasons

Pretend you are a golf novice. Ask any avid golfer why golf is his
primary sport and you will most likely get an eloquent, emphatic and
endless expose on the virtues of golf. You have just pushed his hot
buttons.

His reasons will probably range from simple to sentimental. He
will have innocent reasons and well-thought-out dissertations. There
are as many different reasons as there are golfers.

The simple: Golf is individual, but can be played with a group. It
is serene and relaxing. Golf courses are beautiful places. Golf is truly
a global sport and provides the opportunity to travel. It can also offer
college scholarships and career opportunities. Golf is a game for life
– a sport that can play a major role in developing character and discipline. Good shots make you feel good. Golf is fun!

The innocent: Golf is a safe sport. Golf is a game that can challenge you to be the best you can be and allows you to enjoy it at many
levels. It gives you the freedom to pick your schedule and your level
of involvement – unlike team sports that come with a fixed schedule
and regimen. Age, sex and size do not matter in golf – anyone can
play and enjoy the game. There are no rules officials or irate parents
screaming about bad calls. It is a game of personal integrity.

The sentimental: Golf bridges the family generation gap. Grandpas
and grandmas enjoy playing with their grandchildren. Kids can beat

their parents. Golf affords you the opportunity to play with and meet people from all walks of life. Children learn etiquette and learn to socialize with adults. Golfers enjoy other golfers' successes. Golf teaches you that life is not always fair – there will always be good days and bad days.

Good stuff! Don't get all teary-eyed just yet. There are also sometimes reasons for concern in introducing your child to golf. Prize money and prestige in professional golf are enticing. Their influence on interest and desire to achieve cannot be denied. However, if fame and fortune are the primary motivators for you and your child, you are setting your child up for heartbreak and failure. External motivations such as these often lead to burnout.

It is key to help your child develop internal desires that motivate her to be her best. Teach your child that it is rewarding to challenge herself and that it shows great character to give maximum effort. Your child needs to know her efforts are enough reward for you. Parental approval should never be equated with a scorecard. Golf is a unique game with unique challenges every time you play. Children need to learn from the challenges and should learn not to take success or failure personally. The nature of the game itself teaches patience and persistence. Enthusiasm for golf will not be sustained if she feels she lets you down every time she plays poorly. If the game of golf can fuel the desire to learn more each day, then you are creating great habits for your child.

Fortunately, there are specific steps described in this book that will help you, your child and golf coaches learn the game in a positive atmosphere. Choosing to introduce your child to golf for all of the right reasons makes you a very special parent, and we are excited to help you on your journey. Should your child be incredibly gifted and have the desire to pursue golf at the highest levels, we will help you recognize that road as well. Smile and enjoy the journey!

Learn to Love the Game

Enjoying golf yourself is a surefire way to jumpstart your child's interest in the game. However, if in the past you have always thought of golf as "a retired man's game" and even now have a hard time calling golf a "sport," don't worry – you do not have to play golf to enjoy golf.

For starters, do you have a friend who absolutely loves golf? Start there. Chances are he would love to explain some golf lingo to you. You will know what a par, birdie and bogey are in no time. Golf tournaments on television are hit and miss. Some avid golfers say it is like watching paint dry while others love to watch their heroes shoot unimaginable scores. Your friend who loves golf can take you to his

club or a sports bar to watch the final round of a major golf championship amidst some other golf fanatics – you'll learn to love the game!

There may be an initial resistance to fall in love with golf. Be per-
sistent in your discovery of the game. Take your time. Watch more
golf both on television and in person, if you're lucky enough to have
an event near you. Pick a top golfer and follow him throughout his
season on tour. There are exciting biographies written about many
successful golfers as well as videos you can buy or rent that chroni-
cle the game and the personalities that play it.

Payne Stewart, written by Stewart's wife, Tracey Stewart, is a wonderful biography. Stewart does a great job telling her late husband's
story and how they realized together his lifelong dream of playing
on the PGA Tour. Authors John Feinstein, James Dodson and Rick
Reilly all have written fantastic books about golf, its history and the
comings and goings of professional golf. You can't go wrong when
you read books written by or about legends such as Sam Snead,
Arnold Palmer, Jack Nicklaus, Babe Zaharias, Mickey Wright and
Nancy Lopez. There are also many great books available about more
recent superstars like Phil Mickelson, Tiger Woods and Annika
Sorenstam. Golfers are so unique and come to the game for various
reasons and from very different backgrounds. Their personal stories
will be inspiring and give you new insights to the game.

Feed your new interest in the game and it won't be long before
you get excited watching Phil, Tiger or Annika on television. Soon
your four-year-old daughter snuggles up with you on the couch asking, "Daddy, can I watch with you?" Voila! A seed is sown.

Before you know it you will be asking your spouse for golf clubs
for Christmas. Your kids will want to buy you the latest and greatest
golf gizmo for your birthday and Father's Day.

Exposing Kids to Golf

Practice Together

Enthusiasm breeds enthusiasm, and your kids will not want to be
left behind. Just as you want to imitate your favorite touring pro,
they will soon be mimicking you. They will beg you to take them to
hit balls.

Remember, kids have short attention spans. Keep your practice
sessions short if you tote them along. Do not be discouraged if their
moments of interest are brief and sporadic – she might watch a couple
of holes, but can't hang with you for the entire back nine. Continue to
invite your child into your golf world – let her ride along with you on
the course and include her in your golf outings as much as possible.
Share your love of the game until she develops a love of her own.

Go to Tournaments

Expose your children to good golf as well as "fun golf." Take them to the local PGA or LPGA Tour event. Get up close and personal on practice and pro-am days, because the professionals are much friendlier then and usually will stop and talk to children. Autographs, used golf balls and tees are easier to come by when the pros are practicing at the driving range or putting green. Help your little one get autographs – remembering that they don't have to be from Tiger Woods or Annika Sorenstam. Often, kids will be excited with any playing professional's "John Hancock." Golf balls and tees are a big deal to an eight-year-old!

Big tournaments to a kid are like a carnival of sorts, with all of the vendors and free giveaways. The kids will be in awe of the clicking leader boards and the exciting gallery. Winning will be the pinnacle for one lucky player that week, but your kid will see all the others as winners every time she sees a good shot and hears the crowd roar. Just romping in the grass with Dad is delightful to young kids. Because there are players all over the course, subconsciously, there is not so much emphasis on winning and losing.

Watch Television or Videos

If you do not have a tournament in your area, watch golf on television. You can get a map out and talk about the area where the tournament is being held. Talk about where the players are from. There are a variety of topics to discuss if you want to make it more interesting for your child. Alligators on the course in Florida will be more interesting to your child at first. As she learns the game, she will learn to appreciate the magic of a holed 40-foot putt or a shot holed out from a bunker. Use the telecast to explain funny golf terms such as "hook" or "slice."

The Golf Channel (More info: thegolfchannel.com) has all kinds of interesting programming in addition to telecasting professional and amateur golf tournaments from all over the world. You and your child can learn about historic moments in the game and your favorite players and participate in Golf Academy Live – a program in which top instructors give viewers golf lessons. It is also a golf news channel, keeping the golfing public the latest results from all the top professional tours. Its also sponsors the National Drive, Pitch and Putt tournament for juniors and produces fun reality television shows such as "The Big Break." The Golf Channel gives the golf enthusiast 24 hours of golf each day!

"Golf in the Kingdom" is a short animated instructional golf video for children of all ages. Golf great Johnny Miller endorses this magical movie – "I wish it had been around when my children were learning to play," he said. It is filled with lively characters and will touch the hearts and inspire the talents of children just learning the game. The whole family will love the illustrations and techniques, golf vocabulary and etiquette brought to life.

Introduce Junior Golf

Discover junior golf together. Take your child to see other kids playing good golf. The American Junior Golf Association (More info: ajga.org) showcases the best juniors in your region. The USGA runs several big tournaments for boys and girls during the summer. If you read about a major event like the U.S. Junior Girls Championship being played in your area, take your child out to see the opening ceremonies or the final award presentations. Your kid might say, "Wow! That looks like fun. I want to do that!" Also, check out the official junior golf web sites of the USGA, PGA Tour, PGA of America, LPGA, NGCOA, GCSAA and the World Golf Foundation (More info: juniorlinks.com).

Let 'Em Caddy

Let your daughter "caddy" for you in an event you might be playing. It's a great way for her to learn the game. Kids are like sponges – they will pick up a lot by watching the game. When they finally get to go on the course, they will feel more at ease, more prepared. The USGA sponsors programs during "Bring Your Daughter to the Course Week" each summer. Older children can volunteer at a professional event as a sign bearer, helper to the caddy master or a group scorer.

Read Books

Exposure is the key. If kids are exposed to golf, they may lose some of those preconceived notions that it's boring. At any age, you can expose your child to golf in a fun and innovative way. There are storybooks for preschoolers available for those of you anxious to introduce your pre K child to the game. *The ABCs of Golf, Count on Golf,* and *Consider it Golf: Golf Etiquette & Safety Tips,* by Susan Greene are excellent read-a-loud books. *Teaching Kids Golf,* by Bernadette Moore and *Tiger's Tips: Beginner's Golf for Kids,* by Don Emerick are also fun introductions to the game. The National Golf Foundation publishes a small rulebook with Snoopy as the main character. All of these are great for children under eight. Emerick's book has nothing to do with Tiger Woods. If your child is a little older, *Tiger Woods: A Biography for Kids,* by Tiger Woods, and *A-Game Golf: The Complete Starter Kit for Golfers for Tiger Woods' Amateur Instructor,* by Earl Woods and John Anselmo, are excellent resources.

Use Pop Culture

Before Tiger Woods, you may have had a tougher time exposing your child to golf, but he made golf cool. Tiger brought kids to the game in droves – he leads the trendy youth movement, and other high-profile celebrity duffers have infused golf with a dose of "hipness." These days, everyone golfs – rap stars, sports stars and television and movie stars – golf is part of popular culture. Show your child how many superstars love playing golf. Inspire enthusiasm for golf in your child and see where her interest takes her.

Use Off-Course Games

Video Games

"Hey Mom, I just got a hole-in-one and beat Tiger Woods!" screams your daughter from the other room. "I have never had a hole-in-one before. That was cool! I love golf!"

Yes, let your guard down and enter the world of video games with your child. The old adage "If you can't beat 'em, join 'em" might be the advice you need when you are talking to your kid about her love of video games. Warning- these games may be extremely challenging! Make a deal–she needs to teach you a few skills on the Nintendo or Play Station. Tell her she is going to give you video game lessons and the deal is the game you use is "Tiger Woods PGA Tour."

There are several golf games available, but the key is now you have entered your child's world. Her expertise in game play will amaze you. More important, the exciting virtual golf will give you the opportunity to talk about the game with your child on her terms. This fantasy play will give you opportunity to introduce other off-course games that will enhance your child's ability to develop early skills suited for golf.

Dice Game

There is a dice game called "GOLO." This fun game is simply golf in a cup. Golfers (and non-golfers) of all ages find the game easy to learn and difficult to put down. GOLO consists of nine dice, a dice cup, the rules of GOLO, scorecards and a pencil. The goal of the game, as in real golf, is to shoot the lowest possible score, or "go low."

The nine dice represent nine holes on a typical golf course. Each die has twelve sides with various scores on each side – some great, some not so good. Each person rolls the dice, and a particular situation comes up on the die. Each die is removed to "score." A player follows the instructions and keeps score on a notepad. Players can play a variety of games according to the number of players involved and the length of time available.

This is a great game to help kids learn about rules, etiquette, and possible scenarios from the golf course. (More info: igolo.com)

Real Golf	vs.	GOLO
9 holes		9 holes
Takes years to learn		Takes minutes to learn
Play nine in two hours		Play nine in minutes
Bogeys and birdies		Nine dice
Go to the course		Course goes with you
No fivesomes		The more the merrier

Stork

Balance is crucial for golfers, and there are a few key ways to help develop your child's balance. One fun way for younger kids is to play Stork with you. The player tries to balance standing on one leg with arms outstretched like a stork. Who can stand like a stork the longest? The child is allowed to wobble if necessary, but you are not. Variations in the game might include switching legs, standing on a curb, or hopping up and down.

8board

Another great tool to use for developing balance and centeredness is the 8board. This amazing tool was designed to learn balance and experience lower body rotation – both critical in a fundamentally sound golf swing. With or without clubs in hand, you can play balance games, swiveling around and maintaining your balance without falling off the board. At first it may be awkward, but in no time both you and your child will have better balance and coordination. Being stationary, it is safer than a skateboard. Don't be bummed if your child masters the 8board before you do. (More info: 8board.com.)

Medicine Ball

This game is designed to address the motor development patterns of children and develop a stronger foundation for golf skills. Use a two-to-four-pound medicine ball, a soccer ball or a large sized koosh ball.

Two people stand a couple of yards apart, side to side, and throw the ball to each other from waist high using a movement similar to the downswing release motion used in a proper golf swing. The palms of the hands should face each other while they are on the ball, and the arms, forearms and hands should mimic the motion of the lower part of a golfer's downswing. The weight transfer should be from back side to front side as the ball is released.

Trampoline

You can also purchase a miniature trampoline and prop it up so a ball will bounce back, allowing your child to play by herself. As you and your kid develop this skill, throw and release in the opposite direction. This will help strengthen the opposite muscle group and give you increased strength and coordination.

Jump Rope

Jumping rope can be fun and is good for timing and endurance; again, another fun way for you and your child to build some crucial skills necessary for golf. Look for adjustable ropes with cushioned handles.

Juggle

Teaching kids to juggle is fun. Learning to juggle is great for hand-eye coordination and is a great way to develop soft focus. Start with two small beanbags, and after a few weeks of practice, progress to three bags.

Play Catch

However simple this sounds, it is not done enough these days. Little boys often get the ABCs of throwing through baseball and playing nerf football with their friends. Teach your daughters how to throw, because they often get left behind. The correct throwing motion is critical to many sports, including golf. Use a mitt and baseball or a fun Velcro-type mitt and ball.

All of these games can be played away from a golf course and can be instrumental in developing a child's range of motion, sense of balance, overall coordination, strength and basic golf related skills. John Mason, the director of instruction for JC Resorts Golf Schools in Encinitas, California is purposeful in teaching kids and adults these fun innovative games that can enhance your golfing skills. He encourages his students to make these fun games a part of their golf preparation. Mason avows, "These off-course games can be instrumental in a student's development and will help dramatically with proper mechanics. They are fun, and I love to do them myself"

Plan a Golf Vacation

Family vacations conjure up different ideals for different people. Golfers can find a golf course just about anywhere they plan to visit – whether it is on a family vacation at the Magic Kingdom, while enjoying a faraway tropical paradise, undertaking an international experience or going all out on a recreational free-for-all. You can make golf a small part of your family plan, or you can plan a family golf school together. Resorts range from the luxurious to the simply affordable.

Popular vacation destinations might be hosting a major golf event – giving you the opportunity to create a trip of a lifetime. For example, the 2008 US Men's Open will be held at Torrey Pines Golf Course in beautiful San Diego, California. A family getaway might include a couple of days at the tournament mixed in with days at SeaWorld or the World Famous San Diego Zoo. Within a 100-mile radius, you have everything from Disneyland and Universal Studios to the Mexican border. There are many kid friendly golf courses and practice facilities in the area to visit if your kid is motivated by the tournament. Challenge yourselves and plan to play the championship course just after the event. Each year, the 15-17 year-old divisions for the Callaway Junior World Championships, one of the most elite junior golf events in the country, play on this beautiful Torrey Pines layout.

The world is your canvas as you plan a family vacation. International golf vacations offer a different view of the game as different styles of courses, weather and customs come alive for your child. There are amazing golf packages available to Scotland and Ireland, golf's birthplace. In the Far East you and your child can share a caddy as you stroll along the fairways admiring wild monkeys swinging through the trees. Kangaroos play along many of the fairways in Australia. Do you think with backdrops such as these, it will matter how well you play? Whether you choose to cross time zones to escape busy school calendars and demanding jobs or decide to vacation closer to home, you and your kids can always find a place to take a swing or two.

No other family activity can add so much to a family vacation. Every family member – from the novice to the expert and anywhere in between – will enjoy planning a golf getaway.

More and more parents want to golf with their kids. Nike Golf Schools offer special parent-child schools in a variety of destinations in addition to their popular kids' camps. Travel agents aside, you can find thousands of web sites specializing in family golf vacations. The Family Golf Association (FGA) was created to celebrate and promote golf as a family activity and suggests golf courses designed for family friendly experiences. (More info: familygolf.org)

Be sure to inform whoever you plan through that you are traveling as a family and that you would like golf to be a memorable experience and an important part of your kid's vacation.

Remember also, these are just a couple of the wonderful resources available for planning your perfect golf vacation. Most important is to make your trip FUN! FUN! FUN! Your child will identify golf with all the fun activities she enjoyed during her vacation. Introducing the game of golf on vacation can be the most fun-filled way to get your child started in golf.

Choosing a Coach

Selecting a coach is a parent's single most important job. Your best teaching professionals will be qualified through either the Professional Golfers Association (PGA. More info: PGA.com) or the Ladies Professional Golfers Association (LPGA. More info: LPGA.com). The PGA of America and The Ladies Professional Golfers Association's Teaching and Club Professional Divisions are dedicated to ensuring proper instruction at all levels and to growing the game of golf. Along with the USGA, they endorse "Bring Your Daughter to the Course Week," "Play Golf America," and many other exciting programs tailored for community enjoyment.

Phases of Development

There are many phases of development for a junior golfer. An excellent teaching professional may be qualified to instruct your child from the raw beginning phase through to top amateur ranking or the professional level. The best instructors understand the different phases of development, and it is even best if the teacher has had experience in the levels of competition your child aspires to reach. There are many factors that are important when choosing the right coach for your child. It is also key to recognize at what point a teacher is not working out for your child.

Beginner Phase

The first phase of instruction is the beginner phase. A student is introduced to the game, its rules, the etiquette and the basic fundamentals of playing the game. Good teachers will work on sound mechanics. Learning the correct way to hold the club and align oneself toward a target as well as proper posture, balance and swing tempo from the beginning will help your child immensely. Great teachers will keep the instruction simple. They will also be dedicated to setting a strong foundation so your child may move from phase to phase of her development with success. The best teachers will give new golfers many areas in which to succeed. Kids need to be encouraged to keep learning at every phase.

Developmental Phase

The second phase is the developmental phase. In the beginning of this phase, your child is just learning all of the nuances of the game – when to putt out and when to leave the flagstick in. An instructor needs to have a high energy level and a high level of commitment to the development of your child's golf game; there should be a strong understanding of your child's golf swing and personality. If your child feels the workload is greater than the reward, you risk your child quitting at this phase. The best instructors are instrumental with proper encouragement and guidance through this difficult phase. As your child progresses through phase two, you should see more self-motivated practice rather than parent-directed practice. This developmental phase is key for building strengths in all areas of your child's game to ensure that her game will withstand the pressure of competition. A good teacher needs to recognize your child's strengths and weaknesses at this point and have a game plan to move into the next phase. It is critical to realize a child's attitude toward the game will evolve during this developmental phase. She may even decide she loves golf, but that she doesn't want to play competitively at all. This is OK! Exposing your child to competition is one thing – forcing a child into competition is another.

Competitive Phase

At some point in the developmental phase, a competitive phase might emerge. There are several different levels of the competitive phase your child might encounter. It might be best to look at each of these phases, from the beginner phase on, as rungs on a ladder. The ladder can go as high as your child wants it to go, but she increases her chances for success if she does not skip any of the rungs on the ladder. Somewhere, the developmental phase will meld into an early stage of the competitive phase. Depending on your child's aspirations and dedication, this phase can be very broad. This phase is the one in which your child might put her nose to the grindstone, so to speak. It is critical that parents and instructors alike help keep this phase fun.

Advanced Competitive Phase

Advanced competition at a national level is stronger than ever, and a good pro will equip your child to compete at this level. Strong, mature junior golfers should be capable of making simple adjustments and should have a good understanding of the demands of tournament golf. Instructors should empower your child to weather the tough times. In the natural growing curve, there will be many times your child is knocked down to the core of her foundation; if the foundation has been properly set, your child will get stronger through the difficult times.

Necessary and Unnecessary Coach Changes

There are coaches that are awesome and may be the only professional your child ever will need. If you have a strong coach from the beginning, your child will build a strong game, move through the phases in a timely manner and will avoid a lot of difficult swing changes as she matures. PGA teaching professional Carl Welty says, "It's almost a sure 'kiss of death' when a really strong player says, 'I'm trying to get my game to the next level'. More times than not, they switch teachers, rip their swings apart, and are never able to get it back to the level of play they once enjoyed." Be careful of changing from pro to pro at this point. Most kids lose out when their parents go on this "find the perfect pro" campaign. That said, it is equally important to be able to recognize when the teaching professional is not working for your child.

When and why are changes necessary? Too often kids initiate changes in their professional when they find it difficult to follow or agree with the instructor's practice regimen. Look at where you started, consider the improvements, and look to the future. Plans for progress should be crystal clear for the student, and a few bad outings, bad rounds or bad tournaments should not be reasons for abandoning set plans. Your child's instructor should be approachable and available to discuss progress, lack of progress, and reasonable expectations your child is striving to accomplish.

Communication and Commitment

Communication and respect are key. There must be a high level of commitment from both the instructor and your family. A strong bond between the team of student, parent and instructor will limit confusion and frustration. An instructor should never allow your child to bring a bad attitude to the practice tee for any length of time. Professionals must insist on a clear mind and clear objections and be willing to work with your child on the emotional aspect of her game. If your kid's instructor is not willing to address difficult learning curves or doesn't recognize shifts in the developmental and competitive phases, then it is best to move on to an instructor who is more experienced in dealing with these advanced issues.

There are excellent instructors who may have limited playing experience, and they may not be qualified to help your child succeed at the next level. Some professionals are honest about their own limited resources, but unfortunately, many do not realize their limitations. Be open and honest about your expectations with the instructor. Each student progresses at a different rate, so you need to be especially careful not to play the comparison game. Truthfully look at your child's efforts over a long period of time. Focus on the long term, and see if this instructor is capable of helping your child reach new goals. Do not rush the learning process at this point. At times, your child is one good performance away from catapulting to the next level. Leave room for patience. There are no guarantees, however, and an instructor is hurting your child's chance of further progress if you can't monitor steady improvements. Ensure due diligence as you prepare to change teaching professionals. Change is necessary at times, but you should not have to keep switching professionals to get your child to the next level of competition. Include your child in the process of choosing her coach.

Certification – What does it all mean?

It is important to check credentials when searching for an instructor. Credentials may look alike on the surface, so it is critical you do research when looking for a good teacher. A good place to start is the PGA or LPGA. However a club professional is quite different than a teaching professional. At times, a PGA apprentice or a LPGA Class B might be a much better choice than even a Class A or Master Professional.

Instructor Qualities

There are specific qualities you are looking for as you search for your child's instructor. There are some excellent teachers who may have some, but not all of these qualities, so you should re-evaluate your child's instructor as she progresses through the developmental phase. A highly qualified pro is someone who loves to teach. A good teacher loves kids and has the energy to teach at appropriate levels – and makes learning fun! Credibility comes with a teacher who has played successfully at some high-level tournament golf or has worked with successful players over the years. You need a teacher who knows a lot about the game and is a good communicator. You want someone who is imaginative, recognizes different personality types and personalizes lessons accordingly. Good teachers know how to set and achieve goals and are willing to meet you at your needs.

Interview Candidates

Interviewing several candidates is always your best option when shopping for a golf professional. Ask for references in both genders as well as in many age groups and talent levels. Talk with other parents, students and golf professionals. Occasionally you will find an excellent reference for a teacher who is neither a PGA nor an LPGA member. Time invested in checking out the instructors cannot be over-emphasized and is worth every hour.

Credentials vs. Results

Credentials are important, but results are equally important in golf instruction. Harvey Penick taught for seven decades and wasn't an "accredited" professional. He coached the University of Texas golf team for 33 years, and among his well-known pupils were PGA Tour champions Tom Kite and Ben Crenshaw. They were only two of the thousands of golfers he influenced over the years. He taught Betty Jameson, Betsy Rawls, Mickey Wright, Kathy Whitworth and Sandra Palmer – women who won more than 240 LPGA Tour events, two U.S. Women's Amateurs and 10 U.S. Women's Opens between them. The men, including William Morris Jr. and Walker Cupper Ed White, account for five NCAA individual titles, two Masters winners, one U.S. Open champion and more than 35 PGA Tour victories. Penick's Little Red Book is a treasured instruction manual to many. Many of his students are now instructors, showing that a teacher's legacy is often the best kind.

Results can be deceiving with children. Beginners might be able to perform with horrible fundamentals, so your child's natural athleticism might make the pro look good, but in actuality your child will stop progressing and be discouraged later on down the road and might quit. On the other hand, you can have an instructor who tries to "make" your child have the perfect swing, and the child never experiences any improvement. Something is wrong here as well. Ask why and how an instructor became qualified – make him give you reasons why he is good at what he does. Who are his mentors? Who does he admire? Does he continue his education? Does he take himself too seriously? Too casually? Is he too rigid? Watch the way he handles people. Who would your child relate well with? Who would you be able to work with? There is really more than one "perfect way to play golf." When the student is ready, the teacher will appear.

Parent as Coach

A golf professional, exasperated and frustrated after attempting to teach his daughter, mumbled as he left the driving range, "I don't think I should teach her. She just doesn't get it. She doesn't listen, and I am afraid I am killing all interest she might have in the game." Parenting kids and coaching them are two of the most challenging roles any adult will ever face. Naturally being a parent-coach makes it a doubly tough assignment.

Parents and grandparents alike have been successful at coaching their kids to stardom. Arnold Palmer, Davis Love III, Curtis Strange and Jim Furyk are just a few of the many golf professionals who were coached by their fathers. Although Earl Woods and Phil Mickelson Sr.

put their sons under the careful eye of golf professionals, they too must be credited with being the most influential coaches in their sons' lives. John Gulbis was not golf professional; in fact he worked for the Sacramento probation department. That didn't stop him from introducing his young four-year-old daughter, Natalie, to golf and coaching her through a great junior career and amateur success. He didn't hand over the reigns to veteran coach Butch Harmon until after she earned her LPGA Tour card.

It's understandable that a parent who is a professional athlete, a coach or a proficient player would want to teach his own child. After all, who better to assess the child's abilities and moods? Experts caution against taking on this dual role, especially once a child outgrows her pre-teen years. Parenting alone becomes a challenging task during these formative years. Adolescence is tough enough for most kids, but when you throw in the highly competitive phase of tournament golf, you are in dangerous waters. The relationship between you and your child can become seriously volatile as she tries to grow through these tough stages of her development. It is wise to avoid this emotional powder keg.

If you do choose to coach your own child because you want to, or because no other coach is available, or to save money on lessons, it's best to limit your coaching to the beginning phase. Keep it fun, or you risk turning your child off forever! When it is time for lessons, you will continue to play a major role in your child's attitude and development. You are still part of the team – you just are not the coach anymore. Go to lessons and absorb as much information as possible (take notes if you have to). You will be an invaluable resource to your child if she understands that you have changed your mindset from teacher to cheerleader. Always show unconditional love. Play with your child. Young children play sports for fun; learning is simply a byproduct. Keep this simple truth in mind, and you will be your child's best "coach" ever.

Whether you choose to teach golf to your child or place her under the careful eye of a skilled professional, remain actively involved in the early years. Sit through hours of lessons and let the coach guide you on when and where to intervene. Your kid will need an extra pair of eyes occasionally and a great sounding board more often. Let her talk, and you listen. Pay close attention to her moods, when she is successful and when she isn't. If you're a golfer, practice your golf game right alongside her. Let your child see your ups and downs, your successes and failures. Spend lots of time together. Play games and help make practice fun. Be involved – do not assume you can turn your kid over to a great pro and she'll be hooked. Children need to experience an emotional involvement if they are to choose golf as the sport of a lifetime. A good parent is clearly best qualified to offer the young child memorable golf experiences.

Getting your Child Interested – Make Golf Fun

If you remember only one keyword for raising a successful golf kid, remember this one – "FUN." As long as a kid is having a good time, self-motivation and golf development occurs naturally. It is your responsibility to help your child find fun in the game. The definition of fun can't be exclusively associated with winning. If your child associates fun only with winning, she will have a difficult time enjoying the game itself outside of her results. Fun must be encouraged in the process of learning the game.

Your kid might be a serious kid, so a pro that is always clowning around and is more outgoing or gregarious might not be the right personality mix for your kid. If your kid is too energetic for a "serious" teaching professional, that might not work either. An environment of encouragement is much more fun for a child. A positive attitude toward effort as much as outcome will help your child fall in love with practice. Good instructors show enthusiasm for your child's interests even in a group of other children.

As you get interested in exposing your children to golf, and as you start down the road to picking their first golf instructor, remember – have fun. This is an important process, but it is a game after all. The ability to make learning golf fun is a key element to your child's future involvement in the sport. If your child has a different personality type than you do, remember, it is her idea of fun you are trying to create. Be in tune with your child, and follow her lead.

2
First Class

Tiger Woods and Annika Sorenstam have raised the standards of professional golf, but unfortunately many future Tigers have been chased away from golf at a young age because of a poor introduction to the game.

Lifelong recreational golfers are likewise lost because their love of the game isn't rooted in the earliest stage of development. Simply the way golf was introduced – boring, legalistic, complicated and too technical – makes them quit. Other times, interest waned because of poor instruction or instruction styles of those trying to impart their great wisdom. For example, an instructor might be teaching his five-year-old beginner student in the same manner as he is teaching his 15-year-old experienced player. Of course, this would be a recipe for disaster.

There are many ways to get your kid to take up golf and many ways to get him to quit. Let us focus on what will ultimately nurture your child's interest in the game, help inspire a desire to learn the game, develop tenacity to keep playing and motivate him to become the best golfer he can be.

"When?" and "How?" are the first two critical questions most parents should ask after considering the "Why golf?" question. These two questions are crucial in assessing your child's development.

The Right Age

What is the ideal age to start a kid in golf? Parents, players, psychologists and coaches will never agree on an ideal age. Ask 10 different professionals and you may get 10 different responses. You may even get the undefined, unsatisfying, logical answer – "Whenever your child is ready." If it makes you feel any better, most sports psychologists agree with this reply to the "right age" question. However, a lot of parents do not really want to simply know the "right age" to start their kid in golf. The question they really want answered is, "What is the "right age" to start my kid in golf so he can win the U.S. Open?"

Sports psychology expert Jeff Troesch says the right age for getting kids into golf or competitive athletics varies widely with each child. "A child develops along at least four major dimensions: physical, motor skills, psychosocial and cognitive," Troesch says. "Identifying where a child is along each of these dimensions is crucial. There might be some who are ready to hold a golf club and emulate a parent or older sibling at an age as young as 3 or 4. This does not mean they are ready for competition anytime soon. I would encourage parents to err on the side of introducing the game too late rather than too early. Let the desire spring from the child and not the parents' agenda. Typically, a child will show healthy interest around ages 8-10." Troesch also adds that children can be younger, but warns, "If earlier, be sure that he is indeed ready."

Great golfers have run the gamut on this age-old question, with Mickelson and Woods still being in diapers when they first showed great promise to Norman having his first golfing experiences as a 15-year-old. Research shows that most touring professionals start golfing some time before the age of 12.

The consensus shows that, if you want your child to reach the top echelon of golf, there is a critical period or a window of opportunity during which your child must be exposed to the sport. If he does not get exposed to the sport at this time, he may not develop to the highest level. This age range still hovers between 9 and 12. However, kids are getting introduced to golf earlier than kids just a few decades ago, and the level of play in junior golf has dramatically improved in the last five years.

The Callaway Junior World Championships recently changed its competitive fields to include a new six-and-under division. The tournament had recently made room for a new seven-and-eight-year-old division, splitting away from the traditional 10-and-under division that had been in place since 1968. Tournament directors have been adjusting the age groups and moving the courses to accommodate the vast improvement of play for kids 10 and under. Still, if your child hasn't been crowned world champion by age eight, don't lose hope. Kids develop at different ages and peak physically, mentally and emotionally at different ages. Several tour stars didn't discover their potential until high school. Although PGA Tour player Paul Azinger started to play golf at age five, he was a senior in high school before he could break 40 for nine holes. Some kids may burn out if pushed into playing too much competitive golf at an early age.

Jumpstart Interest

Starting with the notion that the most important part of becoming a good golfer is to begin playing young, how do you jumpstart interest with your child in this relatively slow-paced game? Common sense dictates that a kid has to have basic comprehension and motor skills before considering any sport. It is key that a child be self-controlled and disciplined to listening before taking lessons, but a love for the game can be spawned before he even takes his first lesson. Just like Tiger and Phil, love of the game can be cultivated right from the high chair.

There are simple ways to introduce kids to golf. Kids love to mimic. Watch golf together, either on television or at a local tournament; play in the yard with plastic clubs and Wiffle balls; go to a driving range or practice facility; go miniature golfing; introduce your child to other children that play golf; read golf picture books or watch golf videos designed for kids; seek out child friendly facilities; or play SNAG (More info: snagusa.com)

No matter how you introduce the game, be sure to make golf fun. If it is not fun, kids will not want to learn how to play. It will be easy to gauge your child's interest once he has been adequately exposed to the sport. Is he smiling when he comes off of the course? How's his overall disposition? Is he asking to go practice? Does he often talk about golf? Always keep it fun, and you increase the chance that your child will want to practice and compete.

Most parents have a system of rewards for good behavior. Ask your child if he would like to earn his own clubs. Let your child earn his way onto the golf course as well. When youngsters get on the course early, they can start assimilating the game of golf. Usually this can happen around six years old, but there are a few kids who can handle playing on the course earlier than this. Playing only a few holes may give a child a great golfing experience. Don't over-do it, and be creative. Play from halfway to the hole or 50-100 yards out, hit alternate shots, or give your child a "real" opportunity to sink a putt for par or birdie. If your child is not mature enough to behave on the course, stick to giving the child privileges on the driving range. There are many games kids can play on the driving range or putting green, making their experience fun and exciting as well. Peter Jacobsen "learned to aim a golf shot by trying to hit that little car picking up the balls on the driving range," he has recalled.

Share enthusiasm, but don't push. Pay attention to your child's lead; and as his enjoyment is continually sustained, all that the game of golf is will be gradually incorporated and repeatedly instilled into him. Show patience as he develops his own interests. Keep it simple in the earliest stages of development, and never "force" him to play. Interest may come and go over the first few years, and that is OK. Every so often, encourage him to give the game another try. If your kid is destined to take up golf, he will eventually show interest. When that happens, you know you've found the right age and that he will most likely enjoy the game the rest of his life.

Right Goal, Right Way

"My daughter is 18 – is it too late to get started in golf?" First of all, it is never too late to learn to play golf, but it may be too late for this person to earn a college scholarship. Japanese sensation Ayako Okamoto didn't learn to play until she was 21 and had a very success-ful LPGA career. Larry Nelson, a winner of two major championships who now plays on the Champions Tour, didn't start playing until he was in his late 20s. Yes, they are exceptions, but you should look at an attainable goal in conjunction with your child's age.

Goal setting is instrumental to success in golf. At every age and at every talent level there are real, challenging and achievable goals that can be set forth. Yes, there are tournaments for kids as young as five, but Jeff Troesch stresses, "having children compete prematurely potentially threatens to create a negative sport experience."

It is vital that parents help children set goals that match their child's interest level and then give the children the tools to give them the highest probability of success. Children may need help setting appropriate goals, but kids must establish complete ownership of the goals they have set. Not all goals have to be competitive in nature, and usually personal achievement goals will stimulate quicker improvement and success.

If a child wants to compete at a national level, he must have proper training and expect to work very hard. The best thing a par-ent can do is prepare a child for the goals and challenges set forth. At every level of competition, a child has the opportunity to reach for the pinnacle. There is a clear possibility for success at any age if small goals and challenges are met with proper preparation. There are many junior golf associations that offer full golf schedules so your child can test himself against his peers. The best in a particular city, region or country can play against each other several times a year if that is your child's ambition.

A child may simply want to play golf for self enjoyment and grat-ification and want nothing to do with competitive play. Social in nature or competitive in nature, parents must accept whatever rea-sons a child chooses to play golf. Most golfers will tell you golf is enjoyed more when played well, so parents need to focus their atten-tion on how to get their child started toward achieving goals that will help him play better.

The best answers to the "When?" and "How" questions are directly related to the goals your child has. There is no one best age answer; so, that should mean there are many questions a parent should ask. These questions are best answered when posed differently. For example, it would be best to ask, "My kid is 'X' years old – what are appropriate goals for him to set?" After setting those goals, it is vital to ask, "What is the best way for us to help him start achieving his golf goals?"

The Right Class

The importance of a child's first golf lesson can not be overemphasized. Once you have a child capable of reasoning and taking instruction, it is vital you nurture this stage of development. Liken your child's interest in golf to a spark that can either grow into a raging fire or be snuffed out before it ever gets started. The first lessons your child has will either fan this flame or could be as detrimental as a bucket of water.

Getting Started – First Lessons

There are a wide variety of golf lessons available in most areas. The majority of facilities offer options ranging from recreational group lessons to private lessons. Options will also vary depending on the level of golfers seeking instruction. Child or adult, if you want to play golf to the best of your ability, you should take golf lessons with a qualified teaching professional. Do your homework, be picky and don't simply settle for what is offered. The right beginning is vital to your child's ongoing interest and achievements.

There are PGA or LPGA golf professionals available at most facilities. It would behoove you to check out a professional before signing up for classes. You do not want to turn your child off to golf should the instructor have a teaching style that doesn't suit your child. Be sure to check references and call around your area to talk with several professionals about their experiences, philosophy, teaching methods and styles. If an instructor has little or no experience with kids, do you really want your kid to be his guinea pig?

Introductory and Recreational Classes

Introductory classes have one objective – to get kids to want to come back for more instruction. Young kids are capable of understanding the basic fundamentals and mechanics, but they must be taught in a fun, innovative way. Many kids take instruction better than adults do. In the beginning, a lot of what is taught may not seem like it relates to the golf game; however, good teachers teach in a way such that kids do not realize how much they are "learning" because they are having so much fun.

First lessons might include playing catch with a Velcro mitt and ball, jumping on one leg, jumping rope, doing the twist, throwing a medicine ball, or more fun, using their clubs. SNAG equipment is great for introducing youngsters to golf using oversized clubs and targets. During this phase of development, they should be giggling a lot. You want your kids to relate fun, laughter, success and rewards to their first golf experiences.

Many parents will often get frustrated with this fun game-like instruction because they are so programmed to expect dry, technical, "serious" lessons. Renowned teaching professional Chuck Hogan says, "Juniors do not relate to overly analytical, adult-oriented teaching styles." There is an enormous amount of information a beginner has to learn; it can be overwhelming for anyone just taking up the game, let alone a kid who just wants to have fun.

To some, it may appear as if no "golf" is being taught, and this could send some well-meaning parents over the edge. After all, "golf" lessons are what you signed up for.

To avoid frustration in this area, ask the instructor to give you a written outline of what is being covered each week. A syllabus is helpful for a very structured parent.

A series of lessons may be outlined session by session. For example: "Fourth session will include rules such as unplayable lies, lost ball and provisional ball. Fifth session will cover standard bunker shots and discussion of golf clubs' lofts. Also, students will learn several games to help practice these shots."

Instructors might assign "homework" for parent and child to do together – hoping for a parent-child discussion of terms such as par, birdie, bogey, handicaps, slope, rating, pace of play, local rules, etc. Parents might be told about the importance of warm-up and asked to do some new stretches with kids. Most important, a good instructor will create a practice routine or schedule that parents will be familiar with and encourage the child to follow.

If you are an accomplished player yourself and have what it takes to relax, back up and be a kid again, then you could possibly be all your child needs to get started. However, if you are pretty analytical, the more "serious" type or know very little about the game, it is best you let your kid learn the game with other kids. Breaking down the game into small, digestible pieces will keep him hungry for more. Don't fall into the trap of trying to teach your child everything you have read, heard, watched and experienced. Your child does not need to know everything you know for a long time, or maybe ever! Let your kid have fun, because, if you do, chances are he will always be yearning for more.

Recreational classes are usually large group lessons offered through your local youth groups – the YMCA, scout troops, in after school programs or through golf facilities. These classes can be a great introduction to the game and its rules and etiquette, but there is usually a high student-to-teacher ratio. The class composition depends on the class itself. A YMCA summer camp class usually has boys and girls grouped together, with kids ranging in age from six to 14. This is not the ideal introductory class, but it can spark your child's interest in the game.

Do not have high expectations for his information retention in such a setting, but if the teachers are well-qualified instructors who enjoy working with kids, are concerned with safety and have good knowledge of the game and its etiquette, your child should enjoy the time spent.

The First Tee, Future Links and the LPGA-USGA Girls Golf (More info: LPGA.com) programs are great introductory recreational programs that may be available in your area. Each of these programs is unique and designed to help your child navigate those early learning stages of golf with other kids who are also just learning. Large group classes should have a minimal cost, and at times a course may offer large recreational classes without charge. Recreational classes are a start, but realize that there is usually very little one-on-one instruction and they are not designed to move students to the next level quickly.

Group Classes

Group classes offer a better student-teacher ratio and are usually tailored so that kids of similar age, interest and ability are grouped together. It is not a good idea to put 14-year-olds together with seven-year-olds. Usually there will be four-five kids, but hopefully no more than eight kids per class. Parents on a tighter budget may find this a good alternative to private lessons in the beginning. Classes are most successful when the kids are within a two-year age range of one another and are at relatively the same playing ability. It is also better for your daughter if there is at least one other girl in a group class. However, the group's students may have skills and talents developing at different paces, so don't panic if some kids progress faster than others do.

Certain improvement and progress may be a result of more effort put forward, and that is always a good example for the group as a whole. Parents might gauge enthusiasm and practice habits a child is developing through his group classes and offer their child additional private lessons as a reward for extraordinary effort. Be cautious in removing your child from a group and opting for private lessons just for quick improvement. Games and competition with each other are often what keeps golf fun in those early stages of development and as junior progresses from one level of play to the next. Improvement by some might prove to be good motivation to others.

A good instructor will help excelling students set new goals and will recommend when they are ready for additional private or semi-private instruction. If the kids have developed relationships, it is best to keep them with their friends even if a big gap in playing abilities has developed. Take note if kids are discouraged, and along with their instructor, offer suggestions to help them experience some progress toward their personal goals. Help them with their expectations. Encourage kids to encourage one another. The environment should be a non-threatening one, and always remember that if a kid is not having fun, he will want to quit. The pro should acquire a good feel for the child's personality traits and be able to recommend the appropriate lesson style. For example, kids who tend to be wanderers are best in a private lesson unless the professional is experienced at dealing with this learning style.

Research shows that girls will stick around longer and enjoy class more if there is at least one other girl her age to play with. LPGA-USGA Girls Golf Programs are popping up all over the country. They are designed for girls between the ages of seven and 17 and are designed to introduce young girls to golf in a fun, positive and more social environment. Their success is a testimony to the fact that girls tend to enjoy the game more when they are initially exposed to golf in a social, friendly, less competitive setting. It would be wise to create a small group of girls your daughter relates to from a larger more recreational program to take lessons together. She will enjoy more individual instruction, yet still have her friends there to play games and learn rules with, keeping it fun

It is extremely important to know if your child works well in a group. Group classes work best if kids can pick up and apply the principles being taught, are social and do not need constant undivided attention. Early instruction often will be the foundation on which they will build. It is vital to their game to have good habits and strong building blocks. Small group classes only work well if everyone there wants to learn golf.

The age-old expression "iron sharpens iron" is applicable in a good group of kids. Kids might work harder just to beat their friends. Group classes can make learning simple rules and etiquette more fun, but just like a traditional classroom setting, goof offs and disruptive kids are distracting to the teacher and those wanting to learn. The consistency and energy of the students and teacher are vital to a successful class.

Consistency is the key to overall development of your golfer. The class needs a teacher who has a lot of energy, shows enthusiasm for every student's progress, uses games and targets, challenges kids, rewards them and ultimately gets students to recognize their own progress and development. It is key that your child be rewarded for his consistent dedication and hard work. Students love their achievements to be recognized!

Ask the pro to give you a "report card" of sorts, explaining where your child stands and how he is progressing in the many areas of the game. You want to see his strengths as well as his weaknesses. This evaluation should cover every aspect of the game: putting, chipping, full swing, bunkers, attitude, practice habits and competition. Within each of these categories are sub categories – under the full swing category, the pro might have fundamentals, short irons, mid irons, long irons, fairway woods and driver. These report cards will help your child set goals.

Semi-private Lessons

During group lessons or while hanging out at the course, your child might really connect with another kid; this is the kid you might arrange semi-private lessons with.

There are several ways to share a lesson with someone. Invite a friend to join your child for lessons or have an interested sibling share lesson time. Kids should be relatively the same age and at relatively the same levels of learning.

A golf buddy for your kid helps in many ways. First and foremost, buddying up keeps your child accountable to someone else for practice and lesson time. Friends hold each other accountable. Second, it's more fun learning, practicing and playing together. If your children get along fairly well, siblings can share lessons now and will golf together for life. Kids can also be good at motivating each other to practice. When kids share the same pro, they can help each other with things they may be working on. Last, it helps you be accountable for taking your child to the course. Everyone is busy, and sometimes it helps when you are obligated to take someone else's kid to the course. Your child will also benefit from this arrangement. Often another parent is able to drive to lessons or to practice when you are not able to go. As kids mature, they can spend hours at the golf course, practicing and playing together, both on and off the course.

Semi-private lessons are less expensive than private lessons, but like everything else, discuss this option with your child. He may like his one-on-one time with his instructor and feel like he can open up more and discuss his game more honestly when he is by himself. Teenagers bask in successes with an audience, but find it very hard to expose weaknesses in front of their peers – they may want private lessons as they get older. If your child is not driving, it may help to schedule half-hour private lessons around the same time period as their golf buddy's lesson so you can still carpool. Semi-private lessons are encouraged and quite acceptable, but it is extremely important to eventually provide private lessons for your child.

Private Lessons

While some might think their kids need to have private lessons right away, it really depends upon the group's makeup and the personality of your kid. Budget issues and their level of interest in improving quickly are two other factors that might influence your decisions. Private lessons can cost between $40 and $100 per hour, but may be worth it for kids who want to improve as quickly as possible. It is common for intermediate to advanced kids to intersperse private lessons with group lessons. Some kids just want one-on-one instruction from the very beginning, and this works as well. If a child's desire is to improve to a competitive level, then consistent private lessons are necessary.

Private lessons are simply more personal. All of the attention is focused on your child and his individual needs. An instructor is better able to figure out how your child learns and then adapt his own teaching style to meet those needs. During lesson time, students can discuss personal goals without the fear of judgement. Students may have concerns or issues about their progress and find it difficult or too personal to discuss in a group setting. Likewise, teachers have the freedom to bring up things they may need to address without embarrassing their student. Private lesson time gives both the student and the teacher time to develop a sense of trust and respect for one another. Both student and teacher can focus on their common goal – making your child the best golfer he can be. They are a team!

It really doesn't matter how your child is introduced to golf, but it is vital to consistently nurture the interest he has developed. Every child will love golf for his own reasons. That's golf. Encourage him in the best way possible. That little spark of interest must be fueled. To keep the flame alive, at times you may have to nudge him a little or bribe him a lot, but always shower him with love. Let him move at his own pace and help him set his goals. Afford him good instruction so he can experience some success; most important, keep golf fun and you will have a child who will be on his way to being a golfer for life.

The Games Approach

Let's face it – a young child attends a golf clinic not to learn golf, but to play the game. As a child develops skills essential to golf technique and mechanics, he is more apt to respond to learning advanced mechanics. A games approach helps kids learn by playing a smaller, shorter version of golf. While simulating some part of the whole golf game, kids will discover skills and strategies along the way. Kids who play putting-green games, games from the bunker and short-game area and driving-range games are better prepared to then put the total game together. This is a perfectly valid method of learning the game. Success will breed success.

Get 'em on a golf course, ASAP! Once kids learn some of the basic fundamentals, it is key to get them playing on a "real" golf course as soon as possible. Par-3 courses are great for kids to learn how to appropriately play the game. Playing games should continue to be a part of your child's advancement in golf. Golf is a game, and there are six steps they will go through as an instructor insures they learn how to play at an efficient level. That means they can go to a golf course, tee it up and play a round of golf abiding by the rules and etiquette necessary for the enjoyment of everyone in the group. You do not have to wait until your child's skill level is "good" or efficient to allow them on the course.

1. Introduction to golf:	
• It is a sport.	• It is a game.

2. Game appreciation:	
• It is different than most other games.	
• It is a game of personal honor, respect and integrity.	
• Golfers play by the rules, and there is game etiquette we learn so that everyone enjoys the game.	

3. Tactical and creative awareness:	
• Personal decisions are required.	• Game management, attention to detail and creativity are required.
• Each hole can be assessed as an individual part of the whole round, and each shot can be assessed as an individual part of a hole.	

4. Personal Choices:	
• What to do and how to do it.	
• Challenges are evaluated and tackled.	
• Wind or no wind?	• How far?
• What club?	• What trajectory?

5. Skill Execution:	
• Small successes.	• This is assessed individually.

6. Performance:	
• Let it speak for itself.	• Do not judge it! It is what it is.
• Am I performing similar to how I do in game situations at the practice area? With friends?	• Enjoy game without putting unfair expectations on your child.

Let the Games Begin

Group Games

Game 1: Around the World, or Two-Putt Pass

> **Develops putting skills**

There are nine holes preferably (but the game can be played with less). The goal is to be the first player to successfully hit the putt at hole No. 9 into the two-foot circle. The first hole features a three-foot putt. A player must make the putt to proceed to hole No. 2. The second hole calls for a six-foot putt, and if the player does not make the putt, the ball must go past the cup, and then the player must make the second putt to go on. Hole No. 3 includes a nine-foot putt and is the same in that the ball must go past the hole in order to have a chance at a two-putt. If the first putt on holes No. 2 or 3 is short, they must start over on that hole.

The game gets interesting because a player coming up to the hole for the first time gets the honor of passing the other players. Should the first-timer either make the putt or accomplish the two-putt under the no-short-putt rule, he should proceed to the next hole. Hole No. 4 is a 12-foot putt; Hole No. 5 is from 15 feet; Hole No. 6 is 18 feet; Hole No. 7 is 21 feet; Hole No. 8 is 24 feet and Hole No. 9 is a two-foot circle by itself or around a hole from 30 feet.

From Hole No. 4, the goal is simply to two-putt. If you are ready to "re-do" a hole because you did not two-putt, and a player who has not played that hole before approaches, you must give him the honor. He will have a chance to pass you should he two-putt. If the player doesn't two-putt, he is now behind you until one of you two-putts and moves on. It is possible that several players can pass before a waiting player takes his next turn. Players have as many turns as it takes to accomplish a two-putt and advance to the next hole. The game is "officially" over when the first player puts a ball into the circle on the ninth hole. Some kids will do the whole course again since there are always players to pass. Depending on your time limit, a great goal is for everyone who started to finish the game by getting a 30-foot putt in the two-foot circle. Some kids will count how many times they completed the course.

This game teaches the foundational truth that you are expected to use no more than two putting strokes in golf. It helps with distance and direction skills and gives players an awareness of subtle differences. Short putts are important. A player can't move on without mastering these. It also gives the instructor an opportunity to discuss "honor."

Game 2: SSS-Point Game – Solid, Straight and Satisfactory

> **Develops hitting skills**

This is fun to play in a large group on the driving range. The instructor is the sole judge and jury. The instructor asks players to pick a lofted club, either a pitching wedge, 8- or 9-iron. Next, the instructor gives the students a target. "Aim at the red (100 yard) flag," he might say.

The distance is not the issue, since many of the players might be of different sizes or abilities. The instructor then calls out a player's name, and it is that player's turn to hit. The goal is to hit the ball in the air (solid contact), straight (alignment) and to a satisfactory distance – based on the instructor's determination. If the player hits it exactly where he wanted to, he is awarded 30 points. If a player tops it, but it goes straight and rolls quite a distance, he should get no points for not getting it airborne, 10 for hitting it straight and maybe five for some distance, giving him 15 points. Another example might be that the player creams it, but the ball doesn't go toward the intended target. That player would receive 10 points for solid contact and 10 for appropriate distance, but none in the category of direction.

The instructor might do a couple of rounds with a lofted club and then have the kids switch to mid irons, giving the kids a choice of anything from a 7-iron to a 5-iron. He can use the same scoring system but switch targets. Later, play the game with a driving club. Players can choose if they want to use a fairway wood or a driver. They love this! The first kid to make it to a pre-determined number of points or the kid with the most points after 10 shots is the winner.

This game teaches kids to focus on several different components of the result. It rewards them for something done well. The game simulates the pressure of everyone stopping and watching them swing – a feeling they must learn to deal with eventually. Kids learn to choose the club they want to hit, and they learn the difference between trajectory and distance with different clubs. It gives them a goal and teaches them the importance of forgetting the last shot and the necessity to focus on the present shot. It also helps them with their math!

Partner Games

Game 1: High Five

> **Develops putting skills**

In this game, two players pick two holes about 20-25 feet apart in distance (novice players can choose holes closer together, say 10-15 feet). One player stands off to the side of one hole and the other player stands off to the side of the other hole. Players should position themselves so their putts do not interfere with one another and they can putt simultaneously. The players will putt back and forth (using the other one's golf ball) until someone holes out. After a player sinks, the players switch holes and keep going until someone sinks again. This continues until one of the players has made five putts.

This game teaches kids to respond to previous outcomes such as putting the ball too hard, too soft or getting less break than expected, as well as to adjust for uphill and downhill putts. Drilling in repetition helps them zero in on a path or target line. Doing this increases awareness and focus. This game is a great confidence builder and is fun for any competitive person.

Game 2: Par Saves

> Develops putting skills

An instructor can call out the shots to be played, or the kids can create them on their own. The game can be played with a two foot circle (target circles can be drawn with gypsum or baseball field chalk to avoid damaging greens). Throw a tee up in the air and let if fall to the ground – whoever it points to, or closest to, chooses the first shot. The player can choose any kind of chip, pitch or bunker shot (if a bunker practice area is available) he wants to practice. Shots should range from bump and run to lob shots to side-hill lies and 40-yard pitches. The player who hits closest to the hole or makes it in the circle gets a letter. Players alternate choosing shots, and the first person who spells out PAR SAVES is the winner.

This game teaches creative shot making and strengthens the imagination. It also stresses the importance of getting the ball close enough to the hole to save par. Practice in pressure situations also can increase performance. The game displays how many different shot options are available and will also help kids realize their strengths and weaknesses. It is also good practice for situations involving varying lies.

Individual Games

Game 1: The Compass

> Develops putting skills

Pick a hole on the putting green and put a tee one putter length from the hole. Go to the opposite side of the hole and again put a tee one putter length from the hole. Next, do the same on the perpendicular line to the hole. There should be four tees in the shape of a compass – north, east, south and west. Go to the first tee, which will represent a putt for birdie. If the player makes it, he is 1-under par. The next tee represents a putt for par. If he misses, it's a bogey and the player is back to par.

The third tee represents a putt for birdie again. Miss it and there is no change in score. Make it and the player is back to 1-under. The last putt is for par again. Adjust the score accordingly, pick up all the tees and move to a different hole and go through the same procedure. The game is over when the player either gets to 5-under (a win) or 5-over (need more practice).

This game teaches players to practice more like they play on the course – with a one-chance-at-it mentality. It also puts putts into perspective and stirs up course-like emotions in a practice setting. It changes the scenery and gives the player many different putts, but doesn't create the false sense of security that develops when players make the same putt over and over. It can create a sense of accomplishment when the player wins the game. It also develops a mentality of putting for birdies.

Game 2: Points for front, middle, back

> **Develops hitting skills**

Take a bucket of 50 balls. Practice this game from different yardage, but start at 25 yards. If possible, increase the yardage increments by five yards with every bucket hit. Practice hitting a pitch so that it lands on the front of the green. If it lands near the intended landing area, the player gives himself a point. The next pick is a landing area in the middle of the green, and finally a landing area at the back of the green. Mentally divide your green into thirds.

Every time the player hits the intended landing area, he gets a point. You may want to start with hitting several to the same intended landing area, but as you advance, mix up the shot selections. Better players can divide the green down the middle, giving them six landing areas to pick from. The goal is to get 30 points before you use up your 50 balls. In the beginning, a player might want to play by counting how many points he gets with 50 shots and then trying to improve on that score. After the first bucket, step back five yards and do it again, and compare scores. Don't forget to repair your ball marks!

This game teaches great distance control and allows for different options with different wedges. It shows players landing areas compared with the actual distance the ball rolls. It is a repetition drill and is good for visual imagery. The game ties the player into the ultimate goal and develops confidence and belief in the short game. For inexperienced players, it also reinforces the concept of repairing ball marks.

These are just a few simple games. There are hundreds of games a player can play. Some simple games apply to the total beginner, but most games are adaptable to the various stages of development. Kids can come up with their own games, and as long as everyone playing agrees on the rules of the game, the possibilities are endless. Skill games, target games, scoring games and match play games – all have different purposes and teach different aspects of the game as a whole at all levels.

When kids understand what to do in a game, they want to develop the skills to play the game. The coach can then demonstrate those skills, practice using game-like drills and individually identify player errors, thus helping to correct them. The key to the games approach is in the game-guided discovery of rules and techniques, goals at hand and the process of self correction. Most important is the emphasis on games and fun.

Once a Week

Usually children start out with weekly classes. Even though your child loved his first class and you had to pry him away, it may require extra effort getting him there for the next lesson. Kids are fickle. One day they love grilled cheese, the following week they tell you in no uncertain terms that they HATE it. Even if your child didn't thoroughly enjoy the first experience, keep going. The key is to be consistent. Do not skip lessons. Keep the momentum going. Once your son has experienced a few successful classes and gets into a groove, he will want to play more often. If there is absolutely no enthusiasm for the game after a series of classes, take a break and consider reintroducing golf at a later date.

Rewards

In the beginning, less is more. Your goal is to create an appetite for the game for your child. If you "stuff" him with golf, he won't develop a desire for more. Take the case of a San Diego woman whose two boys loved their golf instructor so much that when they were misbehaving, all Mom had to do was mention that their golf lesson privilege was in danger and they immediately shaped up. She also told the instructor that her kids had much better than normal attitudes, kept their rooms cleaner and picked up after themselves in the bathroom. She was perplexed by their recent turnaround in behavior and asked if the instructor had said something to the boys. The coach said she had. "I told them it was a privilege to be able to play golf and that their mother sacrificed a lot to afford them with lessons and the opportunity to learn the game," the instructor said. "I also told them they had to be more organized and more disciplined in their daily routines and thinking because good golfers are disciplined in everything they did. If they weren't going to give their best efforts, I wasn't going to waste their mother's money." This mother was not a golfer, but she allowed someone else to kindle her boys' interest in golf. She went on to set up a rewards system so that the boys could earn more lesson time and get to go to the course more often. Good grades, extra chores and other good behavior earned them precious practice time.

One Day at a Time

Most professionals don't start out as superstar phenoms. There are exceptions, but most start to play golf, like it, like the environment and then hang around golf courses and driving ranges more often. They chase birdies and eagles and somewhere along the way break par. They can't get enough. The final destination is not important to most kids – they just start hitting that white ball and chasing it down the fairway, and some of them never stop.

Finding a Course

Okay, so your six-year-old is all excited because he loves his golf classes. He thinks he is really good and he wants to take you out to show you how he can play. It's the weekend and he wants to go play golf with Daddy. Driving range outings are nice, but he wants to play "real" golf. You know he can't play 18 holes or hang for five hours on a regulation-size course. To encourage his enthusiasm, though, you tell him you will find a place for the two of you to play golf together.

Some parts of the country are better than others when it comes to having a viable option for you and your son. If you want to play on a weekend, it is best you try to make a tee time. Most par-3 courses do not reserve tee times. Executive courses, depending on their popularity, have reservations like regulation courses. Many courses will not allow singles to make a tee time. Juniors are usually permitted to play without a parent or guardian, but in some cases are not permitted to reserve tee times. Often juniors and singles must put their name on a "walk on" list, and the course starter will work them in on an available-only basis.

Par-3s or pitch-and-putt courses are a great place to start. They are child friendly. They are not overwhelming for your child, and your kid can really start to sense "playing" the game and using the rules and course etiquette all together. Greens fees are usually $5-$10.

Executive courses are usually a little longer than par-3 courses and will have a few par-4s on the layout. Executive courses can have a total par ranging from 58 to 62. These courses are a great introduction to the longer holes, yet still give kids and beginners a chance for success and positive experiences. Greens fees will usually be $10-$25.

Municipal courses are also great places to take your children. They are usually less expensive and a bit more child friendly than an expensive daily fee course or exclusive resort courses. Always honor the etiquette of golf and the dress code, and teach your child to respect the course. There may be a little more lenience on the dress code issue at a municipal course, but it's best if you train him early that blue jeans are not acceptable for golf. Courses are usually par-70 to par-72 and will challenge golfers of every level. Greens fees on municipal courses vary in a wide range. There are usually discounted fees for city residents, seniors and juniors, as well as for twilight golf. Fees are usually much less than other daily-fee courses.

Country club golf can be a blessing or a curse. Unlimited usage, course availability and possible instruction are wonderful benefits that come with being a member at a country club. It is awesome when you can play the course with your child and "make up" your own tee boxes. Hopefully the club is kid friendly and encourages children to take up the game, practice, play and spend lots of time at the course. Children will be children, and unfortunately, many times club members only notice what children do wrong. Too much stress related to their behavior or constantly being "in trouble" will turn kids away from golf quickly. Respect should be mutual at the golf course, and kids need their time spent at the course associated with fun.

Junior memberships are available at private and public courses. These are a great way to receive cost breaks on practice balls, greens fees and lessons. The golf shop pros usually make junior members feel special. Good programs have many benefits, but one of the best things is that there are usually other young golfers around to practice and play with. Hanging around at the golf course with friends is a great way to keep your child out of trouble!

Driving Ranges and Practice Facilities

There may be days when playing is simply not an option. Whether you couldn't get a tee time or you don't have enough time to get a full round in, there is still no reason why your child can't practice as scheduled. The last thing you want is for your child to lose the momentum of his enthusiasm due to bad weather or challenging circumstances beyond his control.

Get familiar with the driving ranges and different practice facilities in your area. Expose him to them all so he will feel comfortable when you take him there. Know which facilities have the best balls and the best grass, as well as which days are mat days, grass days. Know whether there is a bunker available, if there is a short-game area to practice on, if there is a putting green and which one has the best putting green. Know the operating hours, so if you are in a particular area of town, you can choose to use a particular venue. Know whether they have lights or not. Mix it up for your child, but if he develops a personal favorite, try to cater to that facility. Driving ranges often offer discount cards for juniors or frequent buyer cards offering some discount on range balls. Range balls could run you as much as $10 a bucket otherwise. San Diego's JC Resorts offers $40 range cards, giving juniors $100 worth of balls.

Home Practice

When playing is not an option, it is helpful to keep your kid enthused by participating in off-course games or allowing him to swing in the yard. There are many training aids now available for kids (More info: golfaroundtheworld.com, or golfstuff.com). If you do not want to lose your beautiful yard, it would be wise to invest in a small piece of turf and some whiffle balls. Most parks prohibit golf practice. Small nets are perfect for after-school practice in the yard and are available in most sporting good stores. Give kids bonus points or award them with course time as they show initiative to practice on their own.

The latest craze in backyard landscape is the home-designed short-game practice area. Phil Mickelson honed his flop shot in his backyard after his dad, Phil Sr., built a chipping and putting green for his kids to practice on. All three Mickelson children have careers in golf. If an artificial turf putting green is not in the budget, your little one will have fun practicing in the hallway using one of those putter trays that spits the ball back at you.

Practice, Practice, and More Practice

Ben Hogan was a ruthless perfectionist, and he hit thousands of golf balls day after day on the practice tee trying to find the secret of the perfect swing. In reality, there can never be a perfect swing, because, like fingerprints, every golfer has a different one. Perfecting what you learn and build over time will only come with practice. Practice is just as important as lessons. It can be a real source of enjoyment and an end in itself.

Schedule a practice session with your child and make it a regular activity, something you'll both look forward to. Be consistent and don't deviate from your agreed-upon schedule unless absolutely necessary. Use the same techniques and games introduced during the lessons. Your child should keep a small journal in his bag to record necessary information from his lesson and also to record thoughts and statistics from his practice sessions. Make sure the coach is giving your child a plan to follow.

Practicing with very young children requires a lot of patience and imagination. Sessions should go a lot smoother when you use the games approach. Do not argue with your child; let him lead the practice. This helps him develop confidence and creativity and trains him to start thinking for himself on the golf course. If you have a question or disagreement with something the coach has told your child, don't contradict the coach in front of your child. Many times it may be a matter of interpretation. Speak with the coach privately. Parents need to edify coaches, and coaches need to edify parents.

Role-play with your child. Ask your child to pretend to be the teacher and offer to be his student. This is tons of fun. Follow your "teacher's" lead. Always highlight accomplishments, not mistakes. Be dramatic in your appreciation for his knowledge and attentive to his instruction. Let him know how smart you think he is and how much he has improved in all areas of his game. Remind him that you are thrilled he enjoys golf, but his skills are not what matter most. Always reward great attitude and character and help him see the valuable life skills that he is learning on the golf course.

3
In The Groove

....

"The harder you work, the luckier you get."
Gary Player, Hall of Fame Golfer, Thinkexist.com

....

A 10-year-old who receives support from a parent for practice and motivation from a coach to learn will more likely grow into a 16-year-old who is still hitting golf balls and enjoying the game. Kids need grown-ups to encourage them and to stay involved in their practice and progress in order for them to get in the groove.

Getting Kids Hooked

Two words: parental involvement. There are many well-known examples on both the men's and women's professional tours of the tremendous influence parental involvement can have. For years, champions have attributed their success and their love of the game to their parents. Generations of great golfers have come and gone, but this is still the most common sentiment found among top players worldwide – among them Tiger Woods, Phil Mickelson, Retief Goosen, Jim Furyk, Payne Stewart, John Cook, Scott Simpson, Seve Ballesteros, Nick Price, Curtis Strange, Davis Love III, Craig Stadler, Annika Sorenstam, Nancy Lopez, Laura Davies, Meg Mallon and Patty Sheehan. Without exception, all of these world-renowned champions recall their early years, when a mom or dad was involved in their golf.

The stories are part of golf folklore – parents who did everything they could to support their kids. Phil Mickelson Sr. built a green in the backyard so his kids could practice their chipping and short games. Earl Woods – "Pop" – trained Tiger how to make birdies, and lots of them, before he reached double digits in age. Domingo Lopez, impressed with Nancy's talent as a junior, dug a big hole in the backyard and filled it with sand so she could practice her bunker shots.

Tom Kite senior, an IRS employee, didn't take up golf until late in life, but dragged himself to the golf course at sunrise in order to become a better golfer and in essence beat his golfing buddies. Kite Sr.'s work ethic and competitive nature soon became qualities that his only son would rely upon, as he would strive to become one of the world's greatest golfers. The family moved to Austin, Texas, and young Tom Kite would soon come under the tutelage of teaching great Harvey Penick. The rest is history, as they say.

Some champions have golf bloodlines. The great golfing legend Arnold Palmer literally grew up at Western Pennsylvania's Latrobe Country Club under the watchful eye of the club pro, his father Deke Palmer. Palmer's grandson, Sam Saunders, is now an accomplished junior player, having medaled in the 2005 U.S. Junior Championship. Curtis Strange, the son of a Virginia club pro often spent 15-hour days with his father. Curtis loved to work at the course doing whatever his dad, Tom, needed, but he really loved to spend hours hitting balls on the range. It is said that, to this day, he can't sleep at night if he hasn't spent some time on the driving range.

Davis Love II taught Davis Love III to golf almost before he could walk, as he too was a teaching professional, at a club in Georgia. By the time Love III was nine years old, he had told his father he wanted to be a pro and by age 18, the dream had become more clear – he wanted to be the best player in the world.

Craig Stadler has passed on the love of the game he learned from his father on to his son Kevin. In 2004, both father and son were on tour leader boards during the same week. Kevin was enjoying a first-round lead in a regular PGA Tour event, while his dad was on his way to winning a Champions Tour event. Jay and Bill Haas are another father-son example – both having simultaneous success on the professional level as well. Bob Tway's son, Kevin, won the elite 2005 U.S. Junior Championship as dad anxiously walked in the gallery.

There are so many second- and third -generation success stories that a popular father-son professional event is held every December. Great golfers such as Jack Nicklaus, Gary Player, Dave Stockton, Billy Casper, Hale Irwin, Al Geiberger, Lee Trevino, Johnny Miller, Craig Stadler, and Jay Haas are just a few who pair up with their talented offspring. There is at least a million dollars in prize money, and the Willie Park Trophy and bragging rights for the year are at stake in this made-for-television charity event.

Willie Park was the first winner of the British Open, the world's oldest golf championship. Park won the British Open four times (1860, 1863, 1866 and 1875), and his son, Willie, Jr., won twice (1887 and 1889).

Simple, modest and humble beginnings can be the sparks needed to get the fire burning. Hitting golf balls with your child, playing games taught in a lesson, encouraging your child to practice, enjoying recreational play with a bunch of other kids or simply watching an exciting golf tournament on television or in person can all be great motivators for a child.

When a mom and dad who have never played golf before take golf lessons, begin to play tournaments and return from the golf course smiling and content, it sends a message to the kids that golf is fun to learn and to play. A non-playing parent can also get involved by volunteering with the junior golf association or local golf program. Anything a parent does to get connected to golf is sure to spark the child's interest.

A parent often shows support by walking around the course as a part of the "gallery." It may be tempting to go to the café with a good book for a couple of hours or get some needed errands done, but most children want your undivided attention and enjoy your presence. More advanced players may want you to take notes or keep "stats" for them.

The bottom line is, lessons alone will not get a kid hooked on golf. Practicing with a parent and developing a family connection to golf will. Whether or not the parent is a golfer is not important; what matters is involvement beyond paying for lessons and dropping kids off at the course.

Learn to Handle Loss

At a parent-teacher conference for second-graders, the teacher was asked how parents could help their kids. The wise teacher replied, "Play a lot of games with your kids, and play so they lose."

Why is it important to learn to handle loss? Face it – golf is a game of failure. There is only one champion. Most tournaments have a large field of players all trying to do the same thing – win! Everyone but the eventual champion will get a taste of losing. In an individual sport like golf, the player is solely responsible for his score and has no control over the rest of the field. In actuality, a golfer has no control over anything else – bad breaks, weather changes, course conditions or somebody else doing well. Personal performance has to be a reward in and of itself. A loss not handled well can weigh heavily on a junior's self esteem and enjoyment of the game, but fortunately, golf, unlike other sports, has many ways to reward its players.

Fear of Losing

Curtis Strange said in reference to wanting to get picked for the 1993 Ryder Cup team, "When you start to think about what it means, to really want it, you can't perform."

Most tour players will agree that fear of missing a cut is the best way to ensure you will miss the cut. The best way to remove the fear of failure is to de-emphasize wins and losses, especially in the early years. That means don't over-celebrate a child's wins, and don't go ballistic after a loss. In either case, compliment the child's effort and ask, "What did you learn today?" Be genuine about it; a child can see through cover-ups faster than you can say, "You're away."

The Three Step Solution

Any junior can follow this three-step process in order to handle a loss without feeling like a loser:

1. **Handshake:** Shake hands with your playing partners at the end of every round, regardless of the results.
2. **Cope with losing:** It's okay to be disappointed and a little hurt. After all, a lot of lessons, practice and effort are invested, but every child copes differently. Some sulk, others verbalize, and still others take their minds off a loss by playing a video game or watching television. A parent should let the child work it out. It may be best to simply make a perfunctory remark or two and stay out of it.
3. **Find redeemable qualities in a lost match or a bad tournament:** Losing doesn't destroy self-esteem; the lack of ability to find redeemable qualities in a bad round or a tough loss does. Did you play your best? Did you stay relaxed? Were you focused on one shot at a time? Did you drive the ball or putt well? Did you have many birdie opportunities? Was your short game as good as it had been in practice? Did you keep a good attitude throughout the round? Did your tournament finish help improve your ranking points? Find something positive, and then say, "You're a winner."

None of these things comes easily or naturally to an eight-year-old that has just played poorly in her golf tournament. That's why it's important for parents and coaches to teach young players to handle losses – the earlier the better. Admittedly, there will be times when the child bursts into tears after playing poorly or losing an important match. Relax. Wait a day or two and reinforce the three steps again. Learn how your child wants to deal with loss. Most importantly, help your child deal with losing in a healthy manner. Nancy Lopez's father told her "You can't win all the time. As long as you are doing your best, that's all that really matters." He also told her, "Don't cry – you won't be able to see the golf ball!"

Reward Effort

In many junior team sports, all players are awarded prizes for their participation and effort, regardless of the results. This is a great practice, but is tough to be incorporated into individual sports such as golf. Developmental programs will be more apt to reward kids based simply on participation, but in reality most junior golf tournaments will award winners ranked from first to fifth. Junior golf has become so highly competitive, even in the younger divisions, that kids as young as six get a clear understanding of winning and losing. Anyone 12 and under is still learning to cope with losing, so be mindful of your reactions. Boy or girl, there may be tears.

Parents need to come up with their own reward system for their child. Far from rewarding mediocrity or explaining why every player deserved an award, even though some may have a higher score, help your child learn to measure accomplishments in improvements and effort rather than simply in wins and losses. Besides, in a sanctioned tournament, players are motivated to play their best because they earn ranking points. Show your child how tournament golf differs from recreational golf. For junior tournaments, only the top five players, and sometimes only the top three, receive a trophy or any recognition. Explain how professional golfers are paid only if they make the cut. Teach them to take joy from the game and the experience, not necessarily their accomplishments or achievements.

Parent-child Practice

Handling a loss can be practiced in an emotionally safe environment. A parent-child session is as safe as it can get. The objective is for the child to practice match play with a bigger, better player, learn to handle loss and find ways to improve.

First, promise you will not say, "Susie, let's go play some golf and I'll teach you how to lose." You're going to be more subtle than that, or perhaps you'll simply keep the game plan to yourself. Admit it – it's frightening to take your 10-year-old to the putting green, knowing she has no chance and that you're about to beat her mercifully. So remember to carry her favorite Jelly Belly. You'll need it.

You can make the match as even as possible, though, by handicapping. In the beginning, learn to adjust your daughter's par to her playing ability. If she can only hit the ball 80 yards consistently, then a hole that is 150 yards must be at least a par-4, giving her two shots to hit the green and two putts. If only her best shots go 80 yards, but she averages 60 yards, you might make it a par-5 at first to build her confidence, giving her three shots to reach the green. The first time she makes a "birdie 4," you have instilled a sense of confidence that can only come from success. As she improves and you find she is beating you all the time because she is now consistently making easy birdies, you adjust the par accordingly. There may come a day when her handicap is lower than yours and she has to give you strokes. Another fun way to play is with mom restricted to playing the hole with only one club, while your daughter gets to play normal.

Match play is fun, and it gives your child many opportunities for victory. In golf, because there are 18 holes on a course, your kid has a chance to beat you at least 18 times. In the beginning you might win more often, giving your child a great environment to practice handling loss. If you play your cards right, the tables will turn and one day you will be the one learning to deal with losing. Parent-child match play doesn't have to take place just on the golf course either. You can set up fun matches at the putting green and chipping area as well. Give yourself ample opportunity to say, "Susie, you haven't failed, you just haven't succeeded.....YET!"

Some parents use monetary rewards to get their kids' attention. Every time your daughter chips it closer to the hole than you do, she earns a quarter. Every time she gets it up and down with one chip and one putt, you might reward her, but tell her every time she three-putts, she owes you! In the beginning, you may have to de-emphasize the results and put rewards toward her efforts. Help her find improvements in her game and set a modest goal for the next match – to win one more hole than the previous match. Kid her a little and stir up some competitiveness. Your goal is to unlock her competitive spirit, which will in turn motivate her to practice. Continue to teach her to replay her good shots and to go over what she did right, even if she loses – especially when she loses. Train her to replay a putt she made or a sensational shot. Emphasize how she never gives up and how you admire her determination. If possible, give her hope and a sense she is close to beating you. If the game is handicapped and she is badly beating you consistently, give her the news and satisfaction that you will have to re-adjust the game to make it fair for you! Tell her you are giving it all you can, but to play fairly, you'll have to change the game. Pick a formula that will allow her to compete hard. Reward effort.

Learning by Watching

Walking, running, opening doors and climbing stairs – a child learns new things every day just by watching Mommy and Daddy. Now replace Mommy (just for a little while!) with a Patty Sheehan SyberVision video. SyberVision golf instruction uses observation, rhythm, repeated images, enhanced computer models, slow motion, and music to enable you to consistently duplicate the variety of shots being demonstrated. Sheehan demonstrates all the fundamentals in this golf video as she hits her driver, fairway wood, a long iron, a short iron, pitch shots, sand shots, chips and putts.

Can a child learn the game watching a video? It's an interesting thought, though it's doubtful players can sufficiently develop this way alone.

Training Videos

Golf involves more complex human motions than an exercise like walking. There is a lot more to golf than just repetitive motion – strategy, for example. But we know many recreational players study training videos and picture books and become pretty good competitors. Greg Norman, the "Great White Shark," studied two Jack Nicklaus instructional books ("Golf My Way" and "55 Ways to Learn Golf") given to him by his mother. Within two years, he was a scratch golfer. Training videos can be great teaching aids for juniors as well because they can slow down the swing frame by frame. Video is great because it captures the swing in motion, something still photographs can't do.

Fortunately, there are a variety of good instructional videos made by teaching gurus David Leadbeter, Butch Harmon, Jim McClean and Rick Smith. Ben Crenshaw's "*The Art of Putting*" is a classic, and David Pelz has a few specific to putting and the short game as well. Children's videos are limited and are directed at a very young audience. These are great to peak interest, but for mimicking, kids will benefit from watching anything that demonstrates a quality golf swing.

Quality golf videos can help a coach become a better instructor and help your child better understand her swing, correct common mistakes, practice more efficiently and play more consistently. Videos can help even a non-playing parent appreciate what the pro is teaching and give him a better understanding of how the child is performing technically.

Television

Try this experiment. Let your kid watch a stockcar race on television for about an hour. Immediately head to the garage with your junior, and, without actually starting the car, plunk him on the driver's side of the parked car. Guess what? More than likely, he'll make an aggressive go at the steering wheel just like he watched the drivers do on television.

On a less dangerous note, get the junior interested in watching an exciting professional golf tournament on television. Children learn by subconscious absorption of visual images, so they don't need much explanation. The 24- hour Golf Channel now affords viewers many different types of tournaments. Keep an eye out for the elite junior events or an exciting NCAA tournament. Your child might say, "Hey, I would like to try that!" or "Wow! That looks like fun – I could do that."

In addition to keeping an eye on the scoreboard or the glamorous celebrities that might be mucking it up, it's fun to watch while pretending to be the roving reporter. Key portions of the telecast worth paying attention to include:

- Player's rhythm and timing
- Player's club selection
- Player's preparation, including pre-shot routine
- Player's short-game expertise
- Player's focus and intense concentration
- How players get themselves out of trouble

- Recognizing that even great players can find themselves in trouble
- Comments from the experts.

To learn from watching televised matches, one has to be an active, thinking participant in the game. Once again, remember that young children have extremely limited attention spans, so don't be surprised or annoyed when your youngster wanders in and out of the television room. Some telecasts are even hard for an adult to sit through.

The plus side of television drama is that it is all neatly packaged for you. Your kid doesn't have to fight the galleries. She has a clear view of all of the leaders and usually the best golf of the day. Television gives you the opportunity to see many different players spread out in several different groups without dragging your child on a 15-mile hike as you scurry from one group to another trying to keep up with the action. It was television and the worldwide broadcast of the 1971 Masters that got 13 year-old Nick Faldo hooked on golf. Thousands of miles and several time zones away, the athletic teenager was mesmerized by "Big Jack" Nicklaus and the rolling fairways of Augusta National. Charles Coody won the green jacket that day, but the seed had been sown as far away as England. The magic of television worked for this champion – 18 years later, the lad from Hertfordshire had gone on to win his own green jacket. His dreams have been expanded over the years, and he actually owns three green jackets. He also has won three magnificent Claret Jugs – the award given to the British Open champion, or as Faldo and the rest of Europe call it The Open Championship. Six majors – not bad from a dream ignited in front of the telly.

Tournaments

Some people swear by the aura created by walking the fairways with the game's best. Professional tournaments can be very exciting. Others prefer the close-ups and ball smacks as seen and heard on high-definition television. Standing next to John Daly on the tee box offers nuances that cannot be seen on television. For instance, Daly's club head speed is intensified when a kid is standing on the tee box. The anticipation of a ball just clearing the hazard or falling into the cup can get lost in the airwaves at times. The momentum change felt with a drained putt or a changing leader board often moves through the gallery. Nasty lies, gnarly rough and wicked bounces from too much spin or a bad kick all come alive for an intense gallery. In person, your daughter can sense how far Laura Davies and Michelle Wie really hit it. Tom Kite was 11 years old when he went to his first professional tournament, the Dallas Open. By the time he got home, he knew he wanted to turn pro.

Golf aside, soaking up the hustle and bustle of a tournament can be a wonderful family experience. On a lucky day, Annika Sorenstam will sign an autograph for your little girl as she reaches out to the girl wonder heading for the press room – a memory of a lifetime for your little one. Personalities come alive. The players are real. Dreams are realities.

Effective Practice

Grown-ups practice to improve; kids practice to have fun. Understand this and there should be no problem getting your 10-year-old to the driving range.

Make a Plan and Stick to It

"Practice with a purpose" may be an overused phrase, but it is so true. Practicing without a plan encourages players to repeat only their best shots, overlooking weaknesses in their game. In the beginning, practice the drills and games taught in class. Once junior has begun playing tournaments, have the coach suggest a plan to enhance her strengths and improve her weaknesses.

Stick to the practice plan. During their junior years, many players have gone through what they might later call a grip crisis. A lot of juniors get started with a baseball grip because it is most comfortable for their small hands, and many pick up golf after a stint in Little League baseball. Even after a few lessons, kids tend to revert to a strong grip – too strong. Talented kids with good hand-eye coordination and good feel will play well in spite of this "dangerous" flaw. PGA Tour champion Paul Azinger has had an amazing career with what most experts will now kindly call "an unorthodox grip." He worked relentlessly to produce a swing that will repeat under pressure. He didn't let naysayers deter him from his plan. One might say he operated under the philosophy of not "How does it look", but "Does it work?"

Other professionals have heeded expert opinion and have waded through the difficult process of making a grip change. Some, like touring professional Billy Andrade, suffer with grace as their games get worse before they get better. He knew he had to make the change if he wanted a future in golf. The experience can be traumatizing, but the key is to stick with it when times get tough. Experts may disagree on many swing issues, but most will agree that it is extremely difficult to succeed without a sound grip and stance. It is easier for your child to make changes early on in a career versus trying to change something she has spent hours and hours ingraining.

Unwaveringly commit to changes in fundamentals such as grip, posture and alignment. Encourage your child to practice until the uncomfortable becomes more comfortable. Old habits are hard enough to break when there is no pressure to perform – give your child some room for failure. Good teaching professionals will assess the limitations created by a flaw and give your child a long-term plan for change. It might take a year of practice to develop competency in the new technique. PGA Tour player Billy Andrade got the support of his Wake Forest golf coach, Jesse Haddock, and made his grip change during the winter months. Haddock encouraged him to stick with it and assured him he would not lose his spot on the team. Andrade was not afraid to use it in competition, and by spring was feeling better about the adjustment. Although he was nervous about the change, he stuck to his plan.

Repetition is key when making big changes in the swing, setup or putting stroke. Jeff Troesch says, "It is a player's goal to become consciously competent. This means they know why they are good. Many players have streaks of brilliance, but they have a hard time repeating their success because they are unconsciously competent. In the beginning, most golfers are unconsciously incompetent, meaning they have no idea of why they aren't any good. Players will generally then move to the next phase, being consciously incompetent. This is when they know why they aren't very good. Better players get stuck in the unconsciously competent stage, never understanding why they perform well at times." The goal is to consciously change actual technique until it is built into muscle memory. Experts suggest concentrating on a problem area for at least a two-week period. Suggested improvements should be practiced during every practice session. Although it is difficult, changes should be played in tournaments as well.

How Much, How Often?

Given a child's limited attention span, it's best to limit practice sessions to 40-60 minutes with frequent breaks. In any case, stop while your kid is still interested. The one thing experts agree on is that children burn out if they are being made to practice by someone else and it's not fun. Otherwise, kids really can't spend too much time playing and practicing golf!

No one can say how often to practice. Davis Love II recalled telling his sons, "I would practice until my hands bled when I was a kid." Davis Love III tells how he would practice for hours, and then go ask his father when his hands were going to bleed. "'Not for a long time yet, son', Dad would say."

Most professionals fondly remember the early days – thousands of hours spent on the driving range, putting and chipping green, standing mesmerized in front of a glass window, or playing with their shadows when they weren't golf course accessible.

There is a long list of champions who will tell you they are grinders, never to be out-practiced by their competition. Legend Sam Snead recalls, "For as long as I have played golf, I have never laid off for more than a few days at a time."

While kids don't necessarily need bloody hands, your child will definitely have callused hands if she is putting the work in necessary to play competitively. Basically, the more hours of effective practice one puts into golf, the more one gets out of it. Be wary of repetitive motion injuries. Every player has to come up with her own practice schedule based on personal goals, commitment and level of interest. The key is it has to be your child's desire to practice for extended periods of time.

Some coaches say a junior who wants to begin competing in tournaments within a year may need about four to six hours on the practice tee per week. This includes private lessons, group clinics, practice sessions and course time. A good rule of thumb is that your child should be putting in at least three hours of practice for every one hour of instruction.

Practice Program

Parents often have to come up with creative ways to make practice fun and, at the same time, achieve a specific objective. Here are guidelines from the professionals that will make practice effective and interesting:

Seven universal principles that make up entire game

1. **Technique** - Swing and putting mechanics are not the only techniques that must be learned. A player must have a solid understanding of a good grip, proper posture and alignment, good balance with proper weight transfer and swing plane theories. All these fundamentals in and of themselves will not make you a good golfer without good rhythm and timing. Tempo is key to success, no matter the technique.
2. **Equipment** – Having properly fitted clubs and a basic understanding of simple club-fitting principles. Knowing what golf ball is best for them.
3. **Practice Programs** – Having clear-cut plans and specific goals set forth by student and professional. "Failing to prepare, is preparing to fail."
4. **Specialty Shots** – Understanding different ball-flight laws. Learning to practice and experiment with the unusual and the extraordinary golf shots – buried bunker shots; uphill, downhill and side-hill lies; knock-down shots; how to fade and draw the ball around trees.

5. **Mental Game** – Preparing your mind to be focused and clear. Positive imagery and mental rehearsal of the game at hand and for the future. Learning to stay in the moment, dealing with pressures of success and failure. Positive self- talk and affirmations.
6. **Physical Conditioning** – Strength training. Knowing when to push and when to back off. Learning to peak.
7. **Nutrition** – What foods can best prepare them to tackle principles 1-6 efficiently. How specific foods may be affecting their performance. The importance of hydration.

Strong and weak points: Make your weaknesses your strengths over time. Be objective. Don't overlook problems like too many missed fairways while focusing on yardage only. Your daughter might say she is a great putter since she rarely three-putts, but she doesn't make many birdies either. Are evaluations honest and accurate?

Over-practice: Giving it your all is a great attribute. You never want your kid to be a quitter, but players have to know when to turn their golf game off. Most players need to recognize fatigue, both mental and physical. Once again, be wary of injuries by limiting practice to short periods. She should mix up her practice to keep herself fresh. Experts also advise not to over-practice the day before a tournament or match. A player's game will ebb and flow – prepare to peak at the right time.

Incorporate mental elements: Simulate tough match situations, and practice playing in a relaxed and focused state. The player needs a par to force a tie, or needs a birdie to win. It is essential to practice needing a tricky four-foot putt to win. She should imagine needing to get up and down to win the U.S. Amateur.

Spice it up: Your child's coach should help her incorporate fun games into her practice routine. She can work on a drill or a technique change, but then she should incorporate her change into "game" situations and have fun trying to improve while using what she has learned. Keep practice fun, challenging, and exciting.

Specific short-term goals: Develop goals that are process -oriented rather than overly results-oriented. Instead of always relating to par, look for other areas of the game to measure progress. For example, did she have fewer putts today? Hit more greens? Hit the middle irons better? Get up and down from the bunker? Find several parts of her game she can be congratulated on.

Measuring Progress

"Great, yesterday you hit seven out of 14 fairways, and today you hit 10. That's wonderful improvement. Good work!" This is positive, encouraging feedback, but be careful not to "over monitor" her game.

Your child doesn't want to be critiqued every time she tees it up. If she has to "measure up" every time she plays, she will be on an emotional roller coaster. If a parent needs to measure success or failure all the time, the child is going to be under immeasurable stress and get lots of mixed messages – there will be no joy in the game. Eventually, she will want to get off this no-win emotional roller coaster.

When you were a kid, how would you have liked it if your teacher prepared a daily report card for you and discussed weaknesses and strengths with you every single day? By all means monitor your child's progress, but do it discreetly. Tournaments are great for measuring progress in all areas of the game. Practice plans should be put together with a goal at least three weeks out.

A parent's primary role at practice is to reinforce the coach's instruction and to simply be an extra pair of eyes to help the child see if she is making progress with technique and preparation. Keeping statistics is important, but you need to be careful not to report in day after day with your findings. Within a few hours of finishing a round or a tournament, you may make her aware of her stats, but you do not want your child dreading that she will be the main topic of conversation at dinner every night. The same is true if you go to her practice sessions; you are not to be at practice as an expert judge, monitoring her results. Let's say that again – **do not judge result**s. When you do discuss your child's golf, highlight the good practice just as much as or more than analyzing a difficult day. Discuss observations with the coach, not with your child. Let the coach figure out how and when to move the child to the next level.

In the beginning you may record all observations; however, your goal is to teach your child to record her observations, either on-course or immediately after practice in a workbook or electronic handheld device. There is great software available to help you organize your child's statistics. There are dozens of websites available providing professional golf analysis software and golf analysis services. (More info: golfstatdoctor.com, ezstat.com, and caddiemaster.com) Round-file notebooks are available in most golf shops.

Your child should learn to record:
1. The date played
2. The course played
3. Tournament or non-tournament round situation and playing partners
4. Weather conditions
5. General comments about round (strange rulings, penalty shots, felt sick, etc.)
6. Specific information about every hole, such as club selected and the outcome of the shot (left, right, short, long)

7. Fairways hit and where (left, center, middle)
8. Greens hit in regulation
9. Percentage of up-and-downs
10. Length of putts attempted, and putts made.

It should be mandatory that your mature child learns to keep notes of her lessons and record observations about every round. Every 5-10 rounds, she should do an evaluation with her coach. Teach her to chart her progress. golfscorekeeper.com, caddiemaster.com and golf-scoretracker.co.uk are all great resources for software.

Playing Partner

Until a child is capable of carrying her own bag, knows and uses proper etiquette and has a basic understanding of fundamental rules, it is best for her to practice with a parent. Other family members or family friends who play golf can serve as a backup when you can't make it to practice. For anyone playing golf with your child, good character, discipline, loads of patience and a sense of humor are qualifications as important as golf skills.

Instead of always practicing alone, you can hold group practice with kids from the same golf class, supervised by a grownup. That way, a group of parents can share supervision. Remember that the goal of practice is to repeat and reinforce what has been taught in class, so even a parent with reasonable skills is fine.

Partners and Pairings

Handling a loss can be practiced in an emotionally safe environment. A parent-child session is as safe as it can get. The objective is for the child to practice match play with a bigger, better player, learn to handle loss and find ways to improve.

First, promise you will not say, "Susie, let's go play some golf and I'll teach you how to lose." You're going to be more subtle than that, or perhaps you'll simply keep the game plan to yourself. Admit it – it's frightening to take your 10-year-old to the putting green, knowing she has no chance and that you're about to beat her mercilessly. So remember to carry her favorite Jelly Belly. You'll need it.

You can make the match as even as possible, though, by handicapping. In the beginning, learn to adjust your daughter's par to her playing ability. If he she can only hit the ball 80 yards consistently, then a hole that is 150 yards must be at least a par-4, giving her two shots to hit the green and two putts. If only her best shots go 80 yards, but she averages 60 yards, you might make it a par-5 at first to build her confidence, giving her three shots to reach the green. The first time she makes a "birdie 4," you have instilled a sense of confidence that can only come from success. As she improves and you find she is beating you all the time because she is now consistently making easy birdies, you adjust the par accordingly. There may come a day when her handicap is lower than yours and she has to give you strokes. Another fun way to play is with mom restricted to playing the hole with only one club, while your daughter gets to play normal.

Some parents use monetary rewards to get their kids' attention. Every time your daughter chips it closer to the hole than you do, she earns a quarter. Every time she gets it up and down with one chip and one putt, you might reward her, but tell her every time she three-putts, she owes you! In the beginning, you may have to de-emphasize the results and put rewards toward her efforts. Help her find improvements in her game and set a modest goal for the next match – to win one more hole than the previous match. Kid her a little and stir up some competitiveness. Your goal is to unlock her competitive spirit, which will in turn motivate her to practice. Continue to teach her to replay her good shots and to go over what she did right, even if she loses – especially when she loses. Train her to replay a putt she made or a sensational shot. Emphasize how she never gives up and how you admire her determination. If possible, give her hope and a sense she is close to beating you. If the game is handicapped and she is badly beating you consistently, give her the news and satisfaction that you will have to re-adjust the game to make it fair for you! Tell her you are giving it all you can, but to play fairly, you'll have to change the game. Pick a formula that will allow her to compete hard. Reward effort.

Team Play

In general, golf is not a team sport. Although most everything golf professionals strive for revolves around personal goals and achievements, being a member of the Ryder Cup team is one of the most highly held honors in their lives. National pride and the idea of coming through for your teammates can drum up more emotional turmoil than trying to clinch a first major. While your daughter might not yet carry the pressure of winning for her nation in the Junior Solheim Cup, an event that proceeds the Ladies Solheim Cup, she may find herself in position to birdie her last hole to win one for her school, her city or her state.

There are occasions when your junior may find herself part of a team. The obvious team scenario would be the aforementioned school golf team. She will be required to play and practice with her team during the school's golf season. There may be a wide variety of talents on her team. Her goal is to stay focused on her game and strive to become the best individual player she can become. Her best play will enhance her team, but she will never be solely responsible for a win or a loss. Distractions in practice will be her nemesis. Reinforce the fact that her practice time is vital to her game and that she should not succumb to goofing off or wasting time. Disciplined practice can be extremely difficult in team situations, but it is essential to a player wanting to progress.

Another form of team play might come at the advanced junior level of play. Certain geographic regions may have a team that arranges matches against other regions in the area. Over the years, there have been many interesting team events staged around the world. At one time the Taiwan Junior Golf Federation hosted a team of San Diego junior golfers to participate in a cultural exchange and team-play tournament.

Players usually qualify to play on a team by earning points in designated events. The Girls' Junior America's Cup, founded in 1978, is a tournament that brings together 18 teams from golf associations all over the western part of the United States, Mexico and Canada. The Boys' Junior America's Cup and the Girls' Junior America's Cup are separate events, held at different locations and on different dates. The philosophy of both tournaments has always been to bring kids together from various states and countries to cultivate new friendships and mutual respect and to promote better understanding of regional history and customs. The tournament is hosted by a different golf association each year and promotes learning about different cultures while demonstrating through golf that players are actually more alike than different.

The American Junior Golf Association (AJGA) top point winners are eligible for special team events such as the East vs. West Canon Cup. The top eight boys and eight girls east of the Mississippi River and eight boys and eight girls west of the Mississippi River are selected to represent their regions and battle it out against one another in an exciting event. The east captain and the west captain pick two more girls and two more boys to complete their teams. Most team play is for juniors in the 15-17-year-old divisions, but there are a few exceptions.

Younger kids get a taste of team camaraderie and sportsmanship at the U.S. Kids' Golf World Championships, held in Williamsburg, Virginia at the Golden Horseshoe Golf Club, the Williamsburg National Golf Club and Kingsmill Golf Resort. The event hosts seven hundred young golfers from around the world and all fifty states. The kids compete in an exciting four-day event, nationally televised on Thanksgiving on Fox Sports Network. During summer, each state holds a state championship tournament with a limited field of 24 players per age group. The individual winners of each age group advance to the World Championship to compete in a two-day stroke play competition, a one-day skills competition, a press day and exciting opening and closing ceremonies. Although the kids earn their way there individually, they are also part of a team competition. Each team total is based on a point system in which teams are awarded points determined by each player's order of finish in their age group.

The highest honor for a male amateur player comes in being asked to play in the Walker Cup. For your daughter, it would be to be asked to join the Curtis Cup Team. Both of these teams are not usually made up of juniors, but while it is rare, an outstanding junior could be invited.

Unorthodox Practice

Seve Ballesteros, a five time major winner, found his golf groove hitting balls with a cut down 3-iron along the sandy beach by his home in Spain. Judging from his amazing flair and Houdini-like ways of recovery, those early days on the beach prepared him to hit a golf ball from anywhere.

Practice away from a course can stimulate a player's imagination and force her to create golf shots beyond her wildest dreams. There isn't a hole or scorecard to remind her that she failed – she has complete freedom to experiment and to be creative. The mind can be used as an amazing canvas if allowed to move away from stringent boundaries, creating infinite possibilities and outcomes. She is allowed to learn by trial and error. Phil Mickelson, a master of the short game, spent hours as a kid making up golf shots in his backyard chipping area.

This kind of creative practice, however, should be encouraged only after your youngster has a good idea of the basic fundamentals. Repeating an imperfect technique or a bad habit on one's own will only make it harder to improve. Putting tracks are great for helping your daughter get consistency with her putting stroke. Fun swing aids may help her develop consistency in her swing. Swing fans or swing poles (weighted poles can be inexpensively purchased at a hardware store) will help her strength development. An impact bag is great to have around the house, inspiring her to increase her clubhead speed. You can make a cheap one by taking an old duffel bag and stuffing it full with sand and old towels, or you can purchase that and many other fun golf aids at a store. (More info: golfaroundtheworld.com.

Right Way

Unorthodox practice doesn't mean your child should be developing unorthodox habits. If fans or poles are too heavy, they will cause her to put unnecessary strain on her arms and elbows. She may also get used to swinging on an incorrect path for her size and stature.

Practicing putts on carpet may help with changing a stroke issue, but it will not address a speed of green problem. Gripping the clubhead and swinging the butt end of the club to hear the sound of the wind is a great practice to warm up and learn to time the release properly, but it's not a drill in clubhead feel. Remember that there are three different areas a child will turn her attention to when training the right way. Separately, she may be focused in on technique, tempo or target. Here are some tips to help practice correctly:

- Practice should always have a purpose.
- Practice can be done anywhere.
- Target training is key – use powdered circles to help highlight success and room for improvement.
- Always have targets when practicing on the driving range. Mix 'em up! Use clubs on the ground or training aids to help with alignment.
- Create her own shag bag from used golf balls.
- Draw lines on the putter and on balls to help identify target lines and proper roll of golf ball.
- Use face tape on clubs to determine whether or not the ball is being hit on the sweet spot.
- Use a removable tape to mark landing areas for chipping and pitching.
- Repetition is good for learning, but must practice a lot with "one shot" mentality as well.
- Play ball out of tough lies.
- Use actual pre-shot routines and don't hit a shot until ready.
- Make practice competitive whenever possible.

And, as always, remember advice given by golf greats Arnold Palmer and Jack Nicklaus. Palmer said, "Practice is the only golf advice that is good for everybody." Nicklaus said, "One must practice with a plan."

Practice Plan

Practice plans or schedules are important for any golfer- good habits can be developed early on and modified as your child develops. Beginners need to understand that improvement comes with practice and juniors who are excited about the game and desire to get better need to understand that their practice is paramount to their success. If properly trained as a beginner and intermediate player, an advanced and national-level competitor should be prepared for intense practice schedules and greater time commitments when the time comes. It is important for your junior to understand that there is always something he can be improving and working on and that golf is a time intensive sport. Your child's coach should be able to help you develop a manageable practice schedule that will work best for your family.

For example, at the national level, there should be time devoted to every aspect of the short game, long game, course management, specialty shots, routines, mental prep, physical fitness and strength conditioning. Many things need to be scheduled into the routine or too often they get left out of your child's training. A beginner might only putt for 15 minutes once a week, while a more eager junior will average more like an hour of putting practice during the week. An advanced or ranked player might devote four or five times that towards her putting. Advanced players will need to read more and spend more time preparing themselves for competition where beginners are still managing more simple and basic objectives. During the school year kids need to be diligent about carving out practice time since so many other areas of life also vie for attention. Time management is a great life skill and junior golfers who pay attention to this are better prepared at each level of development. Summer schedules are less academically demanding, but tournament golf may require more time than school. It is not uncommon for juniors with high ambitions to spend 8-10 hours each day at the golf course during their summer months. Your golfer, with the coach's help, should be making her schedule- parents should not be demanding a rigorous practice schedule just for the sake of having one.

Schedule time for:

- **Putting**
- **Short Game**
  - Chipping
  - Pitching
  - Lob shots
- **Irons**
  - Short
  - Mid
  - Long
- **Woods**
  - Fairway
  - Driver
- **Course Play**
- **Course**

- **Bunker Play**
  - Green side
  - Fairway
- **Specialty shots**
  - Uphill/Downhill Lies
  - Flop shots/ Backspin
  - Difficult lie shots
  - Hook/Slice around objects
- **Management**
- **Scoring**
- **Mental Game**
- **Physical Fitness**
- **Lessons**
- **Down Time, REST**

Times Not To Practice

1. Do not let your child practice when she is overly tired. Fatigue makes people sloppy. It also creates an environment ripe for errors, creating a loss of confidence.

2. Do not let your child practice when she has lost interest. Bad habits will creep in when your child has an "I don't care" attitude.

3. Playing in bad weather conditions for prolonged periods can cause your daughter to alter her swing. However, it is good to expose kids in small doses to the game in windy, rainy and cold conditions. This will help them be better prepared for future less than perfect playing conditions.

4. Do not let your child practice if she is really struggling with her game and it seems progress is a way off. It might be more damaging to let her continue than to pull her away for the day. Encourage her that tomorrow is another day and sometimes all she may need is a fresh start. Frustration is one state that nobody can perform in.

Drills and Games

Hitting on the range doesn't have to be monotonous. There are literally dozens of games one can play to keep practice interesting and productive. Practicing golf should be a myriad of games within a game. Games will help keep kids from getting too mechanical. Kids can simulate play against anyone, but of course it's usually them and the top player of the day paired together, dueling it out in their imaginary round.

Tom Watson's "How to Get Up and Down from 40 Yards and In" is and excellent resource for short-game drills. Good instructional books and videos are filled with fun games and drills to help keep practice interesting.

Practice and Perfection

So your junior has perfected a slice. Anything can be ingrained if practiced enough. There are three ways to groove a shot – practice, practice and more practice. Dr. Bob Rotella says, "The biggest canard in golf is that practice makes perfect." Perfect practice won't even guarantee perfection in golf, but theoretically it will get a player closer to mastering her performance. The goal with practice is to be aware of what you are practicing at all times. Effective practice will move your child closer to her goals. Strong golf requires strong character and strong discipline, especially as one practices. It takes patience not to just hit ball after ball going the wrong direction. It takes fortitude to look for a feeling that isn't quite right, a move to change. To practice in a sloppy manner is to guarantee sloppy play. Golfers will always make mistakes, no matter how much they practice. Kids at the highest levels of competition these days acknowledge that personal awareness and practicing techniques the right way will increase skill. As their skills increase, chance decreases. One would think that because there is always an element of chance involved, perfection would be impossible. While Tiger Woods and Annika Sorenstam are inspiring a generation of golfers to practice properly and showing that golfers are getting closer to the perfect score, there are many more golfers who have become too self-critical and are destroying their games with unreal expectations.

It's vital from the start to learn proper technique from a pro or someone who is knowledgeable. Otherwise, the player will end up reinforcing a bad stroke hundreds of times. Pick specific things to work on, and feel the relationship of certain body movements to where the ball is going during a practice session. Your child needs to learn to read the golf ball and have a good understanding of cause and effect. The sooner your child can learn the ball-flight laws and understand their language, the easier it will be for her to self correct and adjust accordingly. In the beginning stages of learning golf, your child's adjustments might be big ones. Golf at the highest level is simply a game of very slight adjustments.

> **Practice doesn't make perfect, but not practicing won't get her closer either**

Players of the 21st century seem to be determined to break boundaries like never before, closing in on what could be equivalent to the perfect game in baseball. Before 1980, there had only been one player to shoot a tournament score of 59, 13 under par; and only a handful of others to shoot 60. Like Roger Maris and the broken four- minute mile mentality, lately, it seems that players are constantly shooting in the low 60s. In the early 1970s, it was Johnny Miller who was always threatening to go low, captivating the world by shooting 63 in the final round of the 1973 U.S. Open. Then in the mid 80s it was Greg Norman who was always lurking around, capable of firing really low numbers, shaking up the leaderboards week in and week out. The emergence of Tiger Woods and the demands for excellence have created a whole new standard of play from both professionals and the game's new generation of players.

With the new millennium there have been a couple of unofficial 58s and a handful of players to match Al Geiberger's record score of 59. It is quite obvious a new standard has been set. Annika Sorenstam is the only woman to have shot 59 and has publicly declared it is her goal to shoot 54 – it has become her mantra and the mantra of many. This new generation of golfers sees no boundaries. To them, eighteen birdies is an attainable goal. They are programming themselves for perfection. It's fantastic that new frontiers are being discovered on the fairways, and we should never steal anyone else's dreams. However, your child needs to proceed carefully down any road marked "To Perfection" and take heed of the simple truths described in the titles of two of Dr. Rotella's books – "Golf Is Not a Game of Perfect" and "Golf Is a Game of Confidence."

Easing into Competition

Fun is the name of the game for most children under 10 years old. Children are showing interest in competing sooner, but a lot of that is because parents are pushing more. There are plenty of tournaments available for the 10-and-under crowd, but be careful not to push your child into competition before she is emotionally ready. It is best to introduce a child to competition, evaluate a child's response to the pressure and proceed with caution. Early success may stimulate interest and motivate practice, but early failure can be devastating and is more likely going to turn your kid away from golf. It is OK to let a child start competing as late as 13 or 14, but she should be prepared to tee it up with kids with several years of tournament golf under their belts. Some children need to be at least 13 to 14 years of age to have the maturity needed for serious competition with peers. In the interim, if the child continues to show enthusiasm for golf, it is appropriate to transition from fun and games to light competition.

Learning about Competition

It doesn't matter whether a parent or coach had the opportunity to discuss the meaning and nature of competition with the child. Children learn about winning, losing and competition from many other sources. Kids get an early sense of competition in the classroom. Teachers and parents alike reward good grades. No matter how hard you try to keep the emphasis on fun and games, children quickly begin to pick up on the competitive nature of sport. As long as there is less emphasis on winning and losing, children begin to thrive on competition.

The more time a grown-up spends with a child on the course playing and match play, the easier it will be for the child to transition from drills and games to competing with peers. She should learn that it's OK to lose and OK to win. A child can also understand this from watching tournaments on television. Point out how a pro can hit a terrible shot, yet still win a tournament if he keeps his composure.

Show kids how players who missed the cut a week ago are in contention to win this week. Explain how tour players who lost their playing privileges worked hard and regained them again through qualifying school. Always highlight the success stories. Unfortunately, golf is one of the only sports in which most fans root for the favorite player. In any case, show your child how golfers display great sportsmanship.

First Competition

No format is better than the parent-child format to ease a kid into formal competition. Fun charity scrambles on shorter courses are a good place to start. Kids will feel like they can contribute to the success of the team, and yet they don't feel the pressure when they miss hit a shot. This type of a parent-child introduction to competition is like striking two birds with one golf ball. The child earns his first participation wings under the emotional safety of a parent-partner. On the other hand, the parent gains an appreciation for his child's efforts and the stage she's in. It is a delicate time for any new golfer.

Parents should be trying to avoid negative experiences associated with competition. It is essential to create positive experiences whenever possible. If a child gets the idea that she is too far behind the competition to ever catch up, she will be overwhelmed with insecurities. If dwelled upon, these thoughts can destroy a child before she ever gets started. At some point, she has to be willing to jump in if she eventually wants to compete. This is why it is so important for kids to play games and practice competition with parents. Putting contests, bunker contests, chipping and pitching contests – kids can't get enough of these games. Be courteous, but always play to win.

4
Fun to Fiery

"The original objective in golf – put the ball in the hole."
Author unknown

Winning is not everything, but winning is important. To keep this in perspective, remember that enjoyment of the game comes first, and then everything else – including winning.

Junior's beginner class is structured around fun and games. For little Michael, simply attending the class is fun. After a few years of golf lessons, he gets in the groove and becomes more proficient. At this time, the opportunity to participate and hang out with friends is a sufficient incentive. Approaching the adolescent years, Michael develops additional motivators – competition and the desire to win.

The natural desire to compete and win ought to be accepted. A kid who steadily improves is likely to want to continue to play and see where his talents will take him. Acceptance of the natural desire to win, as opposed to emphasizing and pushing for a win, is in line with sports psychologists who advise parents to de-emphasize wins and losses.

Learning to Win

Learning to win starts off the course, with learning to learn. Hall of Fame professional Louise Suggs said, "The most important factor in becoming an accomplished golfer is the urge to play the game and to play it well."

Winning not only requires giving your all during the round – more important, it means giving maximum effort preparing for the tournament. Start by becoming aware of your current strengths and weaknesses. Shut out unnecessary objectives, and practice focusing on a few critical ones. Jack Nicklaus was driven by his desire to be the best he could be. He didn't get caught up in the results; he was more interested in the process. "There's no reason not to be prepared," Nicklaus said. "Being prepared gives you confidence. Couple that with being patient, disciplined, and understanding your abilities. You never know what's going to happen when you start playing for real, but at least if you're prepared to do your best, that's all anyone can ask of you."

Raising the Bar

In "Training a Tiger," Earl Woods clearly depicts how he deliberately led Tiger through every phase of development. Tiger eagerly met each challenge and learned to be the best at each level of competition before he set his sights on the next level. Many kids get ahead of themselves and want to skip a few rungs on the ladder. In the end, the desire to take a shortcut will short-circuit your son's career. Your child should be competitive and win a few times at the local level before putting him in tougher fields on the national level.

In golf, players are competing against a field of other golfers, but more important, they are playing against the course. Your son could be winning tournaments all summer long shooting 77s, but there is a kid in the middle of the state who doesn't get to compete much who is shooting 70 every time he tees it up on his tough home course. Both boys have a challenge. Your son needs to lower his score no matter the competition, and the other young man needs to get to a "playing field" to hone his competitive skills.

If there are not a lot of tournaments around for your child to play in, you need to set goals against the course. The goal should be to watch the handicap drop like a rock. Compete whenever possible. It is best to put pressure on him and get him used to competition, so if that means throwing him into the men's club, do it. Challenge your child by taking him to difficult courses and making him play from the back tees. More important, have him play an easy layout and see how low he can go. He needs to get comfortable making birdies.

If it is his goal to compete at the highest level possible, don't sacrifice golf development at the altar of easy wins. Often a kid loses motivation to improve, and sometimes even to play if he isn't constantly challenged. If your son is by far the best player on his high school team, beating his nearest competition by five strokes or more every time he tees it up, don't let him get caught up in his victories. Challenge him to reach self-improvement goals every time he goes out with the guys. Otherwise, he will get a false confidence and his game won't stay sharp.

He needs to be constantly challenged. If your child is winning every time he tees it up in your local junior golf association tournaments, it is time to get him signed up and playing in the American Junior Golf Association events. It is tough competition to get into these events, but if your son is a low single-digit handicapper, he should have no problem qualifying for their regional events. There are a couple of other junior golf tours that also afford intense competition at a high level. The International Junior Golf Tour and The Future Collegiate Golf Tour give kids an opportunity to shine amongst their peers.

Becoming Assertive on the Course

The Merriam-Webster dictionary defines assertion as "the act to state or declare positively and often forcefully or aggressively." A player might be the nicest person in the world off the golf course and displays excellent sportsmanship as well. To win matches and tournaments, though, the player has to show assertiveness in his game. Being too careful or making tentative shots in a round may indicate the need for a talk with the coach about a more aggressive game.

Knowing when to take a risk is one of the most valuable skills your son can learn as he develops. Nicklaus calls it "knowing your abilities." Bobby Jones once said, "The greatest improvement in my game in the last five years has been a growing disposition for calculating a different situation, and an increasing distaste for the taking of reckless chances." Assertiveness in golf is an acquired skill; it's like knowing when to accelerate in a sharp turn if you are an Indy 500 driver and when you have to just drive the course.

There are many programs available at local community centers that offer assertiveness training for kids. Seeing your options clearly is the first step. Practicing martial arts is a great way to develop assertiveness.

Confidence and cockiness are two sides of the same coin. Assure him that he will be a champion if he builds both – cockiness within and confidence outwardly. If little Michael does not improve his golf as a result, at least he will succeed in gaining new respect in all other areas of his life.

On the course, your son should always walk with his head held high and his shoulders back – he needs to walk with the confidence of a touring professional. Tell him you shouldn't be able to tell whether he is shooting 68 or 78 by his body language. In the beginning, you'll be able to read him like a book. A hung head, tight facial muscles, rolling of the eyes or indifference will send negative messages to his brain. Walking tall and with a bounce in his step will build confidence. The old adage "Fake it 'till you make it" holds true. He should zero in on himself and not the competition.

Broadening the Definition of Winning

By definition, there is only one winner in a golf tournament – the champion, the player with the fewest number of strokes after a certain number of holes. If there is a tie, then there is a "sudden death" playoff. Just the name should tell you how important winning is to golfers. Match play tournaments are different. They are more like tennis tournaments, where there can be a sense of winning in each round. There is still an eventual champion, but as a player progresses through each bracket, he can advance even if he doesn't play his best golf. If competition is to be beneficial to kids, they have to be taught to broaden their definition of winning and success.

In golf tournaments, victory may be taken away, but one doesn't want to give it away. A kid who shoots a personal best 72, but gets beat in match play by someone who actually shot a 73 has to consider his efforts a success, even if the outcome of the match wasn't what he wanted. Your son should consider it a success even if he finishes back in the pack, because it was his first time to make a cut in a major tournament. A junior who reaches the semifinals for the first time is a winner. That's not to say the junior should stop striving. In fact, he should enter the competition preparing to win the tournament. There is no substitute for tournament experience. True champions are the most gracious in victory and defeat.

"Children should be encouraged to compete against their own potential," says Dr Alan Goldberg, a renowned sports psychologist. Measure their accomplishments and continue to create "new comfort zones." One summer day, your son might be thrilled with the fact he broke 90, but within the year he might break 80. Teach him to stretch his dreams to tap his potential.

Winners are also those who handle failure better. There is a widespread belief that great players were successful throughout their careers. Actually, champions probably just coped with their setbacks and losses better than their opponents did. In her illustrious career, Nancy Lopez never won the U.S. Open. She never let her disappointment in that unfulfilled dream squelch her desire to be one of the best women to have ever played the game. In a sport in which a missed putt can cost a player thousands of dollars, attitude can make you or break you.

Until 2004, Phil Mickelson carried around the unfavorable title of best player on Tour who had never won a major. Mickelson has had a fairytale career, winning a professional tournament while he was still an amateur and a student at Arizona State. Still, the media was relentless and constantly reminded Phil of his "failures" in the majors over his 12-year career. His 20-plus victories were often overlooked in the light of having not won a major – all the impressive top-10 finishes meaning nothing as article after article was penned. It takes thick skin to be at the top of any profession, but especially in sports, where athletes are always fair game for criticism, fair or unfair. Some athletes can handle it, and some can't.

Mickelson entered the 2004 season with a swagger in his step and a twinkle in his eyes that his fans hadn't seen of late. He initiated his own renovations. Mickelson worked his way back into form – mentally and physically. The changes he made to his game – playing more conservatively, picking more opportune times to go for the heroic shot, managing his game and the course better – paid off royally. The story of how Mickelson claimed his green jacket and then slept in it is legendary. He used his defeats and frustrations as motivation to reclaim his position as one of the best golfers of his generation. He continues to hover near the top of the world rankings, set records and win championships.

I Don't Want To Win

We want to believe winning makes a golf kid happy and that losing makes him sad. Peel away the superficial emotions and you may be surprised to learn that your kid sometimes feels conflicted after a win – happy, anxious and even guilty. Conversely, after a loss he may actually feel secretly happy and relieved.

Timothy Gallwey, author of best-selling book "Inner Game of Golf," ascribes possible reasons why a player could become conflicted about winning. The challenge for parents and coaches is that these reactions to winning are natural for most kids:

- "If I win and become the champion, I'll have to remain champion or disappoint myself and be criticized for not living up to expectations."
- "If I beat my friend Harry, he'll be angry with me."
- "If I win too much, I won't be able to keep my friendship with fellow players."
- "I won't put in my maximum effort. That way I will have an excuse if I lose."

De-emphasizing wins and losses, especially during the early years, is a first step toward combating these attitudes. Encourage giving maximum effort, and always celebrate the effort, whether the child wins or loses. Playing without expectations is one of the hardest things to do, but it is the best way to experience your best golf.

Find a quiet time away from the bustle of immediate competition and talk to your child about these pre- and post-match emotions. For example, while you chaperone your son to and from lessons, tell him what you know about fear of losing and fear of winning. Help the child understand that these are natural reactions.

Explain how he can overcome these negative attitudes by focusing on each shot, rather than on the final score. Let the child know that giving maximum effort is your only expectation of him and that you will celebrate his effort regardless of the results. We want to raise healthy and balanced athletes. Kids should never question, "Am I loved?" nor "Will you still love me if I lose?" At the core of who they are should be a feeling of unconditional love and support, through failure and success.

Playing a Friend

In local competition, kids invariably have to compete against friends, which can be hard on them. Constantly remind your child that the nature of golf is competition against the course. At times, it's tough for youngsters to play against their buddies. Help them understand that it's all about doing their personal best. Golf is the only sport in which players help their opponents. Professionals compete day in and day out against some of their best friends. Friendly competition ultimately keeps them stronger and will push your child up the ladder of success.

Playing against better players, yet possibly losing the game, will ultimately be better for your child's long-range success. The beauty of golf is that it affords you the opportunity to play your own game even if you are paired up with someone of greater skills. Help your child understand that giving maximum effort in a match is a way to better himself as well as the other player. He will be less anxious about competing against friends. After all, "compete" comes from the Latin word "competere," meaning to seek together.

The Next Phase

A few years of fun and games have gone by and now your child is entering the competitive phase. In the beginner and development phase a coach's primary focus is to get the child interested in golf and to teach the basics. While the game should never cease to be fun, the next stage – the competitive phase – requires more effort and offers fresh challenges for a coach. Coach, parent, and most importantly student must agree to move on to the next phase.

Competitive Phase

The competitive phase will generally start during the kid's pre-adolescent years. In this phase the coach should be able to impart a higher level of skill and demand discipline. Working with kids through their teen years poses a unique set of challenges. The coach should have a successful track record teaching kids at both the beginner and development levels. Changing coaches is not always necessary as your child progresses to the competitive phase and should be considered with caution. Your child has developed a relationship with his coach, and it is important to consult him before deciding to move in another direction. Jack Nicklaus is a great example of the fact that one coach may be all your child needs. Jack Grout started teaching Nicklaus when he was 10 years old, and was the only coach he needed for forty years.

A coach for the competitive phases should satisfy a couple of requirements. The coach should have appropriate certification or experience with good golfers. He should have the ability to be creative and make practice enjoyable. Key considerations for the selection process should include:

- **Commitment:** Look for a coach who teaches golf full-time. Coaching at this level demands greater commitment. Being available for special pre-competition course lessons is important. An adolescent may need emotional attention, outside of golf practice, to prepare him mentally for competition. There should be a high level of commitment to your child's improvement and to him achieving his goals – they're a team! Having a coach who has had playing experience is a huge bonus. The coach will have personal experiences to share. "I have been there – this works, and this doesn't" is powerful teaching. A coach who has been a player through high competition can relate better to his students. Players need to know what to do when everything doesn't go according to plan, or when things aren't perfect.

- **Emphasis on mastery:** The best coaches focus on simply making a player better, rather than making the player better than a certain opponent. All-around development – psychological, physical, tactical and technical – is more important than a good-looking record full of easy wins that will later crumble in the face of higher-level competition. The ability to guide kids toward performance goals is extremely valuable. Continuing to lower his stroke average month after month is more important than chasing rankings. The goal is to build a strong foundation – something that will hold up under pressure.

Advanced Competitive Phase

This phase represents the advanced regional and national levels of junior competition. It is likely your junior will be spending more hours than ever with the coach in lessons, practice and tournament preparation, either in person or by phone. Your son needs to be very clear on what role he wants you to play. By now, the on-course role of the parent may have diminished considerably. He still needs you for a chauffeur, for support and for encouragement. He may also want you to be an additional set of eyes and ears, but he is more in charge now. Keeping an additional set of stats on the course is one way your child may want you to stay involved. Nothing fancy – just something he can compare his own notes with when he goes to record them.

Some kids want little parent involvement, while others still want their parents to be actively involved in their games. At this stage, a strong child-parent relationship is extremely beneficial for several reasons. The child will be testing his ability to cope with the added responsibilities, and it's important the parent allow him to do so. You need to trust each other to stay within the boundaries set. Parents will most likely travel to tournaments for moral support, but need to respect whatever role the child has given them. A player needs to learn what he is capable of.

Strong coaches will demand responsibility out of your child. Parents have to allow them to succeed or fail on their own recognizance. At this level, most players are responsible for pre-tournament check-in. There is a reason most events won't let you do it for them – they want the kids to establish some responsibilities.

At this stage, kids should arrange their own practice round schedules. Your son should be telling you his daily schedule – he needs to let you know what time he expects to be at breakfast, finished with breakfast, how much time he wants to hit balls and to putt. Managing his time for himself throughout the day is a good start in managing his responsibilities. It should be his call if he is going to have post-round practice, and he should let you know about how long it will be. It isn't your job to remember his notes.

When you first start traveling to tournaments, you can help him put together a checklist of things to remember, but after a few events, he should be preparing for the event by himself. He may forget to pack sunscreen or a hat at first, but he should become disciplined early on in managing the small details.

Discipline is the key for success in any tournament. Is he working on what coach wants him to work on or is he off on his own tangent? It takes discipline to stay on track. The coach should be instrumental in going over all the pre-tournament details with him before you leave for an event. Keeping a player in a solid, calm state of mind is just as much of a priority as being physically prepared. It would be wise to discuss these things with his coach when he first enters the competitive stage. He should be proficient at handling himself and all of his personal details by the time he gets to an advanced competitive level. If his coach isn't demanding self-discipline, check the coach's track record with players at this level. Be unabashed in asking about successful protégés at this level of competition, and talk with other parents to see if this is a priority to coach. At a young age, Earl Woods insisted Tiger take care of all of the details, including making the hotel reservations.

Coaching kids, especially teenagers, has unique challenges, to say the least. Again, it is necessary to reiterate that advanced players don't necessarily have to make a coach change. At times this may do more damage than good. Sometimes, the goal isn't to fix a swing, but to give confidence. A great pro can get the best out of a student and show him how good his swing really is. Good coaches are capable of fueling a dream. However, for a variety of reasons, kids may burn out in the competitive or advanced competitive phases. Sometimes coaches burn out, too. Current continuing education credits and recent protégés who have reached the top at regional, national and collegiate levels indicate the coach is motivated and excited. If your kid's coach is excited, the odds are your son will be, too.

From One Coach to the Next

Golf development aside, a parent may have to find a new coach because of relocation, scheduling issues and so on. Whatever the reason, try to make the switch from one coach to the next amicable. Be honest with the coach when you switch.

The toughest transition for a kid is often from the fun and games of the beginner and developmental phases, lasting two to four years, to the more technical and demanding competitive phases. Ideally, your child has a coach who understands his learning style and will incorporate the fundamentals and techniques learned at each level. The foundation should be rock solid if the teacher has taken a slow, deliberate course of action. If there are flaws in the foundation, it will be necessary to rebuild during the competitive phase. This is a tough time to rebuild, but can be done and will be necessary for future, long-term success. Some players are more comfortable going with feel, and others tend to rely on strict attention to positions and theory. If changing coaches in the competitive phase, it may be difficult for a player who was always taught to be an overly mechanical, technique-minded player to relate with a new coach who is extremely feel oriented.

The best players can have a learning style that is dominant in one area or another, but even the best players have learned to balance the two extremes. Tom Kite is a grinder, constantly working on positions and mechanics; Ben Crenshaw is a feel player, relying on rhythm and tempo to help him recover from swing woes. Both players learned the game from the same pro, Harvey Penick. Although these two Texans have very different learning styles and approaches to the game, both have amazing amateur and professional resumes as their legacies.

The transition could occur over a year or more. For some, the transition is never truly complete. Lee Trevino, a unique swinger of the club himself, told Domingo Lopez, "Leave Nancy alone. She's great just the way she is. Let her dance with who she brought to the dance." What a great way to say "Leave it alone!" While veteran players usually went with one swing and whatever worked, modern-day players seem more apt to search for "perfection." There is a trend to have more than one coach as well. Few players can play well with several coaches. "Too many cooks in the kitchen" is not good for anyone's game.

A player might have a swing coach, a putting or short-game coach and possibly a mental-game coach. It is critical the player stick with one swing philosophy. Occasionally, a player may work with more than one swing coach, but only if coaches share the same ideas. Putting and short-game experts will usually focus all their attention on helping a player master the art of putting and improving his skills with the wedges. Mental-game coaches will help with visualization, imagery and self-talk and will give your child tools to help with the emotional ups and downs of golf. Over the years he may choose coaches that complement his primary coach, but each one should bring something different and useful to the player-coach relationship.

Breaking the Mold

In the late 1960s, Dick Fosbury, a high-schooler from Oregon and an avid high-jumper, shattered the Olympic record, clearing 7 feet 4-1/2 inches. More significant than winning the Olympic gold medal was the way in which Fosbury won this event.

For decades, virtually all high jumpers were coached to use a method called the straddle. The jumper kicks one foot up and rolls over the bar with the face down. The straddle method depended on leg strength. Dick Fosbury was taught to use the straddle method when he started high jumping. But his jumps were mediocre at best. He began experimenting with a scissors method, popularized by children leaping fences.

Eventually, he refined this technique and actually started to jump up and over backwards, knee, chest and face to the sky. The technique needed less leg strength, produced higher jumps, and was so revolutionary it got its own name: the Fosbury Flop. The Flop earned Dick Fosbury the Olympic gold.

Golf is no different. Some of the game's greatest improvements came about because a coach or player chose to break the mold and experiment with unorthodox techniques. Of course, advances in clubs, balls and swing assessment have made them practical.

Don't be duped into thinking that there is only one way to hit a golf shot. Good golf shots come from many different swings. Some are pretty and some are not so pretty. There are no pictures on the scorecards. Players seem to fall in one of two categories when describing their swings – either they swing on one plane or two. Jim Furyk and Julie Inkster have two-plane swings, while Amy Alcott and Ernie Els swing on one plane. Keeping the swing as simple as possible is best, but the ability to have consistent, repetitive motions is what really counts. Hitting fairways and greens in tournament play are the goals. History has shown that unorthodox techniques have proven to work. Although they might work, the fact that they might be a little different, "Helpful Harveys" of the world will feel inclined to give their two cents' worth. A child with an unorthodox swing will need to turn deaf to the endless advice of well meaning people.

Bedrock fundamentals won't change: a solid grip, nice posture, good balance, proper weight transfer and so on. Still, there is tremendous room for innovation in technique and tactics. Your child needs to know what works for him.

Measuring Abilities and Success

"You can't manage what you can't measure." The point of this famous quote by management guru Peter Drucker is that effective management requires feedback, knowing that you are progressing toward your objectives. Regular measurement is key to continuous improvement.

Drucker's theory is applicable to managing anything that has investments in time, money and effort, including junior golf development. Win-loss records and junior rankings are some ways to measure a junior's progress. However, just as in the beginner and development phase, experts advise against over-emphasizing winning, losing and rankings during the competitive phases.

When competition rankings and points are used as the sole measure of progress, an unreasonable burden is placed on the coach and the junior. Easy wins will be emphasized over golf development. We know this is true because many youngsters with sterling results and high rankings in the younger divisions seem to suddenly hit a brick wall at the higher echelons of competition. Junior competition is an essential part of golf development, but by measuring the ability to hit good golf shots and many areas of the game, you encourage the development of solid fundamentals and an all-around game. Lower scores will follow suit.

Moving Forward

There are a few steps to measuring sure progress on the golf course. These basics are the foundation with which a good golf game is built. They are the same steps all good players will turn to when evaluating their progress and proficiency. Quick and fun ways to measure valuable skills and proper progress are essential for a coach. They can be the greatest means for a coach determining into which level a new student fits. Using variations of this simple outline will help determine when a kid is ready to move from one phase to another. It will be easy for your son to develop by practicing "families" of drills.

Putting

Step 1 is to learn to take two putts or less. This can't be over-emphasized. Bobby Jones said, "Old Man Par – he never gets down in one putt, and he never takes three." Putts are 50% of your total score on an even-par scorecard. In a game in which par doesn't mean what it used to, players can't afford to be satisfied with two putts per green. A coach can test in three different areas: short putts, mid-range putts and long putts. It is also necessary to teach kids how to read greens. Good players need to recognize the slope or break, speed and grain of greens.

Once your child can consistently make three-foot putts, he should be able to make 25 three-foot putts with his right hand only and then do the same with his left hand only. A good putter should be able to make 50-100 three-foot putts in a row from the same spot. A great putter will move those putts around and not putt them from the same spot. He then needs to be able to consistently two putt from 20 feet. As he improves, he will start making more of these. He needs to be proficient from 15 feet, 18 feet, 21 feet, 24 feet ... and eventually be able to two-putt from any distance on the putting green or the fringe.

Distance control drills and tests can help the coach determine whether this is an area your child needs to work on. Nine years after turning pro, Annika Sorenstam began working with Dave Stockton Sr., a Champions Tour star and one of the world's best putters. Although she was one of the top female players in the game, she realized putting was a weakness she needed to address. Throughout January and February of 2001, the two visited the practice green twice a day, working to develop a smoother stroke and a better feel for speed.

Use gypsum or baby powder and make three-foot circles around the hole. Your son should be working to make it into those circles from every possible area on that green. Mix up the distances; he should putt left-breaking and right-breaking putts. He needs to putt both uphill and downhill too. There are only two things that really matter in putting – distance and direction. The circles will help your child focus on getting good at these two things.

Juniors should incorporate the drill Phil Mickelson uses. Let's call it "Phil's Drill," although he didn't invent it. He attempts to make 50-100 putts in a row from six feet. Each putt is from a different spot on the green. He usually follows the compass – north, south, east and west around the cup. Your child should start from two feet, then move up one foot at a time. This drill is any easy way to monitor improvement and instill confidence. The key is to stay faithful to the drill, execute consistently and use the results to see how good he is.

Finally, it is critical to get a feel for the greens on the course your son is going to play. Too many players skip putting-green warm up. Annika Sorenstam always goes to the putting green first in her stringent pre-tournament warm up.

Chipping, Pitching and Bunkers

The next step is to develop the chipping, pitching and bunker play. If a player has mastered his club selection and has consistent execution, he is on his way. Measurable goals include knowing what club to hit for certain shots and understanding how the lie and loft will affect the ball. Pitch and run shots are basically made with a club in the wedge family, and chip and run shots are done with the 9-iron through 6-iron. However, Tiger Woods was one of the few players who started using a fairway wood to chip with as well. This shot is very similar to a putting stroke, and the technique used with all these clubs doesn't vary much. Mastering this shot comes with mastering the landing area. Good players will know where they should land it and how far the ball will roll once it hits the green.

As with putting, use circles to highlight success. Coaches can make six-foot circles, three-foot maximum length putt, to help evaluate skill level. Have your junior chip from various spots on the apron to the circle. He should be evaluated in two areas: whether he hits the designated landing area and whether he gets the ball in the circle. Players should be able to recognize the proper trajectory with a chip and run. If a ball lands one-third of the distance to the hole, it should roll two-thirds. Your son may want to play the chip to land one-quarter and roll three-quarters. Coaches need to test players on landing areas, speed of greens and the ability to read the green by sight. Great players will "feel the speed" of the green by "feeling the texture" of the green with his feet.

Lay a rope down or use a white powder line and see how many times out of 50 he hits his landing spot. The landing spots must be consistent, but the trajectory of the shot and the roll also need to be consistent. The percentage of balls hitting his mark needs to be increasing with every practice session.

Pitch shots, flop shots and bunker shots are an important part of this family – cousins, so to speak. A new golfer's first goal is to be able to pitch it up on the green in one shot from 35 yards, 45 yards, 50 yards and so on. Depending on the age and strength of your child, by the time you hit 65 yards, he might be making a full swing. The first goal is to hit it on the green from anywhere 50 yards and in with one shot, then two-putt and make 3 on the hole.

The flop shot is a favorite shot for kids. When Phil Mickelson first came out on Tour, he showed how critical this shot was to saving par. Throughout his career, he has demonstrated that he can pretty much get up and down from anywhere. It's been said Phil wouldn't need a drop – he could get up and down out of a trash can! Unlike the chip and run, this shot allows for little movement of the ball once it lands on the green. The lob wedge or 60-degree wedge helps to "lob" it up next to the target. It is the shot to use when you need to go up and over something and there is not a lot of putting surface between the flag and trouble. This shot takes a lot of practice to master, but once a player understands the technique, most find it really fun to play.

Bunker shots are also fun to practice when a player understands the technique. A lot of amateurs freak out when they hit it into a bunker, but often the pros would rather hit from a bunker than have a difficult pitch around the green. In the beginning, getting out in one shot is the No. 1 rule. Golf courses fill their bunkers with different sand; as time goes by, a player will recognize the different types of sand. The green-side bunker shot is one of the only shots in golf where the ball shouldn't come in direct contact with the clubface. The first thing good players will note is if there is a lot of sand or very little sand under and around his golf ball. The sand wedge is designed specifically to help move the sand toward the intended target. The sand basically pushes the ball out – if the sand isn't getting out of the bunker, chances are the ball isn't either. If there is little sand in a bunker, this is more of a specialty shot. The player adjusts the length and speed of his swing and plays it more like a pitch shot. As your child improves, he should zero in on distance control. He should also experiment using different wedges from the sand.

For top-level bunker practice, a player should play from many different lies and use the six-foot-circle game to measure success. Sand saves are an important statistic to golfers since most courses are beautifully designed with these hazards strategically placed between the tee box and the greens. Encourage your son to have a positive mental attitude when he finds himself in one, and stress how important it is to his game to be efficient from the bunker. The average of all of the best bunker players from all of the major tours is a 75% save average; however, before he beats himself up too badly, the worst of the best players in the world is about 12%. While players would prefer to be on the green in regulation, sometimes a bunker is the best place to be. Bob Tway snatched the 1986 PGA Championship out of the hands of Greg Norman by holing an amazing bunker shot on the 72nd hole of the tournament.

From 150 Yards In

The third point of measurement would be to evaluate your skills from 150 yards in. Young golfers might take two shots to get it on the green, making the hole a par-4 for them. Par is the number of strokes a golfer with expert ability should need to play a hole from tee to green without mistake under ordinary conditions, always allowing "Old Man Par" two putts. The computation of par is mostly dependent upon the yardage of the hole. However, allowances should be made for the configuration of the ground, difficult or unusual playing conditions or the severity of the hazards.

The first goal of a golfer is to be able to consistently hit the green from 150 yards out. Kids should always practice hitting at targets when they are on the driving range. A fun game is to pick targets, figure out what club you need to hit it there and then hit. See how many times out of 10 your son is able to hit his target. He only gets one try. In the beginning, the results are hard to stomach, but his confidence will grow as he gets better. This game will help your junior as he improves and his goal changes from not only hitting the green to getting his ball close to the hole. Learning to control trajectory, distance, and spin are critical to the development of his iron play. Better players know how far they carry each club and how far the ball will roll. This is another area of her game in which Annika felt she needed improvement in 2001. Dave Stockton Sr. accompanied her to the driving range, where they arranged cones from distances ranging from 35 yards out to 165 yards. Annika fired away at them, concentrating on the accuracy of her irons. Since then, she often holds the No. 1 ranking in Greens In Regulation (GIR). A player's GIR percentage will develop out of the skills mastered in this stage of development. The best players in the world do not hit every single green in regulation in a round of golf. The average is usually somewhere between 12-14 for the best players in the game. That is why it is key to stress to your child that he needs to work on his putting and his short game.

National Golf Foundation General Yardage to Calculate Par		
PAR	**Men**	**Women**
3	Up to 250 yards	Up to 210 yards
4	251-470 yards	211 to 400 yards
5	471 & over	401 to 575 yards
6	576 and over	576 and over

The Driver

Once your child is making progress in the first three steps outlined, it is time to evaluate the tee shot. As you can tell by the chart above, at the highest level, there is a premium put on distance. Your teenage child should be able to at least get the ball out there 225 yards to have a chance to compete at a high junior level. Due to amazing advances in technology and equipment, players are hitting it farther than at any other time in history. The leading driving averages for the longest hitters in men's professional golf are routinely over 300 yards.

However, the driving statistics are made up of many elements, and distance is just one of them. The tee shot often sets the tone for the hole, so it is a key element of the game. Ball striking is a new statistic kept on tour; it takes the driving-average ranking, the driving-distance ranking and the greens-in-regulation ranking and calculates another ranking. Lately, the best players in the game are those who hit the ball a long way.

Kids are well aware of the attention and glamour the long-ball hitters receive. It is important to note that while a long ball may give an advantage, it is also vital to keep the golf ball in play and avoid unnecessary penalty shots. Accuracy of drives is another statistic that comes into play when evaluating the driving game. It's just as important for your child to keep track of how many fairways he hits each round as it is for him to focus on the yardage of his average drives.

Have him create small fairways in his mind when he is practicing on the driving range. With the driver, a player wants to learn how to take one side of the golf course out of play. Fade or draw, it doesn't matter. Jack Nicklaus took the left side of the fairway out of play, while Billy Casper took the right side out of play. He should chart drives in the beginning and discover what his natural shot is. He will have a tendency that shows up more often and is easier for him to hit. Play an imaginary round on the driving range and see how many fairways you can hit on the driving range. If he hits 14 out of 14 drives just the way he wants to, then his confidence will soar. Like every area of his game, his golf coach should help him develop his long game and address any issues he needs to pay special attention to. Club fitting, strength and conditioning and tempo are key areas of focus when trying to get more yardage off of the tee.

Is Junior Making the Grade?

Here is a simple grading scale to help you evaluate some of the key fundamentals necessary for a good golf game. Kids relate to grades. Help him understand that to play nationally ranked golf, he must begin to compare himself to the standards set in the game and those that will help him score well:

Putting

1. Short Putts times 10 - the objective is to see how many three-foot putts in a row the player can make. More advances testing can put the putts on trickier terrain if the coach chooses.
   Results: 10/10 (A+); 9/10 (A); 8/10 (B+); 7/10 (B); 6/10 (C+); 5/10 (C); 4/10 (D+); 3/10 (D); and less than that he needs to improve
2. Six-foot putts with tee boundaries – the objective is to putt five golf balls, trying to make as many as possible. A player receives two

points if he holes it and one if he hits the putt within the boundaries. Set boundaries by placing a tee a couple of inches on both sides of the cup on the far side and one tee out past the cup about 12-18 inches. Advanced players can test additionally on uphill, downhill and sidehill putts, both left-breaking and right-breaking putts. Results: 10 points (A+); 9(A); 8(B+); 7(B); 6 (C+); 5(C); 4(C-); 3(D+); 2(D); 1 (D-); 0 is a 0

3. 36-foot putts – the objective is to get the ball within a marked two-foot circle. There is a second circle of three and a half feet. The player hits five golf balls from approximately the same spot and is scored accordingly: a made putt scores 20 points, a ball coming to rest in the inner circle receives 10 points, and a ball going in the outer circle receives five points. Advanced players can choose to putt from five different areas of the green. As always, advanced players can be tested on uphill, and downhill putts, etc. **Results:** 60 points (A+); 50(A); 40(B+); 35(B); 30 (C+); 25(C); 20(C-); 15(D+); 10(D); 5 (D-); 0 is a 0

4. The two-putt experience from 30- 40 feet – the objective is to pick two putts from a desired distance – one that breaks left to right and the other right to left. If grading more than one student, put tees down to mark the original spot where they hit from. The goal, like usual, is to two-putt. Play one hole at a time. If the player makes the putt, it is 30 points– a two-putt is 20 points, and a three-putt is 10. Results: 60 points (A+); 50(A); 40(B+); 30(B); 20 (C); 10(D); 0 is a 0

5. Putts per round – course evaluations. Grade your putting perfor-mance on the course. Give five points for every putt under 36 and subtract five points for every putt over 36. If a player has 36 putts, his points are 0; if he has 30 putts, his points are 30. **Results:** 35 + (A+); 30 (A); 25 (A-); 20(B+); 15 (B); 10(B-); 5(C+); 0(C); -5(C-); -10 (D+); -15 (D); -20 (D-); -25 or greater, no grade

Now take all of your grades and make an average. Use the 4.0 grade scale and divide the total grade points by the number of grades: A+ = 4.25; A = 4.0; A- = 3.75; B+ = 3.25; B = 3.0; B- = 2.75; C+ = 2.25; C = 2.0; C- = 1.75; D+ = 1.25; D = 1.0; D- = .75

Chipping

1. **The Chip and Run** – the object is to chip the ball in the marked three-foot circle. There is an outer circle of five feet. Chip five balls and total the points. A holed out chip is worth 20 points, balls chipped to the inner circle are worth 10 points and those to the outer circle are five points. Ultimately, this test should be done from nine, 12, 15, 18, 21, 24, 27 yards and 30 yards until your child maintains an A average. **Results:** 50+ points (A+); 50(A); 40(A-); 35(B+); 30 (B); 25(B-); 20(C+); 15(C); 10(C-); 5(D); 0 is a 0

Pitching

1. **35-yard and 50-yard pitch shots** – the objective is to hit a landing spot on the front, middle or back of the green and have the ball stay on the putting surface. Divide the green horizontally into three equal areas with a white powder line or some rope. The player must hit the pitch in the approximate direction, have solid contact and land the ball in the proper area. The player will get only three balls for each distance. Each ball is worth maximum 20 points, giving a player a possible 60 points per yardage. There are 120 points possible in this test. It is up to the coach testing to evaluate each pitch and the merits of the points awarded. This same test can be used with different yardage and different lies as a student progresses. **Results:** 120+ points (A+); 110(A); 100 (A-); 95(B+); 90 (B); 85(B-); 80(C+); 75-70(C); 65(C-); 60 (D+); 55-50 (D); 45-40 (D-); below 40, no grade

Greens in Regulation

1. **GIR** – the objective is to hit the putting surface in the number of strokes as allocated by "Old Man Par." Beginners can regulate that number based on what it would take them to reach a green hitting their maximum attainable yardage. A "scratch" golfer or zero-handicap golfer is a player who consistently plays to the par set forth by the golf course
   Results: 13+ GIR (A+); 11-12 (A); 10(A-); 8-9(B+); 7 (B); 6(B); 5(C+); 4(C); 3(C-); 2(D+); 1(D); 0 is a 0

Scoring

In the end, golf is a game of scoring – a round made up of pars, birdies, bogeys and other. Although Annika Sorenstam is not the leader in the rankings for birdies made, she does have the leading scoring average. How can that be? She doesn't make a lot of bogeys, so when she does make birdie, it means something. The secret to her success is being consistently accurate and occasionally brilliant. The PGA Tour has many different calculations of scoring average. The Tour keeps track of your weekend scoring average versus your before-the-cut average. Your scores are also calculated according to the field and the course. It is really quite interesting to study the numbers, but it's most important that your son understand his numbers. The bottom line is he can't lose sight of the fact that the way you win golf tournament is by shooting the lowest score.

1. **Keeping track of pars** – making par is the proving ground. A great scale to check your child's scoring ability is to check how many pars

he is making on average. If he makes a lot of pars, but is failing to score well, he is making too many bogies or others.
Results: 17-18 pars (A+); 15-16 (A); 13-14 (A-); 12 (B+); 10-11 (B); 9 (B-); 8 (C+); 6-7 (C); 4-5 (C-); 3 (D+); 2 (D); 1 (D-); 0 is a 0

2. **Keeping track of birdies** – the ability to make birdie is usually the mark of improvement. There has been a change in mentality over the last couple of decades. Earl Woods trained Tiger early on to make birdies, and lots of them. The more comfortable your child gets being under par early on, the better. Before Tiger was a teenager, it was nothing to him to shoot several under par. The scale below shows what might be acceptable for a top junior player. Even though tour professionals are making more birdies than ever and would grade differently, if they simply had four birdies a round and nothing higher than par, they would be happy. Shooting 68 day in and day out is a score many of them could live with.
The scale: 4+ birdies (A+); 3 (A); 2 (B); 1 (C)

Finally, a coach might help him evaluate his progress by giving him skills checks every three months or so. Quarterly evaluations help him focus on short-term goals of improvement and can also serve as motivation to move toward long-term goals. In a quarterly progress report, PGA professional John Mason uses, he records his comments on the following:

● Rules and Etiquette	● Trouble Shots
● Putting and Chipping	● Playing the Course
● Pitch Shots	● Playing Tournament
● Full Swing	● Mental Training
● Club Distances	● Physical Training
● Practice Routine	● Diet

He gives the junior either a mark of 1, 2, or 3: 1- needs work, 2-good, or 3-outstanding. This type of honest evaluation will keep your son moving in the right direction. Grading the skills and simple evaluations will help identify a player's strengths and areas where more work is needed.

5
Competition

Why does Haley hate sports? There may be many reasons, but competition is definitely not one of them. One of the big myths is that children hate sports because of competition. Just ask any child who is good in a particular sport if he would like to compete and the answer is invariably a resounding, "Yes!"

The reason competition gets a bad rap is because children are thrust into tournaments before they can become reasonably good for that level of play. A child will enjoy competing at every level – rookie to elite – provided she develops sufficient proficiency to sustain a good record of improvement. Winning championships should not be the only motivating factor for your child. Lower scores are a great way to measure progress and induce improvement. However, if a child is constantly paired in tournaments with kids her age who are far superior in ability, there is a chance she may become embarrassed by her play and lose the motivation to improve. Experts suggest that, in golf, skill and better scoring, rather than winning, will motivate a young child to continue wanting to improve and compete. Competition is tougher than simply teeing it up with Dad. Golf is uniquely different. It's been said that, "Golf is harder than baseball – you have to play your foul balls."

Is Junior Ready?

Most parents and coaches don't want to hurt or pressure their kids and risk burnout. However, in every sport there comes a time when the junior has to face competition. In golf, to test skill levels, kids will eventually play against other kids about the same age. However, it is best to put competition into perspective. The legendary Bobby Jones said, "I never won a major championship until I learned to play golf against something, not somebody; that something was par." In reality, the true test is against "Old Man Par" and the golf course itself. It is the fundamental nature of sport that one must beat someone or something. Golf is the only sport in which the most feared opponent is you.

Losing hurts, and though winning feels good, some children become anxious when they do well because it means they have to live up to their own expectations. It might mean they have to play with "better" players the next time – the fear of not meeting expectations or embarrassment supercedes the desire to win. The thinking process goes something like this: "If I play well and beat this kid, then I'll have to compete with her every time I tee it up or disappoint myself and be criticized for not living up to expectations." While the fear of success is often an issue, the fear of failure is also a real problem.

Fear of failure will often keep a child from playing her best. The anticipation of failure becomes a powerful distraction and can get in the way for even the most prepared golfers. For some, failure is a great motivator, but for many, failure can be devastating. It has often been said, "The most successful people are those who handle failure best." It is most helpful for parents to help their child focus on the process rather than the outcome and to give her positive reinforcements for the efforts made. In a competitive environment, it is easy to get wrapped up in tournament results, but it is essential you keep failure in proper perspective. It is harder to give "failure" a foothold if she is focused on the learning process and the individual steps it will take for overall improvement – shot making, fewer putts, lower scores and subtle progress.

Kids need to be taught early on that it is not about beating so and so, but about improving scores. Winning will take care of itself if your child learns early on not to pay attention to the tournament record of her fellow competitors. That's why players with better ability might have a hard time getting into the winner's circle, often losing to less competent opponents. Better players may let their guard down against a lesser-known player in match play or get distracted if paired with a poor player. Match play is a different animal for top golfers. Quite often, it may give underdogs who have nothing to lose a chance for victory. Underdogs, if able to relax, often rise to the occasion and play their best golf. Also, better players may draw the best out of an opposing player, so you never know what can happen in match play especially. Mostly, golfers are spread out among many groups and are usually playing many people at one time. It is essential your child learn to play the golf course, not the kids in her foursome. So the question is, "When is a child mature enough to handle competition without too much anxiety?"

The other issue to think about is the child's level of competency in the sport. Consider a crossover scenario in which a 14-year-old soccer player switches to golf. She has been playing competitive soccer for several years and may be mentally mature enough to handle the stress of competition.

Should the young lady take a few golf lessons and jump straight into competition? It depends. Most people would say probably not, because, although mentally prepared for competition, she is clearly not ready from the perspective of technical ability. However, crossover athletes are often capable of competing faster if the child determines to improve and wants to see at what level her peers are competing. If close technically and she has the desire to play, absolutely let her play! Competition will let her know what she's up against and how far away victory might be. In her case, competition will motivate her to practice harder and may reveal she is closer than she originally thought. It will also tell her how much work she has to do to reach the next level or her next goal. Clearly, both technical competency and mental maturity must come into play when deciding if junior is ready for competition.

Technical Competency

As parents, we are unabashedly biased when it comes to judging the technical ability of our kids. After all, little Lauren is the best golf player in her age group, right? The rest of the world may think otherwise. Judging technical readiness for competition is best left to an experienced coach.

A child should definitely be familiar with the game of golf, its basic rules and etiquette and have had some basic instruction before ever attempting to play in a junior golf tournament. That said, your child does not have to be perfect in any of the above, but must be mature enough to play the game in a safe manner. At minimum, your child should be able to get the golf ball airborne, have a system that she can properly keep her score, know the differences in putting, chipping, and full swing and have some distance control. In some peewee competitions, parents will help kids keep score, are available to help with rulings, and will guide them through the course as they reinforce etiquette. Older kids are expected to know the essentials of golf and are held responsible to be at a basic level of mental and emotional maturity. They too should be able to get the ball airborne consistently, know the rules and etiquette of the game, know how to hit different shots and have a sense of distance control. Players should know how to keep score accurately and be able to keep simple stats. If your child is a new competitive golfer, many organizations may put her in a novice division to see how she scores in comparison to other girls her age. If her coach authorizes that she can forego the novice bracket and is capable of stepping right into her age division, she may be allowed to move right up. This is a critical step for most juniors. Be mindful of the fact it is difficult for both novice and experienced players alike when they are paired together in an important tournament situation. It is very distracting for a single-digit handicap player when she arbitrarily gets paired with a player who shoots over 100. It is not the end of the world, but it is not the optimal tournament situation.

A child expecting to compete should have an understanding of the different aspects of the game, and although a junior does not have to be 100% proficient in any of the listed skills, she must be practicing and striving toward competency in such skills in order to compete.

Mental Maturity

America's Funniest Home Videos televised an episode in which a three-year-old, frustrated with a computer challenge game, sobs and screams at the monitor, "I want to win! I want to win!"

Psychologists say children eight years old and under are not mentally mature enough to handle the rigors of competition. Between eight and 10 years of age, children can be eased into competition. This is also the time when children need to be taught about handling success and failure. Some kids develop the maturity necessary to want to enter and win competitions early on.

Competency Chart

1. **Putting** (measure percentage made from each distance / for long putts average number of putts)
   - 10 putts from three feet
   - 10 putts from six feet
   - 10 putts from 20 feet
   - 10 putts from 40 feet
2. **Chipping** (measure average distance from hole for each shot)
   - 10 chips to 15 feet
   - 10 chips to 40 feet
3. **Pitching/lob** (measure average distance from hole for each shot)
   - 10 pitches to hole 20 feet on green
   - 10 pitches to hole 40 feet on green
   - 10 lob shots to hole 10 feet on green
4. **Sand** (measure average distance from hole for each shot)
   - 10 sand shots to hole 15 feet on green
   - 10 sand shots to hole 30 feet on green
5. **Swing/ball-striking consistency** (measure distance from target for each shot, and for driver, the number of shots in the fairway)
   - 10 shots from 100 yards to target
   - 10 shots from 150 yards to target
   - 10 shots from 180 yards to target
   - 10 shots with driver down a fairway (or between targets)
6. **Specialty shots/creativity** (measure percentage of successful shots)
   - Five shots low (under tree/obstacle)
   - Five shots high (over tree/obstacle)
   - Five draws/hooks (around tree/obstacle)
   - Five fades/slices (around tree/obstacle)

Since 1997 and the preeminence of Tiger Woods, children seem to be much more prepared. Parents are painstakingly preparing their children to succeed. Many are doing their all to walk in the footsteps of the late Earl Woods. Where there used to be the one or two exceptionally talented and mature youngsters, tournament officials are seeing trends of amazing competition at the peewee level. National tournaments are available for the eight-and-under crowd. Scoring has dropped dramatically – it is not uncommon to see juniors regularly break par.

Talented young teenagers are routinely breaking par on regulation length courses. This trend has produced female teenage superstars emerging to the highest levels of the game. Michelle Wie was just 14 when she was allowed to compete in the PGA Tour's Sony Open. While she shot 72-68 and missed that cut by one shot, a year later, at 15, she was runner-up in two of the four LPGA Tour tournaments she competed in; one of her second-place finishes was to Annika Sorenstam in a major championship. Her peers don't like the fact that she has chosen to skip the major junior events to focus on her celebrity appearances in professional events.

Unlike in tennis, a player must be at least 18 years old to play professional golf. Wie chose to forgo college golf to pursue her dream of playing professionally. Although she is not an official member of the LPGA Tour, she has accepted multi-million dollar endorsement contracts and is now eligible to accept money for her golf achievements. In the meantime, another young phenom is making history of her own on the LPGA Tour. Paula Creamer is 18 and fearless. She won her first LPGA Tour event before she had even graduated from high school. Creamer will most likely be the youngest player ever to win over a million dollars on the LPGA Tour, for a while anyway. If the 2005 U.S. Women's Open is foretelling the future of women's professional golf, the youngsters have arrived. There were a record-breaking 18 teenagers in the field. Amateurs – teenage amateurs – led or held the lead for most of the championship. A once-in-a-lifetime holed bunker shot from South Korean Birdie Kim left 17-year-old Morgan Pressel and 19-year-old Brittany Lang tied for second. Most definitely, there are more and more success stories of kids performing well beyond their years, leaving LPGA Tour executives contemplating their age requirement.

However, it is still more common for children to develop an intense interest in healthy competition at about the age of 12 or 13. In the early years, kids should be taking lessons, playing games and learning to score. Kids should learn to enjoy the game for the game's sake, enter tournaments if they want to compete and find peers to measure personal progress. If your child is comfortable with the stress of competition and wants to pursue golf to a higher level, it's time to begin the new journey into the world of competitive golf.

Having the mental maturity to face competition is less of an issue for older kids that cross over from other sports. Many talented young athletes may excel at several sports. Encourage your child to continue playing other sports she enjoys for as long as possible. Golf doesn't offer much strength conditioning, and a player can learn valuable skills from different sports.

Hall-of-Famer Patty Sheehan at 13 was one of the top junior skiers in the country, but didn't take golf seriously until she was older. Japanese superstar Ayako Okamoto was a famous softball player before turning to golf in her early twenties. For example, skills she learned as a pitcher in softball served her well as a golfer. A pitcher has to learn to concentrate on every pitch. In golf, players must concentrate on every shot. Jack Nicklaus has always played many sports.

If your daughter chooses to focus on golf as her primary sport, she may have to eventually abandon high-level competition in the other sports she enjoys. Injuries and valuable practice time are the two primary reasons a child may have to scale back from additional sports. However, some kids enjoy the cross training, and it helps to keep golf fresh, preventing burnout.

Pairings

Pairings are an important aspect of tournament golf. Sometimes, they can be intimidating for the new competitor. In stroke-play events, players are competing against the entire field and not one individual. More experienced players are seldom upset by a particular pairing. Most tournaments have a random draw, but others may pair players according to an established ranking. In either case, tournaments will either send players out in threesomes or foursomes; it shouldn't matter who your child is paired with. Most 72-hole tournaments will have set pairings for the first two rounds, and then players are paired according to score. Match-play events will have a stroke-play qualifier to determine the ranking and who goes into which bracket. This determines who gets to play whom. In tournament situations, the pairings may be published online, mailed out, given out at tournament check- in or displayed at the tournament site.

Tournaments will often use a split-tee format – teeing half the field off the front nine and the other half off of the back nine. A tournament may also use a modified shotgun format. No matter the method a tournament committee decides to do its pairings, most tee sheets will give the first and last names of each player for each group, the tee a player is expected to start on and the time a player is expected to start play. Times are usually in 7-8 minute intervals. Players are solely responsible for making it to their tee time at least five minutes prior to their tee time, unless otherwise stated by the tournament committee. In match play, the pairings will show the brackets and tee times for individual matches. If matches are to be played both in the morning and the afternoon, all the times will be listed. If a player misses her tee time, she will be disqualified from the event. Unfortunately, there are too many instances to mention in which a well-qualified junior was disqualified because she went to the wrong tee or didn't make it to the tee on time. There are no exceptions under the rules of golf.

So your junior has honed his technique, practiced, and is now entering her first tournament. You pay the entry fee, put life on hold for a day or two and drive 60 miles to the tournament site. Hours later you and your child are studying the scoreboard and the competition. One of two realities will hit home. One, she may realize she was way out of her league and isn't quite ready for that level of competition. Or two, your daughter evaluates her finish and is inspired by her performance in relationship to her competition. How you and she handle this first tournament experience is critical to her further development. Regardless of performance, it is essential that she can take away something positive.

There are many different types of junior golf tournaments – ranging from one-day local events to multiple-day junior tours to national match-play championships. Players should start competing on the local level before considering competition out of the area. Local tournaments are the best format for "rookie juniors" to get started. If your child blows away the competition, it might take a few regional events for her to get an accurate sense of how she fairs against comparable competition. Most national championships and highly competitive junior golf events require specific qualifying in order to play.

As your child improves and sets challenging goals, the road becomes more defined, yet much more complex. The American Junior Golf Association (AJGA. More info: AJGA.org) is the premier organization established to bring top junior golfers together for competition at the highest level. Membership alone does not guarantee participation in their events. Players must earn spots in order to compete and have the opportunity to showcase their competitive skills. The AJGA tournaments are followed closely by college coaches and are the best exposure for your child if she is interested in playing collegiate golf. In addition to the AJGA, there are also quality tournaments run by the International Junior Golf Tour (IJGT. More info: IJGT.com) and the Future Collegians World Tour (FCWT. More info: FCWTgolf.com). Listed below is a great guide to help you understand the quality of competition represented at the top levels of junior golf and at what level of play your child is ready for:

Level 1 - Local Tournaments

Age divisions vary, but the most common divisions are eight and under, 9-10, 11-12, 13-14 and 15-17. Listed scores based on 18-hole scoring averages.

- **Boys** – 110 and below: Ready for local golf course and country club tournaments. Top finishers in the older divisions will most likely shoot in the 70s. However, it has become more common to see kids in the 11-12 division breaking 80. Although high handicappers are welcome to play, junior golf organizations will try to pair kids according to skill levels. Kids will place according to gross score, and handicaps are not used. Regions with a lot of talent may separate the older age groups into flights, have mandatory qualifying for top tournaments or simultaneously run a novice division.
- **Girls** – 125 and below: Ready for city and county association tournaments. Depending on the region, older players are capable of shooting in the 70s. If there are enough players, there might be a separate novice division for the girls; otherwise novice competition may be co-ed.

Level 2 - State and Regional Tournaments

Based on 18-hole scoring averages.

- **Boys** – 89 and below: Ready for state golf association, PGA sectional tournaments, and depending on the school and region, could play high school golf. A wider range of competition is available, but parents should not invest a lot of money into traveling to a lot of expensive tournaments at this stage. If possible, plan a fun family vacation or school break around an IJGT event at this level.
- **Girls** – 95 and below: Ready for high school golf, but depending on the region, there may be a wide range of skill levels. Take note of the advice given above. Invest money in lessons and clubs at this level.

Level 3 - National Tournaments

Based on 18-hole scoring averages.

- **Boys** – 76 and below: Ready for USGA junior events and national tournaments such as those provided by the AJGA. Pay attention to quality of fields and if tournaments are nationally ranked.
- **Girls** – 80 and below: Ready for USGA junior events and other national tournaments. Play in tournaments that are nationally ranked.

A great website that lists many of the local and regional junior events in each state is juniorgolfscoreboard.com.

Junior Ranking Defined

The Golfweek/Titleist Performance Index (Titleist Sagarin) and the Junior Golf Scoreboard are considered the top two national-ranking services for junior golf in North America. These two complex systems compile results from hundreds of junior golf tournaments and utilize scientific methods to rank male and female junior golfers. The junior ranking system is used by most college coaches as a tool to evaluate talent all over the country. Players have to play in tournaments that qualify for the Golfweek/Titleist Sagarin Ranking System or the National Junior Golf Scoreboard to be considered in either national ranking. The AJGA, IJGT and FCWT all have specific rankings subject to their tournaments, but they also tie into both the Titleist Sagarin and National Scoreboard Rankings.

The junior ranking system is a good tool and is a necessary part of junior golf if your child wants to play golf at the highest levels. These rankings allow junior golfers to market themselves and assess their playing skills against other golfers from different regions.

Planning a regimented tour schedule not unlike touring professionals is quite expensive, and some families pay a high price to be included in such rankings. In 2003, the AJGA piloted a financial assistance program called the Achieving Competitive Excellence (ACE) Grant Program. The goal of this program is to help junior golfers who have the talent to compete nationally, but not the financial resources to play in AJGA events. If financial aid is needed, check with the individual tours or tournaments to uncover your options.

A computerized ranking system is far from perfect, but there are many complex variables when comparing thousands of kids playing in golf tournaments all over the country. Ranking and selection committees would inevitably be accused of playing politics and of power mongering if there were not some system in place to help them with the fields for the more prestigious invitationals. As stated, the computerized ranking systems aren't perfect, but at least no one can accuse it of bias against a specific player.

Each system uses different criteria to compute a player's overall ranking. A mathematical formula based on individual scoring, strength of field and strength of finish adjusts rankings. Strength of field is an average calculated by using the power rankings of each of the players playing in the event. Power ratings used by the Sagarin system are calculated using a player's record, stroke differential and connection to all the other players in the database. Each junior is usually rated over a season of play, at least four events or over a 52-week period. For the National Junior Golf Scoreboard rankings, national events are rated highly, but to be fair to kids who may not travel a national circuit, all multi-day stroke play tournaments also count. Fall, winter and spring tours such as the California Junior

Tour, designed for the highly competitive player, are tied into the National Junior Golf Scoreboard as well. Tournaments that acquire a national power rating become more prestigious and are more attractive to youngsters trying to get noticed on the national level. The PGA (More info: PGA.com) also runs competitive junior events all across the country.

Most tournaments are set up so players compete in specific age divisions. Many junior events require that your child is under the age of 18, but several tours allow players to play prior to their 19th birthday provided they have not yet enrolled in college. While rankings are earned by playing sanctioned tournaments and are earned regardless of age, some rankings only compare players to other players with the same year of graduation. Proof-of-age policies are in place for all tournament play, and the year of high school graduation are vital in all records to help college coaches know who is eligible for recruiting.

Rankings can't necessarily measure a player's skill level. They don't guarantee future performances, but they do measure scoring in relationship to competition. Top-ranked juniors have successful tournament track records and show an ability to compete at the highest level of junior golf and possibly collegiate or professional golf. In some cases, rankings are simply an assessment of a player's past performance and at best an unbiased record of their tournament scores over an extended period of time.

Top Junior Ranking Systems

1. **Golfweek/Titleist Sagarin:** This is a time-tested ranking system for a majority of the national, state, regional and sectional tournaments. This ranking system measures quality of field through its power rating averages, achieved when higher ranked players compete against one another. Power ratings to evaluate quality of field are important for this system and its mathematical calculations. Tournaments consider it an honor to receive Titleist points for ranking, and numerous top junior tours link up to the Titleist Sagarin system database.

2. **National Junior Golf Scoreboard:** The Junior Golf Scoreboard is an information service created in 1998 as a valuable resource for junior golfers and everyone interested in competitive junior golf. The number of rounds played and the strength of the tournament determine the quality of a player's record. An event that includes National Junior Golf Scoreboard recognition gains prestige. While both systems have pluses and minuses, the ideal ranking system, if there is one, should be some combination of the two. Juniors should be ranked 1) nationally, 2) nationally by graduation year, 3) in their state by graduation year and 4) in their state overall.

3. **AJGA Performance-Based Entry:** In 2003, the AJGA abandoned its tournament selection process, which was based on the strength of a tournament application and resume, in favor of a performance-based entry process. This enables 12-18-year-old members to earn their way into AJGA Open tournaments based on performances at the national, regional and state levels. This process guarantees all deserving juniors an opportunity to play and an important opportunity to be recognized for their talents.

Lists

Fortunately, there is plenty of room at the top of the ranking mountain. There are a variety of ranking lists at the national, state and local levels. Rankings, points and honors earned in various tournaments may be used to name players to regional teams, for invitationals or for tournament exemptions for national or international events.

Each list has different uses. For instance, the AJGA will use points and Titleist Rankings to select team members for its prestigious East vs. West Canon Cup. The AJGA will also include rankings and point systems from other top junior golf events to determine postseason honors such as the Rolex Junior Player of the Year and their Rolex Junior All-America teams. Junior golf organizations will use point systems and lists to assist program directors in selecting players for team events.

Perks

Obviously, there is no guarantee that a No. 1-ranked junior will win the next tournament she enters, but earning a high ranking sure has its perks:

- **Entries to tournaments:** If the number of entrants exceeds the field limit, the tournament committee may bump out lower-ranked players. The AJGA Performance Based Entry Exemption clearly defines a player's status. Players with the highest status will gain entry. Many high-profile tournaments are restricted to a qualified number of ranked players.

- **Special opportunities:** A highly ranked player may be asked to play in junior-ams with tournament sponsors or other high-profile amateurs. Corporate executives pay to play with possible future stars while supporting the event itself. These are awesome opportunities for players to network and develop relationships that will benefit them down the road.

- **Special exemptions:** Top players have the opportunity to compete in professional tour events. Top players also become eligible for regional and national team events like the Junior Solheim Cup or Junior Ryder Cup.

- **Consideration in pairings**
- **Financial benefits:** 1. Colleges consider a player's rank on and off the golf course when awarding athletic scholarships. Grades and SAT scores are also a means by which to measure. Golf coaches from top programs at top academic schools will give greater consideration to a better student with a lesser ranking. Being a high-ranked player with good grades and SATs puts your child in good place as colleges recruit. 2. Top ranked players might be given equipment by the leading club, shoe and golf-ball manufacturers. There are restrictions under the guidelines of the NCAA and the USGA – the governing body of amateur golf – but travel and other expenses can be covered as well. A player who wishes to turn professional should know that a history with a good junior and collegiate ranking might help secure some sponsorship.
- **Goal setting:** Rankings provide short- and long-term goals for the young competitor. Consistent improvement in ranking means the player, her coach and her parents are all doing something right. If a junior's ranking is uneven or going down-hill, it's time to re-evaluate.

The Inside Skinny

Understanding how junior rankings are computed can help parents and players pick which and how many tournaments to play to earn a good ranking. The basic premise of the Titleist Ranking is that a player improves her ranking when she wins or has a top finish in a good quality field. The National Scoreboard is more inclusive of regional and local events. The AJGA has compiled a list of hundreds of tournaments included in their Performance Based Entry System. The AJGA members will fall into one of three status categories:

1. **Fully exempt** – These players have first priority into all AJGA Open tournaments. On average, 20-30% of the fields are filled with fully exempt players.
2. **Tournament exemptions** – A player earns a tournament exemption with a top finish at the state, regional or national level. Players with multiple tournament exemptions have the highest priority. On average, 40-60% of a field can be filled with tournament-exempt players.
3. **Performance stars** – Players earn performance stars to assist them in gaining entry into an AJGA Open tournament. AJGA.org gives complete, official and up-to-date information on Performance Based Entry (PBE). Players and parents are also encouraged to call the AJGA Player Services Department at (877) 373-2542.

A parent should help a junior wade through the myriad of tournament choices, and both must research the number of points and ranking values given to certain events. Your child's golf coach might be of some assistance, but only if he has chartered these waters before. In-depth research and proper planning according to personal preferences and budget considerations will be most beneficial. Don't wait until your child is a senior in high school to try to figure out these systems. Your child's tournament record and scoring average become most important during her sophomore and especially junior years of high school if she wants to play collegiate golf at a top program. At times, it might be best to travel to a smaller site in order to earn valuable stars to help gain entry into a more prestigious tournament.

The USGA qualifiers are often talent-loaded in some regions, and it is best to travel to a smaller qualifying site to give your child better odds of making it into the main event itself. She can't win if she doesn't qualify to play. There have been years when top-ranked juniors played well but didn't qualify to play in the U.S. Junior Girls Championship because there are only so many spots allocated at each qualifying site. It is best to do as much research about the junior golf scene from the internet and from players who have successfully made it through this chapter of their golf career.

The exposure factor is key for competitive golfers. Expose your child to competition at many levels. Playing in national junior divisions is great for 10-12-year-olds, but is necessary for the 14-16-year-old. Evaluation of play isn't always measured in wins and losses, but in rankings moving up from top 100 to top 50 to top 25.

Recreational play, long-term skill development and mental maturity are important considerations when discouraging younger age groups from competing for rankings. Younger children can gain tournament experience by playing in local tournaments that don't count toward rankings. Most local junior golf organizations have year-end awards, recognizing the highest achievements and accomplishments of its players. Once a kid develops a level of competitive maturity, the national rankings race can be an exciting goal for the junior.

Competition helps build confidence and can rack up participation points and when Hayley wins, presto! Junior's name will jump up in the rankings list. Lower scores and top finishes will move your child to the top of her class. It's important to verify player records and report any inaccuracies.

Welcome to the race. To improve ranking, enter tournaments that offer a good chance of winning against slightly stronger opponents. Play as many tournaments as possible but don't burn out. Keep it simple – don't over-manage ranking. Enjoy the learning experience. Have fun.

Ratings and Handicaps

Handicaps are a determination of skill level for golfers of any age. They are what allow golfers of all abilities to compete on a fair playing ground. Your child should understand course ratings, slope and the handicap system so that she can easily measure her abilities. Check out the chart to help identify your child's playing level, and use the guide to help pick out the appropriate level of tournament involvement. As soon as your child can play nine holes and has the desire to track her score, sign her up to get an authorized handicap index score. Use the appropriate tee boxes so she isn't discouraged. Watching a handicap fall is one of the most exciting thrills for an avid golfer. It is also a great source of motivation and is one of the best measuring tools for improvement.

Goal Setting

Ten-year old Haley says her goal is to keep improving her game, whereas her classmate Alexis has a dream to win the U.S. Open. Provided they practice well and develop and accomplish short-term goals regularly, there is a chance Haley will continue to accomplish her goal and Alexis might one day win the women's most coveted USGA title by becoming the U.S. Women's Open Champion. There is a critical difference, though, between Haley's goal and Alexis's dream.

Process Goal vs. Outcome Goal

Haley has committed to performance-oriented improvement relative to her own capabilities. If Haley practices smarter and harder, it is likely she will get better. She has good control of the potential and successful outcome of her goal. Haley progresses from novice competition to intermediate and then on to more advanced.

By age 16, Haley's continuous improvement earns her national recognition and possibly a golf-club sponsorship deal. She concentrates on high-performance training. As her focus is still on improving her game, at 18, she continues to improve and is a college player. Within a few years she is able to win several tournaments, including the NCAA Championships and U.S. Amateur. She works hard and continually improves, inspiring her to play at the professional level after college, thus accomplishing a goal she began working toward when she was 10. She refined her performance goals over the years and is good by now at setting and realizing goals as she habitually goes through a planned process. Haley wins several tournaments her rookie year and is named the LPGA Rookie of the Year.

Obviously, achieving such accolades was not entirely accidental for Haley. She put that possibility in the back of her mind as one of the desirable outcomes of her hard work. Other outcomes she hoped for were to maintain a healthy weight, make the junior high and high school teams, achieve a top-10 national ranking, develop travel opportunities, earn a college scholarship and sign a sponsorship deal.

Haley's goal was always centered on the process – improving her game. In the event that one or two desirable outcomes didn't pan out, she would still feel like a winner – not because her friends and parents tell her so, but because in her heart, she knows she is accomplishing the goal of improving her game, and, as a result, achieving many other desirable outcomes.

On the other hand, Alexis was just lucky she won a tour event. Granted, Alexis worked very hard from early childhood and was focused on the dream of winning the U.S. Open. However, unlike Haley, who had a great deal of control over her goal, Alexis only "believed" she had full control of the outcome because she worked harder than anybody else she knew.

It is commendable that Alexis was strong and confident in her beliefs, and she does deserve to win. In spite of that, we know Alexis had, at best, only partial control over the outcome, simply because there are too many other players who practiced just as hard as Alexis did and believed just as strongly that they would win the U.S. Open

A long-term outcome goal like Alexis's has too many external factors that can undermine the result – for instance, moving to a new town, making it necessary to switch teaching professionals. Or there may be a lack of financial support due to changed circumstances; an unexpected injury might occur; or Alexis might face an opponent who is just too good on that final day. Things beyond her control will happen.

Assume that, for whatever reason, Alexis is unable to win the U.S Women's Open, even though she wins and has success in other prestigious events. She might naturally feel like a failure because she was not able to fulfill her childhood dream, something she had worked toward for many years. Alexis didn't realize her success came in the process and that specific outcomes can't be forced.

Table 5.1

Junior Golf Rating General Characteristics of Various Playing Levels	
+40	Player is just starting to play golf and is learning the basic skills of putting, short game and full swing. Someone else helps with rules, etiquette and scoring.
+35	Player is only slightly more advanced than a +40 player. Player is still learning to coordinate swinging motions when hitting the ball. Can get the ball airborne, but may need playable distance. Player is learning etiquette and to keep own score.
+30	Player is now beginning to manage all aspects of the game. Ball contact is better, but still not too consistent. Getting closer to hitting par 4s in regulation. Player understands scoring and is more comfortable with course etiquette and rules of the game. Player has limited success in all areas of the game and moves at a better pace.

Table 5.1 (Cont.)

	Junior Golf Rating General Characteristics of Various Playing Levels
+25	Player is able to control shots better and has a much better sense of distance control. Reads greens now and is better with short game around the greens. Player will make regulation pars, but is still inconsistent. Course management is still weak, but getting better. May still have blowup holes, but will consistently break 100. May even enjoy a birdie now and again. Player can keep score unassisted, has a good pace of play and has an understanding of the basic rules.
+20	Player is getting better at moving the ball from the tee box to the green in regulation. Is improving in all skill fundamentals and learning new shots as well. Driver shots and ball-striking have vastly improved, and although may not be able to execute all of the time, player has a good understanding of what she should be doing. On the verge of consistently breaking 90. More par chances, but occasional mistakes hurt the scoring. Needs to fine-tune short game. Player can identify strengths and weaknesses in game. Player can take a serious look at competition, especially at the local level.
+15	Player may have a string of pars and is capable of making a birdie. Starts to pay attention to actual ball yardage, including knowing exact distances for ball carry with each club. Putting scores should drop below 36 and players should be acquiring less penalty strokes. Consistently breaking 90 and eyes set on the low 80s and high 70s. Starts to develop short game to a higher level – a stronger up-and-down mentality. Learns how to work the ball and to control trajectories. Should always use golf etiquette and play according to the rules of the game. Report scores accurately and step up practice time if player chooses to reach for a single-digit handicap. Starting to recognize opportunities to play more aggressive and to realize when a risk outweighs the benefit. Player is developing more spin and power and is much more aware of own swing. Is starting to think better and coach self on the course in a more mature fashion. Learning about self-control and the mental aspects of the game. Competitive scores may be higher than non-competitive scores at this level.
+10	Player has a dependable swing and good short game and is a decent putter. Player has added variety in shot selection by using lobs, knockdown shots, draws and fades with some success. Player is developing a game plan before she tees off and is consistently capable of making pars and birdies, but still has a few holes where she either scores a high number or a string of holes where she doesn't manage to score par. Player demonstrates solid fundamentals and is only a mistake or two away from good scores. Feels more comfortable competing at the higher levels. Should definitely compete on a local level and should start to enter regional events and get a feel for stronger competition. Starts to seriously track statistics such as putts per round, fairways hit, and greens in regulation.
+5	Player has a very dependable swing and consistently executes most shots. Player's fundamentals are sound and player has a good understanding of the game as a whole and in its parts. Player will keep more accurate statistics and know exact distances from the hole on every shot played. Clubs will be checked and fitted properly, assuring that a player has the best equipment for her body build and physical strength. Player consistently breaks 80 and is always on the verge of shooting par or sub-par rounds. A player at this level will not let mistakes ruin a round and is getting better at recovering from a poor shot. Players are less swing-minded and more target-focused. Players at this level are good golfers and can focus on the higher levels of competition.
0	Player has good visualization and anticipates success. Player will frequently have outstanding round, made up of outstanding shots. Player is capable of hitting most shots. While even the best player's average GIR is 13 or so, par golfers get up and down when they miss greens, or make more birdies. A scratch golfer is consistently good in most areas of the game. Should compete at the highest level of play possible and should attempt to play in the National Championships. Fine tuning all areas of game.

Misconceptions about Process Goals

There are two common misconceptions about process goals. One is that they are less ambitious and thus encourage mediocrity. Not true. A player can be as ambitious as she wants in setting a process goal. The difference is that there is a high degree of correlation between a player's effort and the successful achievement of a process or performance goal.

For instance, Haley can choose to increase her driver's yardage by 35 yards. This is ambitious for Haley, but if she is well coached and works hard, there is a high probability she can achieve the goal because, ultimately, it is up to her. Many of her process goals can be directly related to her statistics. Statistics will help Haley measure her progress. When she does achieve her process goal, she may also experience a desirable outcome – winning the nationals.

The other misconception about process goals is that "improving the game" is not a clear or real goal. Ask yourself two questions: Is the goal measurable? Can the long-term goal be broken down into short-term goals? If your answer to one of these questions is, "yes," then the goal is clear, and it's real. In this case, "improving the game" can be measured – by Haley improved her ranking. The goal can also be broken into many short-term goals: improving driving accuracy, doing 10 extra push-ups in a conditioning routine, and so on.

"Having fun" is another completely valid process goal. At first it might not appear to be a goal at all, and even if it is, how can fun be measured? Ask that of toy manufacturers. These guys know that when a kid picks up a toy his single-minded goal is to have fun. Toy manufacturers routinely use a scientific method called the Likert-type scale to measure fun when studying which of the many toy models has the best potential in the market. For our purposes, we could link "having fun" to a short-term goal such as, "I will engage in an activity I enjoy for three hours each week over the next month." We have just found a way to measure "having fun."

"Improving the game" and "having fun" are different from do-your-best goals such as, "Next year I will try to do the best I can." This goal can neither be measured directly nor can it be divided into measurable short-term goals.

Setting and measuring an outcome goal may be simple – "I want to win the U.S. Open when I grow up" – as compared to a process goal. However, experts recommend, and sports-psychology literature clearly indicates that process goals, when correctly and consistently utilized, allow a player to achieve greater success than either outcome or do-your-best goals. Process goals allow a child to build on immediate successes – a player doesn't have to wait until the end to feel fulfilled or successful.

Still, children are natural dreamers. A dream can be a great source of motivation to work hard. Always encourage their dreams and help them understand the difference between a dream and a process goal. Children should be taught to chase process goals and enjoy each accomplishment. That is the practical way to make children feel successful, whether or not all dreams come true.

Finding a Tournament

It's great to be a golf kid – tournament opportunities couldn't be better, you have a devoted parent or coach driving to and from competition sites, and when the vehicle is equipped with a rear-seat DVD entertainment system, life can't get any better for a golf kid.

There are tournaments and leagues that cater to every skill level – rookie to advanced – and include all junior age groups from five to 18. The best place to start looking for tournaments is at your local golf club or community junior program. Chances are the club runs tournaments and links with a junior competitive structure. Contact the golf organizations involved in junior competition to find tournaments that match set criteria:

- USGA: There are national, sectional and district offices for tournaments and USGA Golf programs in your area (More info: usga.com). Golf programs revolve around three seasons: spring, summer and fall, but in geographically mild climates, tournaments are also available in the winter months.
- Local junior golf associations
- The official junior golf site of the USGA, PGA Tour, PGA of America, LPGA, NGCOA, GCSAA and the World Golf Foundation. (More info: juniorlinks.com)
- Junior golf organizations and tournaments (More info: golfhelp.com)
- PGA Junior Circuit (More info: pga.com).
- American Junior Golf Association (More info: ajga.org)
- International Junior Golf Association (More info: ijgt.com)
- Future Collegians World Tour (More info: fcwtgolf.com)
- All-Star Junior Golf Tour (More info: allstarjuniorgolftour.com)
- National Junior Golf Scoreboard – players are able to search by state (More info: njgs.com)
- Golfweek/Titleist rankings (More info: golfweek.com)
- State-level high school interscholastic federations usually direct high school tournaments. For example, the California Interscholastic Federation (More info: cifstate.org) manages school tournaments in that state. Hook up with the school coach or your local school board to learn more.

If you don't find an appropriate level and format in your area, consider organizing a tournament. Just make sure there are enough kids who want to compete, and contact the LPGA or PGA for support. With a little legwork and some financial savvy, you can have a junior competition or organization to call your own.

Picking the Right Tournament

After the coach and type of class, picking the right tournaments to enter determines whether a player is going to be self-motivated to practice and compete. First, make a list of performance or process goals for the year and write down all the desirable outcomes that are possible once each goal is accomplished.

Recreational Play

Charlotte, a 14-year-old, moved with her family from upstate New York to Southern California. As there are no ice hockey rinks in her new town, she hopes to learn to play golf, the sport that is popular there. Charlotte's process goals are having fun and making friends. Her desirable outcomes are recreation, fitness and having friends to hang out with outside of school.

For her age group and beginner level of play, Charlotte would want to join an LPGA*USGA Girls Golf Program – a program designed for beginners ages seven to 17. This program will introduce girls to golf in a purely recreational and social environment. If she becomes more interested in the sport and wants to compete, she should contact her local junior golf association and the Southern California chapter of the PGA to see what tournament options she may have.

Game Development

Consider the example of a junior who is seriously into competitive golf. Ten-year-old Courtney has spent the last few years learning golf with a professional coach. Along the way she competed in a few junior golf camps and parent-child tournaments, and she can't wait to get into tournaments. She should play in local events and look for possible opportunities to play in larger national events to measure her talent against girls her own age. Courtney doesn't have to play in many tournaments outside her region, but it would be great experience to play in a few PGA section sanction events out of her immediate area.

If Courtney maintains a good scoring average, she should continue to stretch her boundaries over the next few golf seasons. Different tournament experiences will be good for her if she is ready for competition. Stay close to home as much as possible at first; your daughter will be more comfortable in familiar surroundings. Adjusting to time zones, different style golf courses, new food and weather conditions are all things that may affect your child's performance in her early development.

Choice Table

Making a bottom-line choice is easy. If a junior simply wants to try golf for a few seasons as one of many sports she would like to develop, then stay local, keep life simple and move at her pace. On the other hand, a junior who has made a choice to develop golf as her primary sport and makes time throughout the year for practice and play will have access to hundreds of tournament opportunities.

With a variety of choices available in tournament golf, picking the right competition can be tricky. A sample format (Table 5.2) to help select the right program or tournament based on age group, current proficiency and process goals can be useful.

The format is not nearly as complicated as it looks. Start by listing all possible golf-related process goals. (Table 5.2– Part 1). Later we will narrow it down to the goals junior wants to accomplish this year, but for now simply list all the possibilities. List the practice times and tournaments (or programs). Include various age groups and proficiency levels available at the local, regional and national levels.

Third, list all possible golf-related, near-term desirable outcomes (Table 5.2 – Part 2), continuing along the same row as the "process goals." Remember the difference: a process goal is one over which one has a fair degree of control. A desirable outcome is a possibility over which one has little control.

Now, for each competition, review the tournament regulations and checkmark all the possible process goals and desirable outcomes. For example, some of the best kids compete in the Southern California Junior Golf Association (SCJGA) tournaments. Participation in these tournaments can help a new player gain regional competitive experience and improve mental toughness; checkmark these two process goals for the SCJGA scheduled tournaments. In addition to accomplishing these process goals, a kid who does well in these tournaments can earn sectional honors and may qualify for national tournaments – a desirable outcome; checkmark this desirable outcome for the SCJGA scheduled tournaments.

Using the choice table is the easy part. For her age group and current proficiency, the junior has to find the best match in the table for the process goals she intends to accomplish this year. This will point the junior to the right set of tournaments and programs and indicate how many hours of practice and match play are needed to accomplish those goals.

Measure progress at the end of the year. Junior is a happy camper if most process goals have been accomplished and one or two of the desirable outcomes have occurred. If not, consider adjusting process goals and practice time the following year.

Table 5.2 Part 1

Choice Table to Pick the Right Tournament Based Upon Process Goals

Tournaments, Leagues and Programs

		Golf camps, Intro programs, & local 1-day tourneys	Local tournaments	Regional/Off season Tours/PGA Series events in addition to supporting local junior golf org.	IJGT/FCWT/AJGA & Regional	AJGA & USGA- National	AJGA & USGA- National
Practice	*Hours per	4	8	18	20	25	25+
	Weeks per year	8	12	44	44	44	44
Process Goals	Skill mastery		x	x	x	x	x
	Travel opportunity		x	x	x	x	x
	Mental toughness		x	x	x	x	x
	Skill improvement	x	x	x	x	x	x
	National competitive experience					x	
	Regional competitive experience			x	x	x	
	Developing endurance						x
	Skill developmen		x	x	x	x	
	Physical exercise			x	x	x	x
	Learning life skills		x	x	x	x	
	Making friends	x	x	x	x	x	x
	Having fun	x	x	x	x	x	x
	Practice	x	x	x	x	x	x
	Process Goals	x	x	x	x	x	x
Age	Current Proficiency	Beginner	Intermediate	Intermediate	Advanced	Advanced	Advanced
14 to 16							

Table 5.2 Part 2

Choice Table to Pick the Right Tournament Based Upon Process Goals

Near-term Desirable Outcomes

Age: 14 to 16

Near-term Desirable Outcomes	Beginner — Golf camps, Intro programs, & local 1-day tourneys	Intermediate — Local tournaments	Intermediate — Regional/Off season Tours/PGA Series events in addition to supporting local junior golf org.	Intermediate	Advanced — IJGT/FCWT/AJGA & Regional	Advanced — AJGA & USGA-National	Advanced — AJGA & USGA-National
*Turning professional	4	8		18	20	25	25+
Making the college team	8	12		44	44	44	44
Making the national team		X		X	X	X	X
Earning a college scholarship		X		X	X	X	X
Making the high school team		X		X	X	X	X
Earning a sponsorship	X	X		X	X	X	X
Top 10 national ranking							X
Sectional endorsement					X	X	X
Earning a national rankendurance							X
Top 10 sectional ranking				X	X	X	X
Earning a sectional rank				X	X	X	X
Understand match rules			X	X	X	X	
Fitness		X	X	X	X	X	X
Social benefits		X	X	X	X	X	X
Recreation	X		X	X	X	X	X

Updating the choice table at the beginning of each year is a great way to get a golf kid started on developing new process goals for the year. It also is a great help in allocating practice and play time and in choosing competitions that can help her accomplish those goals.

Periodization

Sports scientists use the fancy term "Periodization" to tell you to your face that your 14-year-old is not going to be able to play her best in each of the ten or so tournaments in which she is registered to play this year. Attempting to train full bore and play the best every day of the year will only lead to injury or burnout, or both.

That's not to say that every now and then the player should have a cavalier attitude toward training or take tournaments lightly. Periodization is about finding an appropriate balance between physical training, drills, practice, play, scoring and rest so the player reaches a peak level of performance at a calculated time. Learning to peak is key to success in tournaments.

Experts recommend picking one or two important tournaments from a player's yearly schedule and planning a 12-week-periodization training around the competition, weeks nine and 10 being the tournament weeks.

Say the player wants to devote 20 hours to training in a week – a typical periodization schedule would be as shown in Table 5.3. Professional golfers typically spend at least eight hours a day at a golf course during their season.

Table 5.3

Hours /Week				
	Week 1-to-5	Week 6-to-8	Week 9-to-10	Week 11-to-12
Physical Training	4	2	1	4
Drills/Practice	8.5	8.5	6	10
Playing	6	8	8-12	4
Active Rest	1.5	1.5	1.5	2

This is a light schedule since it usually takes four hours or more to play a competitive round of golf. The weeks after the tournament are called a period of active-rest. This is not an exact science; the purpose of discussion is to point out that players need to plan peaking. The player should rest and have some down time between tournaments, but in many cases, players do not have the luxury of more than a day or two. Children are more resilient, and it is only when they are older that the physical strain starts to take a toll on their bodies. She should push hard leading up to an event, but then back off a bit so that she will not over-train or get fatigued.

At first glance, this schedule may appear impractical. Come on, what kid would want to drill and train the week following the Nationals? However, the junior should be encouraged to stick to some sort of schedule. Pay attention to mental alertness and freshness in addition to physical health. She will thank you for it when she decides to play college golf or join the professional tour, where mental and physical demands are much greater.

It takes planning to coordinate the logistics of tournament golf. It's easier to break down her year into seasons. You have the spring/summer season and the fall/winter season. For example, you might plan one local or regional tournament a month during your fall/winter season and two to four per month during -your spring/ summer season. A top-ranked junior will usually play 12-14 events a year, not counting high school golf. The girls' high school golf season in many areas is from early September through early or mid November. The boys' season usually is from the early part of March through mid May.

Tournament Travel

Teenage players love competitive golf because it gives them a chance to travel and see peers on a regular basis. Some events will provide local housing if junior needs to travel independently. At the higher echelons of junior competition – regional, national and international circuits – albeit rare, a local club or organization may even pick up a portion of the travel tab. If there are several competitors from a certain region or friendships have been established, parents may take turn chaperoning the kids.

Itinerary

There are hundreds of junior tournaments, so it shouldn't be difficult to find nearby tournaments for a beginner or intermediate-level junior player. As a junior advances in the rankings race, tournament travel is inevitable.

Crisscrossing the country, meeting new people and learning about other regions is both fun and educational. A junior has to be prepared to adjust to different time zones, weather conditions and foods and to live out of a suitcase for periods of time, because the schedule can get hectic. Always allow a day or two to adjust for jet-lag. Players who travel extensively during the school year need to bring their schoolwork with them and leave time to complete their assignments.

Housing

If a parent chooses to accompany the child, he might stay with friends or in a hotel. Even if the tournament is within a three-to-four-hour drive from home, it may be advantageous to arrange an overnight stay so the player is better prepared for her round. Tournaments sometimes offer recommendations and discount deals at hotels near the tournament site.

Tournaments may also offer private housing and transportation, including airport transfers for all players who live more than 50 or 60 miles from the tournament. Players can stay at the homes of other players or with members of the host club. In this case, the host family assumes responsibility for providing meals, local transportation and general supervision. Often, tournaments may pitch in by providing lunch and transportation to and from the tournament site. It used to be much more the case 20 years ago, and there is a rising trend to use private housing once again. Rising hotel costs are making it cost-prohibitive for parents and coaches alike to accompany their juniors to big tournaments. In any case, private housing is limited and must be requested ahead of time.

Most tournaments carefully screen host families, but it is a good idea to verify this with the tournament director. A player who stays with a host family should be instructed to behave appropriately so the visit is a pleasant experience for both the host family and the player.

Practice Partners

Good chemistry, integrity and skills that complement your child's are important factors when choosing friends. Golf is an individual sport, but your child will develop lasting friendships with the juniors she is competing against. Mutual respect is a common denominator among players – golf is the only sport in which competitors often help each other with challenges in their games. Often, friendships will grow out of practice rounds or being paired together often. Depending on how social your junior is, she will spend some time with other junior competitors before and after a round, during practice rounds, possibly traveling to and from tournaments and maybe even lodging together. Sharing room expenses is a great way to cut costs when traveling on the national tours. Obviously, having a friend that she can get along with easily is nice in general, but can also help junior relax during tournaments.

Next, encourage your child to play practice rounds with better players and players that will not distract your child from her game plan. Also teach your child that she, too, should always use her best golf etiquette and not be a distraction to anyone she is paired with. If she is not a chatty kid, make sure she doesn't play with someone who talks the entire round. Prepare her to play with all personality types and discuss how she should handle the different personalities she may face.

Advice for the Golf Traveler

Dear Miss Marta:
Our family recently planned a family vacation at a posh golf resort. Upon arrival, the front-desk attendant informed us, "Your children will not be allowed to play the championship course. Would you like day care?" I appreciated the courtesy, but was irked that she assumed my children didn't know how to play golf. In fact, both my children have been playing for years (and they're eight and 10) and are quite accomplished golfers. In fact, my one child is a much better player than my wife is. My children had been so excited to play the course, so they were quite upset at the comments. After some bantering with the attendant, we asked to speak with the head golf professional. In the end, we enjoyed a week of great golf on all the courses at this beautiful resort. However, it was difficult to disguise my annoyance with the resort as we negotiated our way through their policies. I think it is discourteous to assume only adults play golf, and I think resorts should carefully consider where children fit into the scheme of a "golf vacation." I also think they should honor some sort of junior rate as well; but that is an entirely different matter! What do you say?
– Irked in Scottsdale

Miss Marta says: Good job in getting the kids on the golf course ready at an early age! Resorts want to make the facility enjoyable for all guests. They need to be more diplomatic, and you need to communicate that your children are golf savvy before arrival. Find out the policies before trekking out to the first tee! Write a letter to management, but spare the front-desk person. It could be the training – or lack thereof. Now, go hit some balls with your kids.

6
Tournament Time

In golf, it's the little things that can add up when it comes to making those long hours of practice pay off in tournaments. For instance, knowing the tournament rules and code of conduct is essential. Checking equipment the previous evening and getting a good night's rest can make a difference on the big day. Arrive at the tournament site early and well fueled, and always complete a proper warm-up routine.

Walter Hagen adequately defined tournament golf when he said, "One thing a tournament golfer has to learn is that it is not the game he played last year, or last week, that he commands in any one event. He has only his game at the time; and it may be far from his best – but it's all he has, and he'd just as well 'harden his heart' and make the most of it." In more modern language, he had better learn how to "suck it up" and "just do it" even when his "A" game has vanished. One of the highest compliments of both Jack Nicklaus and Tiger Woods is when reporters tell of how they won a tournament in spite of playing their "B" or "C" game. True champions find ways to win.

Translating Practice to Tournament Play

When the top juniors and collegiate players turn professional, they discover in a hurry that qualifying school is the most intense golf they have ever faced. Players who have practiced at a level beyond what's needed to simply win the next junior or collegiate event are usually the ones who can make a smooth transition from top amateur competition to the professional level. The players in Q School who have learned to play well under stressful circumstances, have taught themselves to peak, and, more importantly, how to win at the top amateur level of the game have given themselves a chance for success. The odds are greater than winning on a lottery ticket, but there are still no guarantees in competitive golf.

As a player moves up the junior rankings to the professional levels, it's important to continually raise practice standards up a few notches. If your child has set his goal on becoming a champion golfer, it is wise to help him set his short-term, mid-term and long-term goals for game improvement. He should strive for a mindset that puts him on a course of "four years ahead" mentality. At 12, your son should look toward the skill levels of the top 16-year-olds in the country. When he is 16, he should desire to be at the level of the top 20-year-olds. At 20, he should be looking at the top players in the 24-year-old range. This mentality will help push him up the ladder of success and encourage the junior to give it everything he's got. If obtained, at 16, your son will get the attention of college coaches, yet will be humble in the fact he isn't where he needs to be yet. Top golfers realize they have to maintain intense practice disciplines in order to keep improving in all areas of their game.

Golfers can only practice to be prepared. Proper preparation, good timing and a little good fortune are the elements of victory. Your son can play a flawless round, shoot 67 and get beat. However, if he perseveres and continues to shoot 5-under par, his day will come. Practice to beat another player is futile. All energies should be spent on self-improvement. Your son can't control the competition, but he can put numbers up on the scoreboard that will get the competition's attention.

Your child needs to focus on the things in his game that will make scoring low easier. He needs to practice these things like his life depends on it. Your son needs big weapons for battle. It will be easier to set new comfort zones for scoring as he continues to strengthen areas discussed in Chapter 4. Say junior needs to work on distance off the tee, getting his approach shots closer, improving feel on the putting green, improving his sand play or improving his up-and-down percentages – it is best he works on these as often as possible and gets to do so in a competitive arena.

Your child needs to develop a repeatable golf swing, a great short game and a sound putting stroke and then ingrain them through dedicated and consistent practice. Annika Sorenstam did a fabulous job identifying changes she needed to make and then with the mentality of a marine in combat, set forth to train. It's good to have a shot to depend on when stakes are high. Juniors need to practice in the blazing heat, the sticky humidity, the wind, the rain and the cold just as they practice in good weather conditions. If you live in climates that provide challenging weather conditions, encourage your child to embrace the opportunity to practice in them. Kids who tend to practice in such difficult climates will have an advantage over kids who never have had to face inclement weather. If you live in a place where you get only poor weather, your child also needs a safe, relaxing place to practice where fighting the weather isn't a constant battle. An indoor practice facility is helpful to allow your child to work on his swing, and it allows him to focus on technique without all the other distractions. Mental practice and indoor practice can allow your child quality practice even when the sun isn't shining in your hometown.

For those of you blessed with great weather most of the year, you need to encourage your child to get out the door when the weather conditions are tough. This is his opportunity to practice in conditions he will surely face in his golfing career. If you live in a mild climate and have the opportunity to drive to a town with more severe weather, **do it**.

Tournaments can present many new factors to worry about. Practicing hard in the weeks prior to a tournament can help junior relegate basic strokes, techniques and conditions to the subconscious. Being more "in-the-zone" allows a player to maintain his natural level of play, in spite of normal distractions and nervousness. Being "in the zone" means being subconsciously competent at your highest level of play. At all levels, players are in the process of learning how to juggle everyday life with the demands of tournament golf.

For key tournaments like the season-ending CIF-State Championship, break away from the normal practice routine. Instead, develop a specific practice plan leading up to the championship. Your son should discuss with his coach what he would need to finish first. For example, he knows players are required to play 36 holes the last day or he knows typically the State Championship has ridiculously long rounds, 5 ½ hours or more. It is going to take strength, stamina, and good concentration to carry his bag in 90-degree heat and 90% humidity. He might work on techniques to help him focus. The course might require he hit a fade quite a bit, and he naturally draws the ball. His coach may suggest a daily routine alternating between grooving a fade in one session, practicing in the heat of the day the next, followed by a conditioning session. He may go a whole week practicing to only play while 100% focused. He arrives early to warm up and goes out to play, and as soon as his mind wanders, he's done. He walks off the course. How many days does it take him to be able to warm up and play 36 with complete confidence he was 100% there on each shot, 100% of the time? It takes discipline to walk away from sloppy practice!

Preparing for the Tournament

You won't find professional players who party all night long and head straight into a tournament or match early the next morning. If they do, it's guaranteed they won't be on the professional tour long, and they will not find their names high on any tour earnings rankings. There are pre-tournament rituals most players follow so they can do their best.

At the same time, tournament preparation does not have to be a regimented boot camp. Rather, it is a set of simple, easy-to-follow routines, like getting a good night's sleep the night before a tournament day. When parents encourage the child to follow a pre-tournament ritual, it becomes a habit. Checklists are helpful so your child stays on task and gets in the habit of being prepared. Soon the child will start to prepare for tournaments without bring prodded.

24 Hours Before His Round

Most tournaments inform players of their tee times by email, via a posting on the tournament website, by postal mail or at check-in. It's always a good idea to reconfirm your tee assignment and starting time the night before the tournament. For final rounds or those after a cut has been made, it is the player's responsibility to find out his tee time; this is usually done by telephone or the internet, or it's posted at the course.

The Rules of the United States Golf Association govern play, unless otherwise stated by the tournament committee. Rule 6-3 states, "The player must start at the time established by the Committee." The penalty for breach of Rule 6-3 is disqualification. However, note to Rule 6-3a provides: "The Committee may provide in the conditions of a competition (Rule 33-1) that, if the player arrives at his starting point, ready to play, within five minutes after his starting time, in the absence of circumstances that warrant waiving the penalty of disqualification as provided in Rule 33-7, the penalty for failure to start on time is loss of the first hole in match play or two strokes at the first hole in stroke play instead of disqualification." Remember, all that said, unless the committee has stated such an exception, your child will be disqualified if he is not at the tee at his tee time. Most tournaments require a player to be at the tee five minutes prior to his tee time. There are times when a tournament will run late on the tee. Your child needs to hang around the first tee and is responsible to be there when they call his group to the tee.

In 2003, PGA Tour rookie Aaron Baddeley had a junior moment. He arrived 40 seconds late for a tee time during the PGA Championship and got docked two shots. Not to think that it would only happen to rookies, PGA Tour Veteran Craig Stadler had a senior moment. Thinking his third-round start time at the Senior PGA was 10:20, when it really was 10:05; he arrived 2 minutes, 20 seconds late to the tee and he too was hit with a two-shot penalty.

Golfers should maintain a high-carb diet, especially when facing tournaments being played in hot and windy conditions: eat whole-grain breads, cereals and pasta, plus plenty of fruits and vegetables. Avoid eating fatty and spicy foods during the tournament. In the same way you encourage your kids to put homework and stuff in their school backpack before going to bed, help them prepare their golf bag the night before. It's key that your child be organized so it is easy to fuel and hydrate his body, helping to maintain concentration and minimize fatigue. Make sure he is in the habit of carrying an extra sports drink, fruit juice or water. Also, by tournament time he should know what snacks he would like tucked away for a needed boost of energy. Sandwiches, fruit, cereal bars, dried fruit, trail mix or plain nuts – all pack well in a small pocket of his golf bag. Forgetting snacks would be as detrimental as forgetting his sand wedge.

Get as much sleep as possible the night before a tournament. Researchers know that attention and focus are critical to playing successful golf, and they also know that high levels of attention and focus are dependent on getting quality sleep and being adequately rested. Your child should learn some simple relaxation and visualization techniques for his bedtime routine, assuring a peaceful night's sleep. These tools will help him with jetlag challenges due to travel or the proverbial butterflies in the belly the night before an important round. Note that over-sleeping if your child has a late tee time can be just as detrimental- you don't want him to show up to the tee feeling lazy or groggy.

Make sure the alarm clock is set and working, and always have your child arrange a wakeup call if he is staying in a hotel. There will be days when he may be tempted to hit that snooze alarm as his clock buzzes at 5 a.m. Juniors need to know that it's okay to lose sleep once in a while. More important is that they not psych themselves out before a round because of lost sleep.

Fueling for Tournaments

Always allow time for a decent breakfast. If your son doesn't like to carry around a lot of snacks in his bag, then he is going to have to compensate by having more to eat at breakfast. Breakfast cereal with low-fat milk and banana on top, three slices of toast and a fruit smoothie provides a good amount of carbohydrates without being too filling. Go bananas, go yogurt and eggs are great as long as they aren't too greasy.

Plan. If you have a 7 a.m. tee time, your breakfast options might be limited. Later tee times will afford your child the chance to eat lighter at breakfast and then have a bigger meal prior to warming up. Salads with chicken, turkey sandwiches or some macaroni and cheese would all be great pre-tournament meals. If your child doesn't feel he can eat enough at one sitting to keep him fueled, then it is necessary for him to graze during his round. The high-carbohydrate plan helps store glycogen in the muscles and liver as fuel for activity. Once again, avoid high-fat and spicy foods.

Remember he may eat breakfast at 7 a.m., start warm ups at 8:30 and not tee off until 10. That's fine if he has consumed a large, nutritious meal, giving food time to be absorbed by the stomach. However, come noon, he will need that light snack packed away in his golf bag; he may even consider snacking every two or three holes. Most courses have snack bars, but it is a good habit for him to pack what he likes, keeping him away from possible distractions at a crowded snack bar.

Kids don't sweat as much as adults do and are less able to cool off. They also absorb heat more easily. These factors increase the risk of dehydration in kids. Give children a squeeze bottle of water or sports drink and remind them to take gulps before, during and after the round. Junior should be consuming fluids well before he's thirsty. It's best if he gets in the practice of taking a swig on every tee box. A sports drink is tasty, will supply energy, and turns on thirst, encouraging kids to gulp frequently.

Before a Tournament Round

The big day is here. Weeks, months and years of preparation might go into a tournament victory. The big question for most tournament golfers is "How do I play my best golf when it really counts?" Do you remember the first sentence of this chapter? In golf, it's the little things that can add up when it comes to making those long hours of practice pay off in tournaments. Being prepared is the best way to remain calm and give yourself the best chance for your "A" game to show up. Once junior has taken care of getting up in plenty of time, eaten well and arrived at the course safely, then it is time to settle into his tournament practice routine.

Every player is different in regard to how much pre-round prep time he needs. Your son will develop his own time schedule, but it is best that he arrive at the course at least one hour prior to his tee time. Many professionals like to arrive two hours ahead of their tee time, giving themselves a good 40 minutes or so to stretch and do some pre-swing warm ups. They have private locker rooms and fitness trailers at their convenience. Your child may want to spend some extra time in the hotel room doing his stretch routine. Some tournaments will request that players check in once they arrive at the facility, just to make sure they have arrived safely. He needs to be aware if there is a mandatory check-in. Whether there is check-in or not, he needs to be aware of the time at all times so that he reports to the tee box at least five minutes prior to his assigned time. Often, there will be a clock on the practice facilities to help players keep track of time. A pocket watch attached to his bag can take away anxiousness in this department. A new experience, a different course and the hustle and bustle of parents, players, coaches and officials can be intimidating for a young child.

If the tournament is running late and now he is thrown off his usual preparation time schedule, he can practice putting or chipping a little longer. However, as in any kind of delay, he shouldn't overextend himself so that he is physically or emotionally spending energy he needs for his round. (In golf, tournament play in certain parts of the country will often have rain delays or disruptions in play due to thunder and lightning. In general, golfers play in the rain, unless the players are in danger due to inclement weather or the course is unplayable.) If there is a delay and it is extremely hot, keep him out of the sun and let him listen to his Ipod in a quiet, shady place. In any case, he doesn't want to be physically spent before he tees it up. Avoid negative distractions such as competitors and parents complaining about the delay, course conditions, etc. While waiting, parents may spend some time getting to know one another. Many lasting friendships have blossomed during tournaments.

If the coach is available, players might like to discuss strategies, game plans, club selections or swing thoughts. Delays are great bonding times for players and coaches – having coach there for moral support is huge in really tense tournament situations. A good coach understands that the hard work has already been done. Coaches will remind players to trust themselves, keep things simple, relax and rely on all the pre-tournament preparation. Positive mental cues and avoiding negative self-talk are keys to getting his round started off well.

Sports psychologist Dr. Deborah Graham says that the most valuable tool a player can bring to the course is a strong mental game; some quiet time right before the round is good for your child. He needs to prepare his mind for the task at hand – achieving complete and total focus on every golf shot played. Famous basketball coach Phil Jackson had his players take a ball into a locker room corner and visualize the game plan. Don't expect your little guy to do that just yet, but make room in the schedule for some quiet time so you establish a good pre-tournament ritual for later years. A trip to the restroom or some time with the Ipod may do the trick.

As a junior develops, competition days will increase. At first, he may only play in one-day tournaments. Then he will play in 36-hole events, and as he matures, he will play in 54- or 72-hole championships. There will be travel to tournament sites in different cities and countries. Travel is an exciting perk for a golf kid, but acclimating to a new city and culture takes some getting used to. Following a standard set of pre-tournament rituals will reassure the junior that every round is, in fact, like any other, allowing relaxed and focused play.

Etiquette

Most sports have some unwritten code of conduct or etiquette. However, etiquette is a word most often heard in relation to golf. Golf etiquette is an essential part of the game, but it's not just about manners. It's so important to the game that it is the first topic of discussion in The Rules of Golf. Etiquette is just as much about safety as it is about a player's behavior on the golf course. Golf is usually played without the supervision of a referee or an umpire, and the game ultimately relies on the integrity of the players. The Rules of Golf states in Rule 33-7, "If a Committee considers that a player is guilty of a serious breach of etiquette, it may impose a penalty of disqualification under this rule."

If etiquette is so important to golf, and it is at the very foundation of the spirit of the game, then what is it? Good etiquette is not snobby behavior. It's simply a way to allow everyone involved in the game to have a good time without hindrance. Translated to a golf tournament setting, good etiquette means players, spectators, parents and coaches accept certain behavioral norms so that everyone can derive maximum enjoyment from the event. Everyone involved in the game should conduct himself in a disciplined manner, showing courtesy and sportsmanship at all times.

The rules of golf etiquette are what they are for several very important reasons. Etiquette protects golfers, since many of the rules relate to safety. Many etiquette rules relate to pace of play, ensuring that the game is enjoyable for everyone. Others are important to the game in that they relate to maintaining the quality of the golf course. Last, but definitely not least, proper golf etiquette simply embraces those "golden rules" you want your children to adopt as keystones of their lives whether they golf or not. Courtesy, respect and integrity will always serve a person well.

Newcomers to the game often learn as they go, but there is no excuse for a tournament player, his parents or his coach not to play by the rules and use etiquette on and around the golf course.

Parent Etiquette

- Until your child can pack his bags and fly to a tournament all by himself, you, the parent, have to help junior prepare for his tournament. Parents should be instilling good preparation habits – but let him help.
- Until he can drive, you will have to get him to the tournament site in plenty of time so he doesn't feel rushed and is ready for his round. Plan your day accordingly – give yourself plenty of time to get ready and map out your intended route to the course. Be sure to consider traffic patterns in an unfamiliar city.
- Resist the temptation to sit on the driving range and critique every swing he makes. Don't be bossy, and be respectful of his prep time. On the course, hemming and hawing and tearing your hair out at every missed shot your kid hits is embarrassing for your child. You don't want your child to walk around with "one-of-those-parents." Over-involved parents are distractions and are annoying to their child, other players and other spectators.
- Try to cheer good shots made by all competitors. Cheering a little louder for your little guy is perfectly acceptable.
- Don't hesitate to have your child removed from competition if he is misbehaving on the golf course. Club throwing, swearing, or damaging the course should not be tolerated. Most tournament officials will not tolerate such behavior, but if it goes unnoticed by the committee, then you need to teach your child a hard lesson. No tournament is more important than teaching a child life lessons.
- No matter the outcome, show love to your child as he comes off of the course. If your child is comfortable with public displays of affection, hug him as soon as he comes out of the scoring tent. A pat on the back and a few encouraging words may be what your child needs most after a tough day on the course.
- Help foster friendships. If your child loses a match-play match, offer to buy the other player and his family a soft drink. If the loss devastates your kid, it doesn't have to be right then, but maybe the next time you see them. In stroke-play tournaments, maybe it's the whole group you're springing for. Billy Andrade and Brad Faxon have been friends since they played together as teens in Rhode Island. Their early respect for one another made a great foundation for a lifelong friendship. They have rooted

each other on to victory as spectators more than once. Faxon was in the gallery when Andrade won the 1998 Canadian Open and the 2000 Invensys Classic at Las Vegas. Andrade was there for Faxon when he won the 2001 Sony Open. "It shows what kind of mutual respect you have for someone who is your friend," Andrade said. "If I'm around and my friends are doing well, I'm going to support them." If the two families live in different cities, the kids may choose to stay in each other's homes during tournaments. Competition aside, some of the early tournaments in a junior's career may be where he develops some of his strongest friendships.

Coach Etiquette

Adhering to social graces guarantees an all-round enjoyable tournament, whether one is a certified coach or a parent who proxies for the coach.

- The Rules of Golf prohibit any sort of coaching during the round, so don't. Coaches are not allowed to give any advice to a player during the course of his round. In the rulebook, advice is defined as "any counsel or suggestion that could influence a player in determining his play, the choice of a club or the method of making a stroke." The note to Rule 8 states that only during team play does a Committee-designated coach have the freedom to advise a player.
- A coach is an observer, part of the gallery. Record observations, but do it unobtrusively, without distracting the players.
- A coach is not a rules official. He should not attempt to make any rulings for his junior or any other competitors.
- Just as parents and other loving members of junior's gallery must do, a coach needs to be careful of negative gestures and body language.
- Hug your junior after the match, regardless of the outcome. Unconditional support and love is crucial for the development of emotionally healthy athletes.
- Put off talking about the round until later. Give the kid a chance to cool off emotionally. Coach may join junior for lunch or a late snack and let him vent before they head off to the driving range or putting green. Both player and coach may need some time to clear their heads before discussing the day's happenings. It might be best if coach ventures over to the scoreboard for a quick update. With very young kids, instead of talking to them about mistakes and improvements, simply make mental notes and incorporate appropriate changes into their lesson plans. Junior and coach together, just as they have a pre-round ritual, need to

come up with a post-round routine that works for both of them.
- When it's time, talk about certain circumstances. How was he feeling? What was he thinking? How did he decide such and such? Praise him for steps well taken and shots well played.

Spectator Etiquette

- Switch the mobile phone to silent mode. Because so many spectators are violating this "golden rule," many PGA and LPGA Tour events are checking cell phones at their gates. Some clubs and resorts have a "no cell phone" policy, prohibiting cell phones everywhere on property. Keep cell phones off the golf course itself, off the driving range and putting greens and out of the dining rooms. If you must indulge, limit your phone calls to the parking lot.
- Be quiet and courteous when someone is addressing his ball or hitting. Absolutely don't yell out to anyone on the course. Someone in your group might not be getting ready to play, but someone on an adjoining tee box, fairway or green might be.
- Be still and don't stand in line of sight of the players.
- Don't talk to the golfers.
- If needed, help look for golf balls, even golfers you don't know.
- Stay in the rough or behind the ropes if the course is roped off.
- Wait for a group to exit a green before getting in or out of the bleachers.
- Cheer for everyone's good shots, not just your guys' good ones. You're allowed to go nuts when your favorite player wins, but be respectful of the other players. In the 1999 Ryder Cup Matches held at The Country Club in Brookline, Massachusetts, the rowdy crowds repeatedly taunted Europe's Colin Montgomerie. Opponent Payne Stewart was ashamed of several of the rude "home team" spectators and had the tournament officials remove some of the worst hecklers from the premises. Stewart loved winning like the greatest of champions do, but he found the unsportsmanlike conduct out of control and not appropriate. Bad sportsmanship is never acceptable.

Player Etiquette

A good rule of thumb for a player is to influence and affect nothing on the golf course except your own ball. A great book on etiquette is "The Unspoken Rules of Golf Etiquette" by Jim Simpson. As many tour players agree, this book is a must read for golfers at every level of the game. It is a great reference for anyone who plays golf or is around golf. Even seasoned players need to reacquaint themselves with the game's etiquette and code of conduct.

Here's the rest of the story on player behavior:

- On the course, wear that beautiful smile as often as possible, but avoid the antics professionals put on for television. Keep your composure even when things don't go your way or according to plan.
- Acknowledge playing partners' good shots. Say thanks or use another gesture such as a nod of the head or a flip of your hand when you are praised.
- Watch your playing partners' shots. Pay attention when your playing partners want to take a drop or need a ruling.
- Always call over your playing partner, your scorer in particular, before picking up your ball. Never assume they know what you are doing; you need to ask about a drop or have them to verify your actions.
- Observe the game's rules in regard to who has the honor on the tee box, fairway, and green unless your group falls behind and you are forced to play ready golf. If you must play out of turn, ask first.
- State your score to your scorer sometime between when you hole out and before you tee off on the following hole. Ask the player whom you are scoring for what he made on the previous hole and record it properly on the scorecard. Settle all disputes before teeing off the next hole. Players may have to consult with other members of the group. Cheating is never an option and is said to be one of "golf's unforgivable crimes" and will always lead to disqualification.
- If there is a disagreement on a ruling or a procedure, call for a rules official or proceed under Rule 3-3 (Doubt as to procedure).
- It's good to be excited for a round well played or an exciting victory, but always remember to congratulate your opponent on a good game as well. You should start a round and end a round with a handshake.

Be sure to sign both your scorecard and the scorecard of your competitor. If a player doesn't sign his card or signs it with an incorrect (lower) score, he's disqualified. If a player fails to sign the card of the player he scored for, his opponent's, that player is disqualified should the blunder not be noticed before turning in the card – and nobody wants that to happen. Stay focused, as the round isn't officially over until all the scorecards have been signed correctly and turned into an official box.

During the Round

While junior cruises the course, there is a lot a coach and parent can observe. A professional coach will go about his business, making notes on technical stuff like fairways hit, GIRs, percentage of birdie chances 20 feet and in, up and downs, whether or not he put himself in good position, the player's rhythm, club selection, etc. If coach isn't around to make such observations, a skilled parent can record such stats to give to the player and coach.

There are many handy tools available to a coach who wants to do more than make mental notes. Golf workbooks, handheld personal digital assistants and the good old scratch pad are all worthy aids to record observations.

If your son's coach is there, he may train you to take such stats and will show you what to look for in his swing should things go haywire. Of course you can't tell him anything during play, but if he asked you after play, you might be able to give him some input. For example, he might ask "Did I look like I was aimed that far right on sixth tee?" His coach might have mentioned to you to keep an eye on his alignment and you did in fact notice that he was aiming right on a couple of tee shots. Such teamwork keeps him from guessing, and it gives you something to do as you plod along the course. In addition to being an extra pair of eyes to validate what's going on, a parent can observe two factors over which he has the maximum impact – on-course behavior and mental toughness. This will also help a parent with all his nervous energy and will help keep him from worrying so much about outcomes. Is junior displaying good player etiquette? Are there aspects of junior's behavior that need to be discussed?

When looking for mental toughness, observe whether junior is incorporating habits that sports psychologists recommend:

- Focus: Complete concentration – did he look to be in control? Or did he appear helpless? Calm? Did he make clear decisions or was he doubtful? Did he waste shots or let shots get away? Or, did he look determined? Was he playing one shot at a time, or did it appear he got ahead of himself or that he was struggling with letting go of missed shots? Did things look easy? Effortless? Did you see a pattern? Always a bogey following a birdie, for example. Did his rhythm appear to be "normal"? Did he look tentative? Too aggressive? Walk faster than normal? Slower than normal? Between shots, what was his demeanor? Shoulders back? Head up? Anxious? Angry? Did he keep looking at you? Was he polite to his playing partners, or was he rude and obnoxious because he was having a bad day?

- Rituals and Routines: Develop a ritual before any shot – hitching the pants and pulling the shirt are two such moves. Follow the same pre-shot routine regardless of the situation. There is a commercial that has quick clips of all the strange things golfers do before they take their swing. It's really funny!

- Breathing: Learn to take deep breaths. He should establish a breathing pattern for emotional control.

- Loosen up: Enhance relaxation by loosening the neck and shoulder muscles – wiggle and stretch.
- Posture: Even if a player is playing poorly, he needs to communicate resiliency through body language – shoulders pulled back, head high and striding with a purpose. He should act like his name is atop the leaderboard.
- Self-talk: Is it positive self-talk? He needs to avoid whining about bad bounces or bad breaks. Berating himself after a mistake will never help. Or if speaking about outcomes he would prefer, "My swing is feeling smoother now! I feel a birdie coming my way!"

There are a variety of established drills that work on mental toughness. We will discuss in further detail in Chapter 10 – The Mental Game. Discuss observations with the coach and determine whether appropriate mental drills can be incorporated into lesson plans. If you suspect family or school issues may be affecting the ability to concentrate, try to get to the bottom of the problem as soon as possible. Pia Nilsson, head coach of the Swedish national golf teams from 1990-99, Annika Sorenstam's mental-game coach, and Lynn Marriott, her partner in *Golf 54* and *Coach For The Future, Inc.*, have an awesome little booklet titled *Golf Parent for the Future*. On page 7 of that book there is a helpful chart giving explicit insight into the areas a parent can and cannot influence. Check out their chart and see if you may be trying to control things you aren't capable of controlling.

Table 6.1

WHAT CAN YOU CONTROL?	WHAT YOU CAN'T!
Your feedback	Your child's emotion
Your body language	Your child's performance
Your attitude	Your child's motivation
Your voice	Rankings
What to focus on	Your junior golfer's focus
What questions you ask	How your child answers the questions

Table 6.2

WHAT CAN YOUR YOUNG GOLFER CONTROL?	WHAT HE CAN'T CONTROL!
Pre-shot routine	Parent's behavior
Body posture	Tee times
Shot selection	Playing partners
Attitude	Score
Reaction to outcomes	Lies and bounces
Practice habits	Weather
Target focus	What others think about him
Grip, stance, aim and alignment	Course layout and condition
Goal setting	Rankings

After the Round

After a player has double checked and signed his scorecard, he may want to immediately head to the putting green or driving range. Let him decide what he is going to do post play. He may have a certain routine, but on occasion he may want to break his routine. It should be the player's choice on what's next for the day. If he finished late, he may want to get some practice in before dark or before the range closes. If he finished in the heat of the day, he may want to head to the pool and cool off before an afternoon practice schedule. If he does return for more play, make sure he reapplies that sunscreen. He might need to refuel before heading out to the practice tee. Or he may feel really confident and not want to practice at all after a particular round.

In match-play tournaments, he may have to play another match. He may want to hit a few balls on the range or putt a couple of practice putts before his next match. The most important thing is that he refuels immediately with some simple carbohydrates. He doesn't want to overeat, and he should plan on grazing a bit more in match two. It is important he is hydrated and has energy so he stays mentally sharp. He should definitely re-apply his sunscreen. If hot and sticky, he may want to change clothes as well.

Once again, win or lose, remember to hug your child. It's natural for parents and coaches to want to talk about everything they observed during the match. Stick to the boundaries you and your child have pre-arranged. If there is a concern your child has with his game before going out for a second match, he will ask either you or the coach for your input. Let him lead; don't push! You will find a better listener when you do discuss the round. Focus on the process, not the result. For instance, instead of pointing out how many fairways he missed, mention that you think he should check his alignment.

For a young child, it's best to simply appreciate his effort and plan other post-tournament activities away from golf. If you're in a different city, maybe a quick sight-seeing trip might take his mind off the round. Kids love trips for ice cream or juice smoothies! Discuss observations directly with the coach and have them incorporated into lesson plans.

Learning from a Match

Golfers are on their own in a round, unless they are playing in a tournament that allows caddies. They can't get help from coaches, parents, or friends. Two factors are extremely important to keep them playing and improving. The first is self-motivation achieved by entering tournaments so that a player has a chance to see improvement in his game. It's important for a player to be encouraged by his progress. It is important that you do not let him focus on winning and losing. The second factor is self-learning. Winning is important, but win or lose, a player has to come away from a match with a "Eureka!" feeling of having learned something significant. Sometimes what seems to be the toughest loss is one that actually teaches him the most – character building at its finest.

Self-learning in golf is an acquired skill. This means a coach or parent has to teach a junior how and what to learn from a round. The last thing you want is a helpless golfer. A player who is 100% dependent on a coach or his parent will never be able to fulfill his potential. There are simple and practical tools to help players learn by evaluating their rounds and especially their tournament play.

His coach can help him come up with a system that will show him tendencies and patterns unique to his game. The Tournament Data Form (Table 6.3) is designed to capture self-rated scores in five areas – scores, fitness, mental toughness, life skills and enjoyment. (Yes, enjoyment. Remember that this is supposed to be fun.) Scores are based on criteria suggested in the form and are on a scale of 1 to 10, with 10 as the best.

All areas except wins are based on subjective guidelines. For example, if a player is in mediocre shape, he would rate his fitness 5 or 6; mentally tough, although not perfect, he might rate himself

Table 6.3

Tournament Data Form	
Maximum score for each category is 10. A total of 45 or above is commendable. Discuss the completed form with your coach.	
Score: Start with a score of 10 for even par. For every stroke under par you would add 0.5, and for every stroke over par you would subtract 0.5. Example: If his score was 74, then his score would be a 9. If he shot a 69, it would be 11.5.	
Fitness: Did you feel strong? Feel powerful? Were you getting good yardage on your irons? Tee shots? Did you have good balance? Was it effortless? How was your overall energy? Were you dragging at the end? Did your diet impact the match? Did you train appropriately with adequate intensity/rest ratio?	
Mental Toughness: How was your ability to recover from adversity? Did you demonstrate strong body language and use of positive imagery? Did you exhibiting a "never give in" attitude with maximum effort? Are you enjoying the challenges, and do you still love the game? Are you focused on the scorecard, or did you maintain a one-shot-at-a-time mentality? Were you able to rebound from a poor shot, hole or score? Did you rally and play well in spite of a poor start? Did you have any "key shots" or "key putts"? Did you use sound judgment?	
Life Skills: Did you treat all members of your group with respect? Did you have to stand up for what you believe to be true when challenged? How was your conflict resolution? Did you respond positively to an irritating competitor? Have you kept your play in perspective? Did you set a good example for others to follow? Were you grateful for all that went your way today? Are you appreciative for all of the volunteers who make this tournament function? Do you see a correlation between hard work and improvement?	
Enjoyment: How memorable was the round for you? How strongly do you desire to repeat your performance? How relaxed were you? Did you enjoy the round? Was it fun?	
Total	

Table 6.4

Tournament Evaluation Form

YOUR NAME:				DATE:	
COURSE NAME:				YARDAGE:	

1.Course setup: Mostly need shots that go left to right or right to left.

2. STRENGTHS TODAY:

3. WEAKNESS/VULNERABILITY TODAY:

4.YOUR SCORE:

Putts	Fwys x/14	GIR x/18	Sand Saves x/x	Front Nine	Back Nine

5. YOUR MOST MEMORABLE MOMENT:

6. WOULD YOU DO ANYTHING DIFFERENT NEXT TIME?

7. THINGS YOU'D LIKE TO PRACTICE BEFORE PLAYING THIS COURSE AGAIN:

8 or 9; displaying outstanding sportsmanship, he should gives himself 10 for life skills.

The Tournament Evaluation Form (Table 6.4) asks players to think about their match with respect to strategy and tactics. Question No. 7 is of the utmost importance because it takes the player past understanding of what happened to an action phase.

Be wary – no one enjoys filling out forms, especially kids. Play becomes "work." If your child is also learning how to record his statistics, it may be too much to handle. Dole out the assignments in small doses at first, but try to get him to incorporate these records and help him realize that they are valuable, measurable tools to help him play better. Perhaps limiting the paperwork to certain practice rounds and one-day tournaments may be one way to make use of this system at first. Rewards for turning in the forms can help. Stir up your creative juices and judge when and how to get your junior involved in this process.

7
Camps, Schools and Academies

Kids' camps may bring back fond memories for grownups, but probe kids today and you'll be surprised. They either love 'em or hate 'em; there is rarely an in-between. If parent and child do their homework before selecting a camp, there's a much better chance the child will want to go back the next year. Aren't most golf schools really "golf camps" for adults? Whether you relate well to the word "school" or not, it is best that you check out facilities and programs that specialize in golf schools when researching golf camps for your child.

Golf camps range from programs that simply introduce the game in a casual way to more intense programs with specific goals and objectives set out for your child. Casual introductory camps will usually have several other activities to keep your child occupied all day, while the intense week- long or resident camps are definitely golf intensive.

If your child is looking for a great way to tune up her game or learn new skills, more intensive instructional settings are offered all over the country. Each year, thousands of competitive junior golfers attend schools and camps for a week or two during winter, spring and summer breaks. There are even three academies in the United States prepared to house your child for a whole school year should you consider that an option.

Benefits of a Golf Camp

Perhaps the most important benefit of a week of golf camp for a young kid is the discovery of what it takes physically to play golf all day every day. Intense exposure to how tournament golfers practice and play round after round may help prepare your child for advanced competition. Golf camps help players develop discipline in every area of the game. Novice and elite players alike can learn new drills and games to help keep practice interesting and fresh. Monotonous practice is a key reason most players get sloppy. A camp can also give your kid a connection to the concept that fun, hard work and dedication are attainable. Some kids have an unrealistic image of what it takes to get their games to the highest levels; the proper golf camp will correct such notions. However, like golf swings, golf camps come in many different styles. Do intensive research if you are considering golf camp, and check references. Camps are designed differently, and you need to make sure your expectations match with the camp's agenda. The last thing you want is your aspiring collegiate golfer in a camp filled with kids half her age who aren't sure they even like the sport. While some camps may have a large number of kids with different abilities, superior camps will separate the kids by talent levels and by age.

An advanced player can focus on mastering a particular shot, improving a specific stroke or working on her greatest weaknesses. It's not uncommon for friends to want to go to camp together, but if your daughter ventures to camp solo, she will have an excellent opportunity to make new friends.

The greatest risk an advanced player takes is that a different coach, albeit temporary, might confuse her with a varied swing ideology. Even if it's only a week, new perspectives on the game can be challenging. However, different insights and a new perspective might be what your daughter needs to catapult her to a new level of play and interest. Often, a kid used to playing recreational golf returns from a week of fun with friends at camp eager to take up competitive golf.

Some camps include talks by experts on topics like mental toughness, physical conditioning, nutrition, strategy and tournament play. Golf schools such as those provided by GolfPsych Golf Systems are exclusively designed for the serious junior golfer wanting to improve tournament performance. (More info: golfpsych.com) The evening activities of most resident camps – trips to the beach, barbecues, camp dances and more can often be the most memorable moments of camp!

Choosing a Camp

The Broad Definition of Camp

It is imperative that you learn the most important thing to know about junior golf camps and junior golf schools – they are not all created equal. Golf camp has a broader definition than golf school, but just because a program is labeled a school doesn't guarantee you quality instruction, either. There are literally thousands of camps to choose from, so the first step is to have a clear idea of what you and your child expect. What level golfer is she? What are her goals? What type of camp should she consider? The internet is a great up-to-date resource, but with so many options, you will still need some help finding a fit for your child.

The American Camping Association (ACA. More info: <u>acacamps.org</u>), founded in 1910, is an association of camping professionals that works to create a model and standardizing influence in organized camping for the young. The ACA has currently accredited more than 2,400 camps.

The ACA accredits camps based on an educational process, providing training and publications for its camp directors and staff. At least once every three years, an outside team of trained camp professionals observes the camp in session to verify compliance with over 300 health, safety and program standards.

As application for ACA accreditation is voluntary. Although you may find that golf is an offered activity at many camps, you won't find that there are many exclusively golf camps, especially any high-quality ones.

Research

Start with online sites such as <u>usgolfschoolguide.com</u>, <u>jrpga.com</u>, <u>juniorgolfscoreboard.com</u>, <u>resortgolf.com</u> and <u>ussportscamps.com</u>. Several top colleges and universities also offer golf camps during the summer. Web sites such as <u>summercamps.com</u> and <u>teengolfcamp.com</u> might give your child a choice of camps a little different from those offered on the aforementioned golf school sites. They will also offer a few more interesting alternatives to traditional golf camps. West Coast Connection offers a variety of travel teen experiences throughout the year, including golf trips on both the east and west coasts. Teenagers with a love for the game who are not playing high-level competitive golf might love an extended golfing vacation with teens from all over the world. If parents were willing to foot the bill, what teen wouldn't jump at a chance to jump on an airplane to an exciting resort with golf clubs in tow? (More info: <u>teengolfcamp.com</u>)

Nike Golf offers several different types of camps for junior, including a parent/child camp. This might be the most sensible introduction to an eight-hour golf camp! You and she can commiserate about blisters and share tales of golf shots gone awry.

Any golf camp or school worth your child's time and your money should provide quality instruction in at least five areas of the game: long game, short game, rules, etiquette and course management. Instruction should be fun, adaptable to any age group and taught in a safe environment. Golf camps afford kids of all ages and skill levels opportunities to make friends in an exciting environment and learn more about the game of golf.

Instructors

The camp director is a great resource, but you need to find out who is actually going to instruct the kids. The first thing you need to know is what the ratio of staff to campers is. For a golf camp, the ideal student-to-instructor ratio is four to six students for each instructor. Too low a ratio can tire or bore the students, while too many can result in a free-for-all. Low student-to-instructor ratios ensure that juniors are getting good instruction in a safe teaching environment.

Next, look and see who makes up the faculty. What is the staff's background? Do they have camp experience? Have they worked with kids in the past? Have they had junior golf experience? Are there PGA/LPGA Professionals running the program? Who are the counselors? What are their ages? Are they college players? If college players are responsible for most of the instruction, make sure the director will closely monitor progress and the quality of instruction. Quality camps will have people with a lot of junior golf experience doing the instruction. It's beneficial when the schedule includes rotation of instructors for different drills. The students can pick up a variety of tips.

Curriculum

The best way to decipher a camp's character is through an in-depth conversation with its director. Try to determine whether the character and program's emphasis is a good fit with your child's personality. A reserved child might do better at a camp that emphasizes instruction over competition, while a star player would probably prefer a camp that offers plenty of competition.

Check the camp curriculum. What is the program for instruction? Does the program offer personalization and allow for junior to work at her own level? Does the instructional program cover all aspects of the game and have a proven track record? Are younger kids grouped with older ones on a continuous basis? Is there a specific program for college-bound players? Do you want golf only? Do you prefer a certain religious influence? Is co-ed OK? These are all questions that only you and your family can ask and hope to find answers to.

Happy Campers

The number of returning campers is the best measure of camp quality. There is currently no way to determine return rate statistics for the golf camp industry. But don't be shy about asking the director of a camp you're interested in what the return rate is. Quality camps will proudly share these statistics. Avoid camps that hesitate sharing this kind of information.

Tournament Tough

Top-level kids need a top-level camp. Kids preparing for national tournaments and top-level competition want to pick camps with programs that have proven instructors. It is vital to have your child's coach communicate with the professionals at camp. Pick a camp that may have similar climate and golf-course conditions as where national championships will be played.

Use camp to determine whether your child is dedicated to the sport and the long hours it requires before jet-setting around the country playing in one event after another. Some kids might decide they don't want to put in the hours of practice or make the sacrifices necessary to play top tournament golf – that's OK! It would be best to find this out sooner rather than later, before you mortgage the house. In any case, top camps will help players address some of the weaker areas of their game and give them a plan of action for improvement.

Getting used to wind and weather is a big part of becoming tournament tough. Advanced players from Seattle may want to practice playing in a Florida camp, where it will often be sunny, hot and humid. Playing different types of golf courses is another real benefit to camp. Good golf camps often offer golf at championship courses. Grasses all over the country are so different. If a player only plays on Bent grass, it will behoove her to play on Bermuda grass before she's expected to compete on it. It is extremely beneficial to intermediate and advanced players if given the chance to play in different regions.

Evening Activities

Many kids will want to return to the camp the following season because of the evening activities and camaraderie. Campers enjoy first-run movies, skits, dances and a trip to the town or beach. If your child is shy, find out if the camp has specific getting-to-know-each-other activities. Make sure there is always proper supervision and that activities encouraged are age appropriate. Be specific about your idea of supervision. Find out if computers and televisions with access to cable or the internet have filters and how much exposure your child might have. It general, it isn't such a good idea to have 12-year-olds hanging with 18- or 19-year-olds.

Accommodations

It used to be dorm was the norm for many resident camps, but now kids are often treated to stays at amazing resorts and hotels with championship golf just a few steps away. From Hilton Head to La Quinta, you wouldn't object to being held "hostage" there! Like the camps themselves, accommodations vary. While many camps will still use a nearby university to house their eager golfers, there are many more on-course accommodations available. Either way, a great roomie and a decent sack are all kids really care about until the early morning rise-and-shine knock on the door.

More Money

Camps aren't cheap. A one-week resident camp can run you from $800 to $1,500 or more. Tuition for a non-resident camper is a little more than half as much. Resident camp tuition should include lodging, meals, instruction, all programs, use of facilities, greens fees, evening activities and club-fitting if offered. Don't assume a bigger sticker price means better instruction. Generally, the higher price buys better accommodations, easier access, cutting-edge facilities or simply a popular brand. No matter the sticker price, do your due diligence on the instruction offered.

Despite all the detective work, you may discover the camp you chose isn't a good fit after all. A camp is more than the golf it offers. The social atmosphere is also important, and that can be hard to figure out beforehand. It might take more than one try to find the best match for your child.

Brand Name Camps

The choice is easier when we limit the short list to famous brand names. The professional brands, such as Arnold Palmer, David Leadbetter, Jim McClean, Rick Smith or the corporate brands like Nike, the International Junior Golf Academy and Fellowship of Christian Athletes all evoke perceptions of what to expect at those particular camps.

Obviously a FCA Golf Camp offers a unique blend of golf and spiritual experience not usually found at a junior golf camp. Most of the camps are for kids 12–18 of all skill levels and golf backgrounds. FCA is relatively new to golf camps, but its purpose is to provide the best in golf instruction and practice in an atmosphere that exposes the camper to the Christian faith and fellowship. At FCA camp, golf is not the primary focus, yet FCA Golf has a hand in the professional side of the golf world as it ministers to golfers in professional events worldwide and on the Nationwide Tour. Kids come home from a FCA golf camp with more than a better golf swing. One youngster said, "Camp didn't just make an impression in my life. It made an impact." FCA camps promise a week of "inspiration and perspiration" and to show players what it takes to have the heart of a champion. There are dozens of FCA camps scattered across the country.

In contrast, Nike has hundreds of camps scattered all across the United States, with its most notable camps held in association with the International Junior Golf Academy. All of the benefits that come with Tiger Woods' endorsement of Nike have helped its programs compete with the top teacher camps, but Nike camps are still a bit hit and miss site by site. Some locations are much better than others; do your homework. The IJGA is partnered with Nike, and it is known for the teaching and leadership of renowned junior golf instructor Gary Gilchrist.

Gilchrist serves as Director of Golf at the IJGA. He has supervised the training of some of the most talented golfers in the world including Michelle Wie, Paula Creamer, David Gossett, Ty Tryon, and Aree Song. His students have won virtually every major junior championship in the United States. When the IJGA first opened in 1995, Gilchrist was a top instructor at the David Leadbetter Academy in Bradenton, Florida. Gilchrist has directed the development of over 75 AJGA All-Americans, many AJGA Players of the Year, two U.S. Amateur champions, three U.S. Junior champions, one NCAA champion and one Public Links champion. Although Gilchrist is now at the International Junior Golf Academy at the beautiful Sea Pines Resort on Hilton Head Island, S.C., he was formerly the Director of Golf at the David Leadbetter Golf Academy. During his time at the Leadbetter Academy, Gary also assisted Leadbetter with high-profile clients including Nick Price, David Frost, Nick Faldo, Mark O' Meara, Ernie Els and Andy Bean. He is also Michelle Wie's instructor (and sometime caddie).

While no one can dispute the records of many of the IJGA alumni, David Leadbetter's Academy is touted as the "Home of Junior Golf" and with its state-of-the-art facilities is still considered one of the most noteworthy junior golf schools in the United States. While the Leadbetter Academy and IJGA seem to continue to attract the talent-laden and pump out great golfers, there are equally intense programs available at Arnold Palmer's Academy and Saddlebrook Preparatory School in Wesley Chapel, Florida.

The Saddlebrook programs are taught at the Saddlebrook Resort, a secluded retreat on 480 acres of lush Florida countryside, 30 miles north of Tampa. Instructors are annually certified and well-versed in Palmer's no gurus/no gimmicks approach. The instructional staff is dedicated to teaching sound fundamentals, but they also instill a fair amount of that famous winning attitude. The student's resulting approach to golf becomes more confident, more aggressive and more fun.

The Jim McLean Golf School is one of the country's top-rated golf schools, and, like all the other "famous" schools, proudly boasts of the success of its students and instructors alike. Jim McLean, one of the top three instructors in the world, has schools in multiple locations, being the most widespread program available. The McLean schools are hosted at many top resort destinations. McClean encourages children to pursue college golf if they are serious about their games. He founded the Future Collegians World Tour and links players to coaches all over the country.

Rick Smith is regarded as one of the PGA Tour's best "sounding boards" for swing advice and has continually been ranked as one of the top five golf instructors in the world by Golf Digest. He also owns and operates his own golf academy. The Academy strives to develop the highest potential in every player regardless of skill level. In addition to being housed at the amazing Tiburon Golf Club in Naples, Florida, Smith's school sets itself apart by having one of the lowest student-to-teacher ratios in the industry – 2:1.

All these schools are rated among the best because they offer quality instruction by a professional staff and have a track record. However, just check out a few of the sites listed under the myriad of junior golf camps and you will quickly learn that these are not the only game in town.

Expecting a celebrity coach to greet you at the camp entrance is about as likely as expecting Sam Walton to wave customers in at the nearby Wal-Mart. Occasionally, celebrity coaches do bop in on sessions. Check and see which schools may actually have their famous namesake in for some instruction. Having the head honcho around might help you choose which program you want to invest in. For the most part, these gurus simply impart their experience and techniques through a camp system of trained teachers, methods and teaching philosophy that mirrors the master's way. So even though you may never meet David Leadbetter personally at the David Leadbetter Golf Academy summer camp, rest assured your child will benefit from the master's signature, writ large in all aspects of the camp.

Kids' golf camps bearing the names of well-known professionals and organizations include:

- International Junior Golf Academy
  (More info: ijga.com)
- David Leadbetter Golf Academy
  (More info: leadbetter.com)
- Arnold Palmer Golf Academy
  (More info: saddlebrook.com)
- Jim McClean Golf Academy
  (More info: golfspan.com)
- Rick Smith Golf Academy
  (Info: wcicommunities.com)
- Nike Sports Camps
  (More info: ussportscamps.com)
- Fellowship of Christian Athletes
  (More info: fcagolf.com)

Additional Resources are available at usgolfcamps.com and usgolf-schoolguide.com.

Time Out

Joe could not wait to spill the beans. His company had named him "Salesperson of the Year" and awarded him a two-week, all-expenses-paid vacation for him and his family at a nice golf resort. He was sure his 10-year-old daughter, Alexa, would jump for joy. She loved golf and had been attending regular lessons for nearly a year.

So needless to say, Joe was extremely perplexed when, after making the big announcement at the dinner table, Alexa paused for a moment and asked, "Do I have to attend golf clinics?" It suddenly dawned on Joe that although Alexa enjoyed golf, she viewed the resort as simply more of the same for her. A vacation should offer a break from the routine.

Joe assured Alexa that the resort had plenty of other programs and amenities for kids, like waterslides and a Kids Club. When they got to the resort Joe and his wife signed up for the golf clinics, while Alexa pursued other activities.

The clinics, under the tutelage of the resort's excellent teaching professional, proved to be a lot of fun. On the fourth day of the family's vacation, Alexa asked if she could come along to watch her parents' clinic. At the course, Alexa made friends with the pro and everyone at the golf shop. By the end of the clinic, Alexa was asking, "Dad, can I play, too?"

Joe broke into a smile and replied, "Sweetheart, I would love to hit a few balls with you at the range now, and maybe tomorrow you can play with Mommy and me on the course." Joe let Alexa hit balls on the range and practiced putting for a few minutes before they both headed for the pool.

Unlike the professional brand-name camps, each of which practices a uniform method of instruction at every location, corporate camps such as Nike or FCA usually have a wide range of instructional styles and bear the local director's personal preferences.

Making Camp Count

Many camps will accept children as young as age six or seven. However, golf camps are pretty intensive and require long periods of physical activity and focused attention. Unless you are sending siblings together, it would be best if a child under the age of ten didn't attend a resident camp. You can gauge a kid's camp readiness by how well she handles sleepovers with friends. Young children will be less homesick at camp once they have gotten used to sleepovers.

Camp sessions can run at least four to five hours, and in many cases include almost eight or nine hours of practice and play time. A kid practicing golf year-round may be physically conditioned for such an intensive schedule. Otherwise, players ought to get acclimated through a more intensive practice program two to three weeks prior to the start of camp. That way your kid stays healthy and injury-free during camp.

Nike camps encourage campers to write down short- and long-term goals and to decide how they will go about reaching the short-term goals while at camp. Experts recommend making self-evaluation notes at the end of each day. Campers can rate themselves on their level of effort, attitude, responsibility, willingness to make changes during a round, focus, improvement and of course, on how much fun they had that day.

It's also a good idea to encourage kids to make notes about camp memories – their accomplishments, tips they learned and contact info for all their new friends. Finally, kids should go home and practice what they learned at camp.

Golf Resorts

"Golf" and "resort" – the two words just go together. There is no way to give justice to what's offered in the way of golf camps. Programs are constantly changing, but should you and your child indulge in a golf vacation at a nice resort, one thing is for sure, there are plenty of options. A beginner can get hooked with the pristine beauty and awesome amenities found at most resorts, and your intermediate and advanced players will enjoy exposure to championship courses. However, great instruction doesn't necessarily come with great golf resorts. Yet, unless a player is preparing for a big tournament, the fun your child will have will outweigh any misguided instruction. The relaxing atmosphere and state-of-the-art practice facilities can help your golf kid get refreshed for the upcoming season.

A one-on-one session with a resort pro might just be the best way to introduce golf to a young child, but only if it is lots of fun. Your child will then associate golf with all the other fun activities that were part of the vacation. It can't be said enough that "fun" is the best magnet to keep children enthused to learn the sport. Family instruction can provide lots of laughs and stories to tell for generations – it also might help keep it low key, if that's what you're after.

Walt Disney World Resorts offers a lot of fun family golf packages. In addition to their summer camps, they also host a Junior Golf Weekend in July, in which beginners to serious competitors are treated to an array of complimentary instruction and a parent-child tournament. Few and far between are the resorts that offer the excitement, the service and the challenge of Disney's five masterpiece courses. Camps offer personal PGA instruction and access to their award- winning courses. Walt Disney World Golf has a commitment to service, excellence, immaculate course conditioning. The PGA Tour holds an event at the Magic Kingdom every fall. Young, old and somewhere in between, Disney does a great job making golf a magical golf experience. (More info: disneyworldsports.com)

The great thing about golf is that Disney doesn't have a lock on magical experiences. Maybe a trip to the spectacular World Golf Hall of Fame and The PGA Tour Golf Academy at the World Village in St. Augustine, Florida would be met with just as much enthusiasm as a trip to the Magic Kingdom. A visit to this ultimate destination will be a history lesson in itself and is perfect for a family stay-and-play vacation.

The PGA Tour Golf Academy offers camps for young people of all skill levels. It is a once-in-a-lifetime opportunity to improve their games at the world's first and only PGA Tour academy. Under the watchful eye of top teaching professionals, juniors will learn about the latest and greatest in technology and training. (More info: resortgolf.com).

Famous names in golf, resort destinations and corporate powers from the hotel industry all recognize the value of your vacation dollar. Many realize you are trying to get more bang for your buck by using your vacation dollar to also help your golf game or that of your junior. After years of successful golf under the watchful eye of David Leadbetter, Nick Faldo decided it was his turn to be the teacher. In 1997 Nick Faldo and Marriott joined together and opened the Faldo Golf Institute by Marriott in Orlando, Florida. The Faldo Golf Institute is dedicated to helping golf students of every age and ability improve their skill, understanding and enjoyment of golf. Since then, the Institute has spread its wings from coast to coast, adding locations in Atlantic City, New Jersey; Palm Desert, California and Marco Island, Florida. It has helped thousands of golfers on the road to improvement. The Institute reflects Faldo's demands for excellence, and the amazing practice facilities provide a learning environment like no other. The commitment he made, as a tour professional, is evidently stronger than ever as his instructional programs and unique methods are earning a reputation as some of the finest in the world. (More info: gofaldo.com).

There are a plethora of options available when choosing the right golf resort. Consider these factors when looking at a golf resort:

- The difficulty of the courses
- The practice facilities (Are there hidden fees? Is it all-inclusive?)
- Child friendly (Is your child welcome? Treated with respect?)
- Cost-saving golf packages. These packages offer room rates that include greens fees and possibly meals. Most golf-school packages offer lessons in the morning and course play in the afternoon.
- Additional non-golf activities (Sightseeing or amusement parks?)
- Dining amenities (If this is important to you?)
- Shopping (If this is a high priority or necessity.)

In addition to using the resources of your travel agent and the many online travel sites, you can comb through the pages of Golf Digest, Golf Digest for Women and Travel and Leisure looking for articles specializing in golf vacations. Because information such as dates, times and tuition are constantly updated, the online resort guides are often your best source. (More info: golfonline.com from the editors of Golf Magazine, golflinktravel.com, golftravelinfo.com and golf.worldsbestdeals.com)

Every golf-loving family can find places to play golf on vacation. However, global resorts specializing in golf serve up a unique experiences ranging from the "total immersion" of a camp to the less ambitious, do-nothing solitude of a beach pad.

8
Gearing Up

••

**"Golf is a game in which one endeavors to control
a ball with implements ill adapted for the purpose."**

Woodrow Wilson

••

The game has changed a lot since the 28th president of the United
States chased a painted golf ball around in the snow. Technology continues to be where the golf companies point when trying to sell you
their latest and greatest. A minimalist can perhaps enjoy golf for a
lifetime with just an old club or two and a few balls. But show me a
kid who's a minimalist and I'll sell you beachfront property in
California for zilch. Make stuff interesting and they'll enjoy playing
a whole lot more.

Golf clubs are the keys to the game. You can buy an old club or
two, but there are dozens of snazzy choices for junior, so invest in a
set your kid will take pride in, and it might be the best investment
you ever make. Choosing which golf balls to hit can be overwhelming
if you dive in scientifically, but kids brand new to the game form an
opinion of preference pretty quickly. Golf shoes and clothes become
as much a part of the game for kids as their new wedge while they
develop their golfing personalities! The good news for golf parents is
the apparel is respectful, the dress code is stringent and it won't give
your child a lot of room for expressions of rebellion. However, in golf,
personal preference is the name of the game and overall confidence
will make or break you. Since marketing experts are always trying to
delve into our wallets and it is their job to help the multi-million dollar golf equipment, clothing and accessory businesses hook the young
consumer, you may find that junior digs in his heels on a must-have
item. It is amazing that your six-year-old can give you a 15-minute
dissertation on why you have to buy a Titleist. As junior grows in the
game, help him have equipment that he will be proud to own, will
help him succeed and will make him feel special.

Virtues of Value

Your little guy just has to have that Scotty Cameron divot tool to
repair his ball marks because he saw his favorite player using one.
Indulge – it won't break the bank, and it would make a great stocking

stuffer. The holiday season and birthdays are the best time to "spoil" your child with those "must-have" trinkets. If golf consumes your child, it will also consume a lot of your expendable income. Help your child learn to make wise choices, and be prepared to pick your battles. For example, a new $400 driver might not be the answer to a struggling game; but maybe a new red Nike Tiger Woods "Sunday Win" golf shirt might lift his spirits. Looking the part adds to the allure and does wonders for self-esteem.

Clubs are the tools of the trade. Younger kids outgrow clubs pretty quickly, so value shopping makes sense. However, poor equipment will do your child no good and may keep him from ever getting excited about the game. Ill-fitted equipment makes it difficult for junior to have success and thus limits the probability of ongoing enjoyment. The days of the garage-sale specials or the infamous cut-down adult clubs should be ancient history if you are going to give your child a fair shot at playing golf. Get an idea of equipment price ranges by browsing online stores. Follow your mom's smart shopper advice. Stay away from the highest priced clubs for beginner play – you usually pay for the brand name anyway. Eliminate the cheap ones, too. A club that isn't made well or has improper balance can be dangerous or lead to injury. For juniors' clubs, there aren't the huge price variances one will find in the adult market. Quality is important, but the sticker price doesn't necessarily correlate with club quality. Middle-of-the-road-priced clubs are a great place to start, but mostly, have junior swing the many different options and let a golf professional help guide you to a set that will fit your needs.

Your kids will undoubtedly want the really cool stuff the pros use and endorse. Chic shoes and clothes are limited in junior apparel, but if your child develops his own style, let him. Establish a way for your junior to earn the extras. For starters, those tried and true chores like mowing the lawn, emptying the garbage, washing the car and babysitting could help junior upgrade his equipment or purchase an expensive head cover or two. Golf outcome-related rewards for young kids are a definite no-no. Telling your son, "Justin, you can have those cool shoes if you beat Matthew in the finals today" is a sure recipe for disaster.

Instead, reward your eight-year-old for getting to practice on time. For a 10-year old, how about avoiding junk food for a week? A great report card should always receive some kudos and a reward if you see fit. As your junior develops, falls in love with the game or becomes a competitive player, offer to buy those high-ticket items when he achieves some practice goals or sees a significant improvement in a certain aspect of his game – for example, his putts per round in tournament play have dropped 10%, or his greens in regulation significantly improved.

Golf Clubs

Golf clubs are junior's most important piece of equipment. As he grows and his skills improve, his golf-club needs most definitely change. A golfer's swing evolves from the fit of the equipment. For safety reasons, plastic or toy clubs are fine for toddlers, but if your child wants to hit real golf balls at a chipping green or on the driving range, the real thing is a must. And just as you would not put your child in adult shoes, you would not want to have them swinging "adult" clubs until they are ready to. At no time in history do juniors have such a great selection from which to choose.

Most junior clubs are designed to be lightweight, forgiving and easy to hit. Properly fitted clubs will reward balance. Better balance will usually produce better golf shots. Clubs that fit correctly help junior learn the right techniques, accelerate and insure improvement and minimize the risk of injuries to the wrists, elbows and shoulders. Since a positive first experience for your young golfer is usually a major factor in his future enjoyment of the game, it is critical you ensure that he is starting with well-suited equipment. Purchasing equipment that is properly designed for your child's strength, size and ability is your first order of business. Don't skimp on taking time to pick out the right set.

Here's the No. 1 tip for buying junior his first set of golf clubs - have him shop with you. You'll want to know these three things:

● Height (H)
● Arm length, armpit to fingertips or from fingertip to floor (A)
● A good idea of his physical strength

There is not one uniform club-fitting system for juniors, or for adults, for that matter. The only thing uniform is that most clubs made for juniors fall into some sort of color-coded system. These color-coded systems only mean something within that brand; you can't cross-reference. Most manufacturers list age and height as the reference point for fitting. There are also different schools of thought about club flexibility as well. There are several variables to consider when properly fitting golf clubs. You will want to consider your child's height and arm length as discussed, but you will also consider the optimum lie angle, shaft flex, clubhead loft, grip size and set makeup when purchasing clubs. An excellent reference for club fitting issues is Tom Wishon's book "The Search For The Perfect Golf Club." It is a must read for any serious golfer. Mike Stachura, the equipment editor for Golf Digest magazine says, "Wishon's knowledge of golf equipment isn't theoretical. It's practical. He understands not just the theory of why and how golf equipment works, but how all golfers can make technology work for them." Most important, he makes that knowledge easy to understand. (More info: wishongolf.com)

For kids, it is best if shafts have been built with lightweight materials to provide the appropriate weight, torque and flex for the younger age groups. Many junior clubs are made with super light, flexible shafts to match the typical swing speeds found in most youngsters. In some instances the shaft is too whippy for your strong junior, no matter what age and stature he is. It is up to your child and the golf professional he is working with, but he may require a stiffer shaft or heavier club weight. Older and stronger juniors may prefer the feel of a steel shaft. Often, junior clubs have club heads with specific perimeter weighting to give junior more success in achieving solid contact.

It is best to have your child with you so he can hit a few balls and tell you what "feels" good. A good professional and club fitter will ask questions and rely on the student's feedback. Give your child several different clubs to hit and strive to get your child to respond to how the club feels, the ease of swing motion, ball contact, ball trajectory and, of course, playable results. Impact tape can tell you whether or not he is hitting the clubface on the sweet spot. He will also let you know what "looks" good or is aesthetically pleasing to him. Your little one might love a club that has Snoopy on the sole. Most kids just getting started do not need more than a few clubs. Junior sets typically will come with five or seven clubs, but many manufacturers also sell clubs individually. It is better to have a few clubs that fit, than a whole set that doesn't. Golf shops will usually have several options available for your beginner golfer. An older and more advanced player will be fitted like an adult by either a professional club fitter or his teaching professional, or perhaps both. It is critical for all golfers, juniors included, to be fit for their golf clubs in that the correct combination of variables be considered to ensure consistent squareness of contact and consistent swing motion. Changes in shaft flexibility, lie and loft angles are important to ball control, and ill-fitted clubs make it impossible for your child to play his best golf. Slight adjustments to lie and loft angles may reduce your child's mis-hits, and a properly fitted shaft often makes swinging well much easier. Table 8.1 is an example of the U.S. Kid's Club Fitting Chart.

Table 8.1

Club Fitting Chart		
Height (H) feet-inches	Approximate Age	Club System
3'5"- 3'8"	3-5	Red
3'8"- 4'4"	6-8	Blue
4' 4"- 5'0"	9-11	Green or Silver
4'10"- 5'6"	11 and up	Gold

If your child is around five feet or taller, you can look at women's clubs as an option, especially if he wants a full set. Many companies offer a ladies petite model, which is a great option.

Grips

Just because you are looking for clubs for your daughter, ladies' clubs are not necessarily the best option. If your daughter is tall and strong and is well suited for a man's club, do not assume she should also have a man's grip. Glove size is a good indicator of grip size, and there is a big difference in comfort and proper hand positioning with even the slightest adjustments. Grip size is a key component that is often overlooked when properly fitting clubs. While length and weight determine swinging comfort, a club has to be comfortable to grip, too. Remember that the grip is the only direct contact with the club.

A faulty grip is one of the most common causes of an incorrect club face position. Ben Hogan said, "Golf begins with a good grip." It is hard to make a good grip if the grip doesn't fit junior's hands!

If hands are too small to grip the club properly, junior is starting from a no-win situation. If an older junior has large hands and is forced to play with smaller grips, then he too will develop bad fundamental habits. There is no one perfect grip for every golfer. Hand size and strength help a professional guide a student to a personal preference that will consistently work well for him. The size of the grip itself is a personal preference and will vary from player to player, giving him lead way in choices in hand placement, hand positioning, grip pressure and assuring consistency in these areas. A simple layer of tape may be all junior needs to help him feel better about how he places his hands on the club. There are different size grips available, and club fitters can also adjust the grip circumference with less or more tape wrapped under the grip itself when changing the grips. A stronger junior with small hands may prefer longer and stiffer shafts or more club weight but prefer smaller (junior or ladies) grips. Everybody's different, and it's important to check this dynamic component when getting fit for clubs. It is very important to have a grip that best fits your child's hands.

This might help you fit your junior properly: junior grips have a core size of 0.50 inches. Ladies grips are also smaller and thinner with a core size of 0.560. To determine which grip best fits your child's hands, measure from his wrist (base of hand) to the end of his longest finger. If the dimension is less than 6.5 inches, use a junior or ladies grip; 6.5 to 7 inches, use a .560-inch grip; 7 to 7.5 inches, use a .580-inch grip; 7.5 to 8 inches, use a mid-size grip and over 8 inches choose a jumbo (your kid has huge hands!)

Lie Angle

Another important but often ignored variable in the club-fitting process for junior is the lie angle. If clubs are made shorter or longer, it effectively changes the lie angle of the club by one degree. Simply put, the lie angle is the angle created between the shaft and the sole of the clubhead. If a club is either too upright or too flat, junior will have to compensate his swing motion to hit the ball straight. Club fitters will check your child's effective lie angle by applying some electrical tape or special marking paper on the sole of his club. Junior will be asked to hit off of a Lexan Lie board so he can determine the lie angle that will allow him to make his best swing. A mark centered on the sole will be the optimum lie angle for his swing. Effective lie angles will change with development, so every now and then you should have your child's clubs rechecked. Heel-end marks and toe-end marks require that lie angle be adjusted so your child does not have to make swing compensations for an ill-fitted club.

Whew. That's enough for the moment. Make a short list of clubs with the correct length, lie angle, shaft and grip that you, junior and his golf professional think will work and are in your price range. Let your child have the final say. He may choose his set according to his favorite color or the brand his favorite player endorses, or he may surprise you and really think the clubs emblazoned with Mickey Mouse are cool. Once the research is done, go ahead and let him have the final say – that will make his day!

Remember that kids tend to outgrow clubs fairly quickly. Consider all the variables mentioned to get a true fit, but it would be wise not to spend top dollar on clubs until you know he is done growing. Depending on the growth of your child, plan to buy a new set every 12-18 months. Relax, in the beginning you can get junior clubs at reasonable prices. Properly fit clubs will not cost you more. However, it might take a little more time and effort to be fit properly and resistance to accept the "one size fits all" mentality. You shouldn't spend more than a couple hundred dollars for bag and all. Most starter sets will come with a driving club, a fairway wood (made of metal), two to three irons and a putter. If the set you want to purchase doesn't come with a wedge, make sure your child has a sand wedge or some sort of higher lofted club so he can be successful from around the green and from bunkers right from the start. Too many juniors are stuck with 9-irons to hit when they need a more lofted club to get the shots around the green executed correctly. It is usually necessary to purchase a specialty wedge separately.

As a junior moves to adult-sized clubs, full sets and competitive play, the sticker price jumps dramatically. Depending on your budget and your child's interests, it may be wise to fit your kid on an off brand and help your child earn upgrades if that is his heart's desire. Technology continues to improve the equipment available, but the stroke average of the average player is not improving simultaneously, proving the clubs themselves cannot perform miracles, and most people do not buy properly fitted clubs. In the golf club industry, what's hot and what's not changes so rapidly that you can usually find a good deal just months after a club has been introduced. At some point in the competitive stage, your kid will want and need the best available. At this upper echelon, you may need to have an extra driver, putter or set of wedges around as well. While traveling, clubs get broken or tweaked, and a top player should have a reliable substitute available.

It would be well worth the investment to have junior fitted properly at Hot Stix Golf. Hot Stix Golf is a company dedicated to club fitting at its expansive state-of-the-art fitting center in Scottsdale, Arizona, but they also offer mobile fitting sites across the country. Many tour professionals utilize the expertise available at Hot Stix Golf in order to fit their equipment properly. All manufacturers are represented equally, and a trip to Hot Stix Golf would ensure an unbiased evaluation of your child's needs so that he can maximize his performance. Too many times golfers change their swings to match their equipment; when in reality, the pros know it is best to match your equipment to your swing for ultimate game improvement. (More info: hotstixgolf.com)

If you have already invested in a good set of clubs, changing shafts might be all that is necessary to get junior's clubs where they need to be. E-bay is a great source for finding a "gently used" set for junior. Make sure you double-check all the key elements relative to a proper fit. A good deal isn't a good deal if your kid needs two degrees upright and he gets four degrees flat, or he wanted steel and you bought graphite. Be diligent and you can find just about anything you want online.

After your junior has made a name for himself in tournament play, he may be blessed with some manufacturer support. Most of the manufacturers have a presence at the top junior events, and of course they are all jockeying for position to woo your superstar. Very few juniors get clubs given to them from the club companies, but that doesn't mean they won't give you special "competitive junior" pricing. Golf club companies are always trying to develop a loyalty between player and their brand.

Golf Club Care

Golf clubs are easy to care for. More clubs are lost than are ruined or worn out. Labels with a name and phone number are great and give you a better chance of seeing his club again. It is important to teach your child to count his clubs every time he goes to and from the course. If a club is missing, he can quickly get someone out to find it. It will also ensure that he never tees off with more than 14 clubs in his bag.

Juniors should learn to care for their clubs and other golf equipment as soon as they learn the game. Kids should know how to clean their clubs and get in the habit of cleaning them after each practice or play session. It is important that junior makes sure the grooves on his clubs are kept clean and that his clubs are always kept dry to avoid rusting. Albeit rare, players have worn out the grooves on a favorite club, especially the wedges. Grips will last longer if they are cleaned periodically with soap and water. Kids should recognize when they need to have their grips changed. If the grips are worn, there is a greater chance of the club slipping or making it so junior has to grip too tight. If your child plays in inclement weather, it is always wise to check his grips. Grips are relatively inexpensive and costs will range from $3-$12 to change. If taught properly, teenagers can learn to re-grip their own clubs. If he chooses a repair shop or the local golf shop, make sure your junior purchases a properly fitted grip and gives explicit instructions on how he wants his clubs re-gripped.

Shafts and clubheads may occasionally bend or break due to manufacturer defect, or through a swing gone awry. A tree trunk or branch may catch a club and snap the shaft. However, everyone needs to be careful when loading and unloading clubs from the trunk of a car. Heavy objects thrown on top of a light golf bag can easily damage shafts, club heads, or putters. It is best not to leave clubs in the trunk in extreme climates either. When traveling by air, teach kids to properly pack their travel bags to ensure the lowest probability of airline baggage damage. If the club broke in a natural motion of making a swing, many manufacturers will replace the shaft and head for free. However, if a bent shaft is due to negligence, it is going to tap into your pocketbook. Shafts are more costly – new steel shafts will cost you $12- $24 apiece. Graphite shafts are at least double that, running $24-$60 per shaft, and some of the high-tech shafts can cost up to $300 or more.

Lastly, you should never tolerate broken clubs due to outbursts of anger. Throwing clubs down at the ground, at a bag, or up in the air is a bad habit and should be dealt with immediately. Unfortunately, the professionals are not always good role models in this area, as they can get away with an occasional outward expression of frustration and unsportsmanlike behavior. Every so often you will watch a tournament in which a player breaks his putter and has to finish a round putting with his wedge. Professionals can easily get clubs replaced, but you should make it perfectly clear that your junior cannot.

Golf Balls

The golf ball industry is a $1 billion-per-year industry. Manufacturers use ball sales to gauge the growth of golf throughout the country. It should use sales to gauge if play is improving year to year. With nearly seven major manufacturers, each producing several different brands, it's no wonder the choices are staggering. Even seasoned golfers have a hard time deciphering descriptions on the cover of the fancy boxes. There are "two-piece" balls, "three-piece" balls, "Surlyn," "balata" and "wound" balls; there are also "liquid-center" and "titanium-center" balls. There are "senior" balls, "ladies" balls, and balls that give "extra distance" or "extra spin." There are golf balls that offer combinations of all of the above. The USGA includes almost 1,900 different balls on its "conforming list." It is no wonder many golfers choose which ball to hit by the look of its box.

How do you and your junior wade through all of the fancy terms and confusing descriptions? A lot has changed since the inception of the game, but it has only been since the early 1900s that the modern golf ball utilized superior aerodynamic dimple patterns. The actual development and the timeline associated with the development of the modern golf ball would make a fascinating unit study for your junior (More info: golfeurope. com). Many changes in standards for ball size and weight have evolved. The USGA regulates the golf ball industry within five major categories of testing – weight, size, initial velocity, spherical symmetry and overall distance. Knowing the science of the golf ball is not your responsibility, but again it is an amazing topic your child might be interested in. The Royal and Ancient Golf Club, the governing body of the rules of golf worldwide, except in the USA, decided in 1990 to adopt the 1.68-inch diameter ball. The Rules of Golf are standardized throughout the world for the first time since 1910.

> **Top Golf Ball Manufacturers**
>
> **Titleist**
> **Spalding**
> **Nike**
> **Maxfli**
> **Bridgestone**
> **Hogan**
> **Callaway**
> **Wilson**
> **Srixon**

Hard, Soft and Distance Balls

In general, golf balls will fall in one of three main categories – hard, soft and distance balls. All of these relate to the most critical element of a golf ball – its core. Understanding the core of a golf ball will help you figure out its performance capabilities. Differences in the core composition and construction will affect spin rate ("control"), initial velocity ("distance") and compression ("feel"). Being the one golf product that is considered consumable, it is the one product that the manufacturers spend most of their marketing dollars on. Most manufacturers' research and development departments are also spending millions of dollars to continually challenge themselves to improve the quality and composition of their golf balls to expand their product lines.

Starter and Custom Balls

Manufacturers also spend millions and millions of dollars to ensure endorsements from the best players. Signing well-know professionals to use their products is the easiest way manufacturers have found to establish strong credibility with the golfing public. Just be aware that success, perceived or otherwise, of pros using a particular brand golf ball will quickly attract your child to use a certain brand and type of golf ball. Also realize that except for the top echelon of players, superstar spokespersons such as Tiger and Annika really do not have the same needs as the average player, much less your junior.

After your initial investment of golf clubs, golf balls will be your next biggest expense. If not familiar with the price of a dozen golf balls, a parent might faint at the counter when sent to purchase a dozen or two. There is no reason beginners can't play inexpensive balls. Do not spend top dollar on golf balls while your child is in the beginner's phase of the game. Pinnacle, Top-Flite, and the Noodle are great starter balls. Any of those or any softly used golf balls found in a bargain barrel are sufficient for the novice golfer. If your child gets excited playing with one of the top brand golf balls, look for good used ones and be sure to buy balls when the golf shops are offering special sales.

The top manufacturers fight for market share as each maker sells many different types and brands of golf balls. They specifically design different brands with a particular playing level or need in mind and market them accordingly. Just as they can with club fitting, Hot Stix Golf can help fit junior to the type of ball he should be playing.

Since golf balls are lost quite easily, teach kids early not to get attached to a golf ball; they can't have favorites. Favorites must be retired and kept home on a shelf. Little ones can quickly melt down if they hit their favorite ball in the lake. Playing with range balls on the golf course is a violation of the rules and a bad habit that should not be encouraged. Golf balls also come in different colors, and many younger kids might like to play with a bright pink, orange or yellow ball. Golfers should always have enough golf balls in their bag. Take note of the course's difficulty and make sure your child has plenty of balls to make it to the final hole. Most competitive players will carry at least nine golf balls in their bag. In accordance with the rules of golf (Rule 6-5), a player must always be able to identify his golf ball. Knowing the make and number of the golf ball being played is key. Rule 6-5 also suggests that a player put an additional personal marking on it so that the golf ball is distinctively different than any other golf ball that may be played. Golfers quickly become superstitious about their golf balls. For example, some players will never play with a number 2 ball. Golf balls are generally sold by the dozen or by the sleeve. A sleeve or pack of balls is normally three balls; often "imperfect" used balls or second-hand golf balls can be bought individually.

Life

Golf balls used to have a short life span, but technology has allowed for much better durability without the loss of feel. In the past, playing professionals typically switched out their golf balls every three holes, while top amateurs and junior players might go nine holes before switching out a golf ball. However, research shows that many of the top brands do not need to be switched out any longer. The development of space-age plastics, silicone and improved rubber has allowed golf balls to be played with a lot longer. The actual shelf life has also increased, with a balata-type ball lasting more than 2-3 years before the rubber windings lose a sufficient amount of tension and compression. Surlyn-wound balls will lose compression slower than Balata, and Surlyn two-piece golf balls will have an even longer shelf life.

Usually beginners hit a ball until they badly damage it or lose it. Once the ball is visibly cut, cracked or is off round, it should be removed from play. According to the rules (Rule 5-3), unless a ball is deemed unplayable, it must be holed out before switching it out for a newer one. Only a few of the companies make a golf ball specifically designed for juniors. Encourage your child to play with many different types of golf balls and see if he develops a personal preference tied to performance. Top competitors will be more particular about their golf balls (and they should be), but don't be surprised how opinionated your youngster will become about his golf balls.

Foot Care

Foot care is critical to any sport, but especially to one that keeps you on your feet for hours at a time and walking at least five miles a round every time you play. For juniors, it is extremely important, because their feet are still growing. There is not a lot of choice in footwear for juniors. Only a few golf-shoe companies make a shoe for the younger golfer. Golf shoes must be comfortable. There are enough challenges in golf without junior having his focus turn to his sore, blistered feet. Your son my not win a tournament because of his good shoes, but he may lose one on account of crummy ones.

Shoes

Does he need fancy footwear? Fancy footwear, no. Good footwear, yes. The mere fact that juniors normally carry their bags and walk the course should be enough to convince you that junior golfers need golf shoes made to support the demands of the body. Believe it or not, worn or poorly fitting golf shoes can affect a score. Poor-fitting shoes cause blisters, slipping, a lack of concentration and possible misery on the links. The next time your junior loads up his gear for golf, check out his shoes. If the shoes are curled, cracked, torn or just plain ugly, new shoes are a must.

If your little one is only a driving-range golfer, a good-fitting pair of tennis shoes is sufficient. Make sure the sport shoe junior wears to play golf in is well designed with a flat bottom, giving him good balance and lateral support for a proper swing. Shoes that put feet high off the ground increase the chance of ankle rollover and do not support a good leg turn or weight shift. If your child is either playing on the course or practicing in the rain on wet grass or mats, it is best that you get him a pair of golf shoes, ensuring proper traction and less slipping. The spikes on the bottom of a golf shoe are designed to grip the ground, helping ensure proper body movements and keeping him from slipping. Competitive golfers should own at least one pair of good golf shoes.

The more competitive your kid is, the more necessary it is to invest in good golf shoes. Pre-teen kids have limited choices, but the options are far superior to what they had 20 years ago. It is good for a kid's self-esteem to "look the part." Young boys no longer have to settle for a ladies shoe to get a smaller size. That option is still a valid one if the style and price is right, but your son can also find a more traditional style if he'd rather stick with a shoe that might resemble Dad's.

Adidas, FootJoy, and Nike all offer great youth golf shoes. While each of these shoe brands has distinctive styles and selling points, they are all designed with the competitive golfer in mind. FootJoy shoes may be more traditional, Adidas more casual, and Nike more sporty, but they will all fall in a typical price range of $30-$50. As junior is growing, don't spend much more than this on junior's shoes. Once your child enters the world of adult sizes, his shoe expenses will increase. Look for quality shoes on sale, and do not spend a fortune on any one pair of shoes, at least until you think his foot is done growing. Even then, follow some general guidelines to smart shoe shopping.

In general, golf shoes need to be well fitted to avoid blisters and toe cramps. Comfort and fit always hold priority over fashion or style. It is best if they are waterproof, have good support and padding and come with a well-made sole and replaceable spikes. Wrong-sized and poor-quality shoes will cause foot problems and can lead to more serious back, hip and growth issues. If your child is having trouble with his feet or complains of foot discomfort, take him to a podiatrist or a foot specialist immediately. It may only be that he needs special orthotics to give him ultimate arch or ankle support, but you can never be too careful. For example, conditions such as shin splints and Achilles tendonitis are painful and can be prevented with proper sport insoles and inserts to help cradle and support the foot, preventing inward rollover and stress on the lower leg.

Golf Shoe Care

Golf shoes should be considered part of junior's equipment. When he buys new golf shoes, tighten all the spikes before playing. The shoes themselves are only as good as the spikes – both are necessary for good balance. While it is best to buy him a shoe bag and some shoe trees to help him care for his shoes, it is also important to teach him how to wipe down and clean or polish his shoes. Prideful ownership is taught and you won't mind buying him those new shoes he's going to need while his feet are growing if you see he is taking care of them.

Spikes need to be kept clean and free of dirt and grass. They will also need to be replaced when they wear down. Normal wear and tear will depend on how often your child plays and practices. Daily golfers should replace soft spikes every other month; weekend golfers may only need to change their soft spikes every six months. Show your child how to clean out his spikes with a tee, divot tool or brush every few holes and to check for missing spikes. It is not uncommon for loose spikes to fall out. Junior needs to know when he needs to replace a spike or two. Soft spikes are available at most golf shops, and the secure gripping Black Widow brand is a best seller.

Unscrewing the old ones and screwing in new ones is easy enough for junior to do himself, but make sure he also cleans out the spike holes in the bottom of the shoe to make it easier to insert the new spikes and that they are secure. It is important to use a cleat wrench to make sure they are tight enough. Soft spikes are required at nearly every golf course and are here to stay. Many PGA Tour professionals still use metal spikes, but with a generation of golfers that only knows the feel of soft-spike shoes, it won't be long before the metal spike is extinct.

Socks

There are more sweat glands on the feet than anywhere else on the body. It is very important golfers wear socks if they are wearing a closed-toe golf shoe. Some juniors will try to avoid socks, thinking it will help alleviate the dreaded sock-tan line, but this is not good for their feet or their shoes. Your golfer should wear cotton golf socks. Moist socks can cause chafing and blistering. Sport socks draw moisture away from the foot, keeping it dry. In extremely hot conditions or when your child is playing more than 18 holes and practicing for long extended periods of time, it is best that he change his socks between rounds.

FootJoy makes great golf socks and leads the industry in style selection, but Nike and Ping also make excellent socks. If the sock tan line is an issue with your youngster, he may opt for the ultra low cut that fits just at or below the shoe rim. You may not like the sockless look, but as long as he wears them, who cares? Give in to junior's personal preference. Socks can be ultra thin or they can provide more golf shoe comfort with cushioning at the toe and heel, but like shoes and apparel they can be your child's way to make a fashion statement.

Apparel

While dress code is not addressed in the USGA Rules of Golf, knowing the dress code is just as vital to your child. Abiding by dress code and etiquette are a couple of serendipitous niceties that make golf a great sport for kids. Many golf courses will not let eager golfers, young or old, play or practice at their facilities if not dressed appropriately. In this day, when a discussion of appropriate and tasteful clothing with a teenager runs the risk of emphatic negotiations or opening a Pandora's Box of attitudes, you may apprehensively ask, "What is appropriate?"

Well, there are some basic standard rules of dress that apply to most golf courses, country clubs and tournament organizations. Many junior golf organizations spell out their dress code explicitly in their rules of conduct. Here are some general guidelines to help you out:

- No denim (Jeans may be allowed at some public practice facilities, but rarely allowed on the course.)
- No T-shirts (Public facilities are usually OK with T-shirts being worn on the driving range, but not on the golf course.)
- Collared shirts required.
- Collarless shirts must have sleeves; sleeveless shirts must have collar.
- Cargo pants or shorts are usually not allowed at private clubs.
- Hemlines on skirts and shorts must be respectable.
  (Traditional private clubs most likely will hold to a standard of no more than four inches above the knee. Another good rule of thumb is that the hem must not be higher than the fingertips as the golfer's arms hang down to their side.
- Proper shoes are required. Either soft-spike golf shoes or a flat smooth-sole tennis shoe.
- Hats worn must have bill forward.

Golf apparel is typically conservative. Standard polo shirts and classic twill sports pants or shorts are perfect. Always check for pockets in pants, shorts, skirts and skorts. One-hundred percent cotton pique always works nicely, but there is an excellent ever-growing selection of cotton blends and micro-fiber options available as well. If shopping for appropriate golf wear is a challenge at your local mall, then try the shop at the golf course or independent golf stores.

Liz Claiborne, Ashworth and Ralph Lauren are great places to start when looking for fashion to meet function. Remember many cute "t-shirts" with golf slogans or reference to golfers may not be acceptable to play in. Although your child may not always like the dress code required, it should not be too difficult to find something appropriate. Golf-clothing manufacturers have been slow to respond to a junior clientele, but a few are now making youthful, junior specific lines to accommodate the young golfer. Outlet malls and online stores are great places to shop for classically designed clothing at reasonable prices. The variety of styles and materials is mind boggling, especially for girls.

Encourage your children to look their best when heading out to the golf course. Since most kids want to emulate their sports heroes, be forewarned that there is neither a dress code for the PGA Tour or the LPGA Tour. The trend on the LPGA is short and shorter, much like tennis apparel. Paula Creamer may get away with a hemline or style of dress that your daughter might not be able to. When Tiger Woods started to wear the mock turtleneck and golf clothing manufacturers followed suit with the trendy style, many golf courses around the country had to re-address their "collar only" rule. Lately, both LPGA and PGA Tour players are stretching the traditional dress codes like a good piece of spandex.

Rain Gear and Golf Umbrella

Competitive golfers play in all sorts of weather. Lightning storms will keep junior off a golf course, but rainstorms in and of themselves rarely stop competition. So if you live in an area that gets a lot of rain or your child is playing high-level tournament golf, he needs good rain gear. As a matter of fact, rain gear is a critical necessity. It is meant to keep your child dry, so Gore-Tex is a must! You can't skimp on rain gear – you get what you pay for.

Head to Toe: Accessories

Accessorizing can be fun. Some accessories, like fashionable earrings for girls, are just for fun; many are useful, and quite a few are indispensable. Accessories are usually what kids remember about the pros they watch on TV. In a sport in which everyone seems to clone one another, accessories are often what might separate one player from another in the eye of the fan. The late Payne Stewart and Hall-of-Fame LPGA star Patty Sheehan set themselves apart by playing in knickers. Soft-spoken Duffy Waldorf is known for the "loud" bold prints he wears week in and week out. Many others may opt for certain colors worn on certain days. Tiger usually wears red on Sunday. No matter the style of clothing or hats worn by the professional, they are most likely embroidered with extra large logos advertising the player's sponsor. For generations, different types of hats, belts, gloves, hair accessories and jewelry are the few simple things that display a golfer's personality and help fans connect with a particular player.

Hats and Visors

Your child should get used to playing golf with a hat right from the start. A regular baseball cap with at least a four-inch bill is fine to keep out the glare and protect skin from the sun. If the cap style is his style of choice, there are millions of styles to choose from. He can wear the hat of his favorite sports team or don the name of his favorite golf manufacturer. Just make sure he wears the bill facing forward at the golf course, since he needs the sun protection and most clubs prohibit wearing caps backward. Visors are also a popular hat choice for juniors. They too come in many styles and colors and give great sun protection while showing-off highlighted blonde locks. Floppy hats do not offer as much sun protection, but also tend to be popular with kids. Wide-brimmed and larger safari hats are best for kids who need extra sun protection.

Sunblock

Just as a hat is a necessary item, sunscreen is indispensable. Kids need to get in the habit of applying sunscreen daily, especially kid golfers. The Australian national motto should be a golfer's mantra: "Slip, Slap, Slop!" They are words of wisdom in the day of a deteriorating ozone layer and rising incidents of skin cancer. "Slip on loose clothing. Slap on a wide brimmed hat. Slop on sunscreen."

Your young golfer feels invincible, yet he is typically ignorant to the dangers of overexposure to the sun. It is your responsibility to protect him from serious skin damage and possible skin cancers such as melanoma that could appear years down the road. Research shows that childhood sunburns dramatically increases the risk of developing melanoma, the most dangerous form of skin cancer. Incidents of melanoma have nearly quadrupled in the last 25 years.

Golfers are a high-risk group and are advised to wear sunblock every day. Slather a high SPF all over the body before leaving home. Golf pros tend to favor the 45 SPF or 50 SPF – both experts and golf professionals alike agree that you need a moisturizing sunscreen that blocks both ultraviolet A (UVA) and ultraviolet B (UVB). UV rays penetrate through clothing, especially light-colored clothing, so be sure to cover junior's back. Sun Precautions is a company devoted to making sportswear with special UV protection fabrics needed for active people who spend hours out in the sun. Dermatologists recommend that golfers always reapply sunscreen, since they play most often between 10 a.m. and 4 p.m., when direct sun exposure is most intense. Keep an aerosol or spray sunscreen in your child's golf bag and remind him to reapply several times throughout the day. A good time to reapply sunscreen is at the turn.

A spray-on type will keep hands from getting greasy. Make sure junior diligently covers the ears, neck, scalp, tops of the hands and of course any other body parts that are exposed to the sun. Excessive sweating and continual wiping of the face will require more timely applications. Sweat-proof varieties, like Coppertone Sport SPF 30+, designed especially for athletes, are your best bet. While it is understandable that your child might not want to wear long sleeves or cover himself from head to toe, it is important that he understands the risks of overexposed skin.

Technology Toys

Each year, the USGA approves a variety of rules changes. It appears The USGA is finally giving GPS (Global Positioning Systems) or rangefinders a place in the Rules of Golf. They will be allowed at the discretion of tournament organizers. Depending on the trends, this advanced technology may be a necessity for your child. Yardage books may be a thing of the past if kids are allowed to use a GPS device. Your child should always check with tournament officials before using one during a competition.

Golf Bags, Pull Carts, and Travel Bags

Golf bags come in many shapes and sizes, but the key to a junior's bag is its weight – the lighter the better. Juniors need a light bag that is easy to carry. They also need sufficient pocket space. Since most kids walk the round, you want to buy a "carry" bag, not a "cart" bag. Kickout bag stands make it easier to put down and pick up the bag and are pretty commonplace these days. Strong, comfortable shoulder straps are essential when choosing a reliable bag. Even though there are not a slew of choices, choosing a golf bag can be overwhelming. There are almost 10 million pages on the web offering golf bags. All that, and it usually comes down to a color or brand preference for junior.

Younger children will need a much smaller bag, and many starter sets come with a stylish "matching" bag. Make sure all juniors have a bag with the convenient double strap. This is a must for good posture and to assure a good fit. A bag that fits junior's back properly will not put extra stress and strain on the back or on one side of the body. A golf bag for the 12-and-under crowd should not cost you more than $75 if you're buying it separately.

Some youngsters may opt for a bigger bag than they are capable of comfortably caring. If they do, be sure to buy them a push or pull cart. Carts have a greater range in quality, weight and price than golf bags do. While some carts are the simple, no-frills type, others are deluxe models with a list of luxury options similar to what you might find when shopping for a car. Important options and special features to consider are the size of the tires, the frame durability, the overall weight, easy maneuvering, comfortable gripping, the brake system, special holders (scorecard, bottle, or umbrella) and storage ease. Prices have a wide range, yet in general you will find that pull carts are lighter, smaller and less costly; push carts tend to be heavier, have stronger frames and tires, and are usually more expensive. In either case you will spend anywhere from $40 to $200 if junior wants to roll his bag down the fairway.

Whether carrying or pulling the bag, convenient, zippered pockets are important to competitive players who need to bring a few extra items with them. Remember, your golfer needs room for a snack, sunscreen, water, tees, balls, markers, a note pad or two, pens, personal valuables (watch, rings, jewelry or keys), a repair tool, a towel, rain gear and possibly an umbrella. Competitive players also need golf bags made to take more wear and tear and that will hold up to the demands of travel. A good sturdy travel bag or travel bag cover is a must for players flying from tournament to tournament. Good travel bags will provide an extra layer of protection and should have additional compartments for extra golf shoes and golf balls. Besides making your junior look like a touring pro, they're invaluable for protecting his equipment from the savage treatment of commercial airlines.

Manufacturers offer a variety of bells and whistles on these babies: Have junior look and try on golf bags to see what fits his body type best. Look to spend anywhere from $80 to $150 for a quality "walking" bag. The good news is these bags are less expensive than the more traditional leather "cart" bags. You may spend a little more if you want a name embroidered ... another great gift idea!

Teaching and Practice Aids

There are many kinds of teaching aids that can make practice sessions more fruitful and much more fun. It used to be that teaching aids were only made for adults, and junior had to adapt or forget it. A plethora of training aids is available today. Thousands of gadgets and gizmos are designed to help improve various elements of the golf swing. From building golf muscles to learning the proper swing plane to adding flexibility, it's all covered, even putting.

In some cases, if junior has to use an adult version of an aid, it is best if he doesn't use it. Swing and putting aids range widely in price. It is best to keep in mind that junior does not need a hundred different aids and that certain items should only be used on recommendation or direction from his teaching professional. Aids often help keep practice simple, purposeful and fun.

Shag Bag

Junior should retire his older, gently used golf balls into a personal shag bag. He can use these balls instead of range balls for better short-game practice. Practicing with the same type of golf ball that he plays most of his golf with will help a player develop a better short game. Pitches, chips and bunker shots will be easier to regulate and control. Beginners can put all non-range golf balls into a shag bag and use this as his supply of golf balls. The main equipment manufacturers offer small leather bags to conveniently hold golf balls in, but junior can also use a small canvas drawstring bag as well. A good shag bag will hold 50+ golf balls. Leather bags with a fancy logo will cost somewhere between $50-$100, and the canvas type will be under $50.

Ball Tube

It is much easier for junior to pick up his practice balls using a ball tube. There are many types of tubes available, and the original shag bag (Bag Shag) is a metal tube with a canvas shag bag attached and holds many more balls than the straight metal tubes. These stick-like tubes hold about 25-30 golf balls and are ideal for the short-game area. Kids can't wait to tear away from the drill and scurry around tubing the balls without having to bend down to pick them up. Cleaning up is fun with a tube.

Whiffle Balls and Limited Flight Practice Balls

Backyard whiffle balls have been around since the early 1950s. They are great for hitting around and practicing without fear of breaking a window. Whether it is a neighborhood baseball game or an imaginary golf course, kids have used them to entertain themselves for hours over the years. Golfers can practice their full swings and these balls won't go but a few yards, but they are fun to hit and can be great for target practice and for drills. If you have a little more room in your yard and have set up a place for your child to practice, you may invest in either practice balls with convex dimples or the latest BirdieBall and StrikePad.

The convex dimple-patterned golf balls create wind resistance to reduce the flight of the ball by fifty-percent. The feel is the same as any golf ball, which helps give more positive feedback than a traditional whiffle ball.

BirdieBalls have a limited distance of 40 yards, but they feel and fly just like a real golf ball. Unconventional in shape, they look like napkin rings, but they have a heavy feel just like a traditional golf ball. They also show true spin and more accurate flight patterns. Junior can see whether he hit a fade or a draw. This makes them effective training devices for practice. The BirdieBall is offered in two different series – the Super White Series and the Pro Series. When buying, choose the Pro Series – it is guaranteed not to break or crack. BirdieBalls are made from a super polymer. A StrikePad should be purchased along with the BirdieBalls to simulate taking a divot, and these may be used anywhere, including on asphalt or concrete.

Miniature Nets and Mats

Introduce golf to your peewee with a portable mini-net. These are 10-17 feet long, eight-10 feet high and can cost less than $100. A home practice center can be set up on your lawn or in a spacious garage in seconds, without tools. Small chipping-net baskets are also available to help encourage your child to practice chipping. Small laundry baskets or trashcans also can be used for pitching practice.

Practice mats are also great for indoor or outdoor practice. Small mats are usually one-two feet long and come with a rubber mat tee. Small practice mats are key to saving your lawn. Your child can hit the ground or brush the grass at impact without the fear of divots strewn all over.

More sophisticated practice centers can also be set up at home if you and your child want to have an area for practice at home. Elaborate setups are available for patio decks, spare rooms or empty garages. Juniors who live in inclement-weather areas might want a home practice center available for those long winter days. If you want to get really fancy, you can set it up with your own computer and video camera.

Remember, nets with a stronger, tighter weave are best for golf practice.

Portable Putting Mats, Greens, Rebound Dishes and Putting Tracks

Putting is one of the most important elements of your child's game. It is also an area of the game in which he does not have to be big in size, strength or stature to see success and feel gratification from practice. Scotty Cameron hit the ball on the sweet spot when he said, "What takes place on the green is a totally separate game."

Practicing the art of putting can be as simple as putting a golf ball down the hallway into an empty glass or taking a soda can and trying to putt it so it rolls end over end to an intended target. Plenty of touring professionals have spent many a night rolling putts across their hotel-room floors. Your child may have an entire miniature golf course set up through the house before you know it – this is a good thing! Kids also love automated putting dishes that spit the golf ball back at them. The only down side to these putting trays is that they are only one-dimensional. Putting mats are great for developing sound putting fundamentals and training golfers to put with confidence. Good mats have squaring lines and can stretch out to at least 15 feet. The great thing about portable putting systems is that they are moveable. Kids can move them from the living room to their bedroom, to the garage or to grandpa's house if need be. The quality of putting mats continues to improve. Many offer adjustable hole positions and different breaks for advanced putting practice. A practice aid is only good for your child if he uses it, so it should be where it is visible and easily accessible. Putting mats come in many different styles and price ranges. Simple mats and trays will cost you less than $50, and more sophisticated systems can run you $250 or more.

Another option for encouraging home practice is the outdoor all-weather putting green. This can enhance your home and is beautiful landscaping. Artificial turf has come a long way since AstroTurf was introduced in the 1960s, thanks to research and advanced technology. A high percentage of tour players have synthetic turf or similar turf practice facilities at their homes today. These good golfers know that excellence on and around the greens can mean the difference between winning or just making the cut each week. Great golfers have great short games, period. A realistic surface is critical for proper feedback needed to practice and improve the short game. Many companies offer beautiful outdoor putting and chipping greens for your yard, but you want to make sure the one you buy is high quality, durable, long lasting and low maintenance. There are many different kinds of synthetic turf, and while most have come down in cost, you will have to decide what is best for your yard and your budget.

Natural grass backyard putting greens are very difficult if not impossible for the average person to maintain. The may be feasible if you are fortunate to have a full time gardener; even so, they are challenging to keep up. Even with daily mowing and the chemicals needed to maintain a quality practice area, it is tough to justify the constant and necessary financial investment when quality artificial greens are so accessible.

Kids can spend hours practicing in an outdoor short-game area or they can spend just a few minutes practicing between homework and dinner. In either case, having a short-game area at home can save you time driving to and from the golf course. Do your research and check out the finished product of previous clients to ensure the quality of their work before making your investment. (More info: <u>puttinggreens-direct.com</u> or <u>theputtinggreencompany.com</u>)

Don't panic if a synthetic putting or practice area isn't in your budget. There are quality outdoor modular putting greens available, many of which offer the benefits and looks of a permanently installed putting green. The new generation of modular putting greens is all weather, easy to set up and easily movable, has adjustable cups and also simulates different slopes and contours. Depending on the size and layout, a modular green will range in cost from $500- 3000, an investment worth its weight in gold if your child takes his putting practice seriously.

Other Putting Aids

There are several hundred putting aids available in the retail market, but a trip to the local hardware store may be all junior needs for some helpful putting practice tools. Putting guru Geoff Mangum's Putting Zone web site has some great suggestions for homemade aids. (More info: <u>puttingzone.com</u>)

Inexpensive Alternatives for Putting Practice

- **The String Guide** – a 12-15 foot string and two metal spikes are great for helping junior realize a proper swing path. With the strings attached to each metal spike, put one spike just behind the cup and position the other as far out as your string will stretch. Place the golf ball on the line of the putt under the string and then make the stroke. The actual club path will become obvious as it will be easy to see if it is off line one way or another.
- **Putter Guides** – A pair of three-inch two-by-fours help a player realize proper swing and show whether there are outside-in or inside-out motions hindering a proper stoke.
- **Electrical Tape** – Placed on the ground laid down in parallel lines, this will also easily show an incorrect motion and help guide a player with a proper swing back and through.
- **Square Clubface Directional Guide** – A small 8-10-inch piece of thin, flat wood shaped into a triangle with a line drawn to bisect the point helps junior see what a square clubface should look like directed toward a target and target line.
- **Baby Powder** – Tie an old shoelace or a piece of string around the top of the powder. Tie the other end to the flagstick and make

three-inch circles to put and chip to. Baby powder will not damage the green. For beginners, use longer string and make a bigger circle. Play games with three or four different sizes. Gives kids better target awareness and a better opportunity for success.

Popular Putting Aids

An improper path is one of the most common flaws juniors struggle with at all skill levels. Most of the putting aids available address issues with path and centeredness of contact at impact (the sweet spot). Players will manipulate the path in many different ways, leading to many different styles of compensation.

The best source for deciphering the world of training aids is your child's coach. Here are just a few of the most popular putting aids on the market, most of them relatively inexpensive. For more information on quality training aids of all sorts, go to golfaroundtheworld.com, practicerange.com or dwquailgolf.com:

- **The Cameron Cube** - This is a small acrylic cube that attaches to the putter and holds the golf ball. Any manipulation of the putter head has no effect on the ball's roll, so a putting path too far outside will send the ball off to the left and a path too far inside will send the ball off to the right. Quite simple. (More info: scottycameron.com)
- **The Putting Arc** - This is a training device laid on the practice green with the putter flush against it. Players allow the putter to follow the track of the putting arc while making a stroke. U.S. Open Champion Michael Campbell credited his improved putting stroke and confidence to his Putting Arc practice. Golf Pros worldwide practice with it. (More info: puttingarc.com)
- **The High Tech Putting Track** - PVC rails help you achieve a reliable and consistent putting stroke. This aid has many features that give you a balanced combination of kinesthetic and visual feedback during putting practice.
- **Fuzzy Zoeller's Putting Peg and Pod** - This aid is designed by veteran tour player and Masters Champion Fuzzy Zoeller - he promises that practice with this gadget will "make a regulation hole look as big as a coffee can."
- **Golf Metronome** - This can be a great help to make junior aware of his optimal rhythm and timing. It clips right on to your child's shirt or his hat and is simple to use. Whether putting, chipping or driving, this will help create a consistent rhythm. It comes highly recommended by teaching experts Pia Nilson and Lynn Marriott, founders of Golf 54 and authors of "Every Shot Must Have a Purpose."

- **Putting Mirrors** – These show proper head and eye position, body setup position, putter position and alignment position prior to and when making a putting stroke. Ray Cook and Butch Harmon have great mirror systems available. This will improve junior's putting, and practice becomes fun.
- **No Three-Putt Cup-Reducing Ring** – This aid has two beveled plastic cup reducers to make the hole smaller. For years, the pros have advocated practicing to a single point. Practicing to the smaller hole makes putting to a standard 4.25-inch cup seem easy. Increased confidence naturally creates a better stroke. Shrinking the cup on the practice green is challenging, fun and makes it easier to find the center of the cup on the course.
- **Laser Pens** – This is a laser that attaches to the putter shaft and shows junior his path. Lasers are also available for full-swing training to help with swing path. Teaching experts Butch Harmon and David Leadbetter both have laser systems.
- **Dave Pelz's Putter Clips** – These putting clips are small aluminum clips about three-quarters of an inch high with prongs on either end that attach to any flat-faced putter with double-sided mylar tape. Clips are meant to give you immediate feedback on the precision of your putter impact relative to the sweet spot. These can be frustrating, but if you have a child who loves a challenge, he'll love them. There are other clips on the market as well. A less expensive alternative is to wrap two rubber bands around the putter on both sides of the sweet spot. The ball will carom off if not hit precisely.
- **Pelz' O'Balls** – These are a new concept in golf balls. Playing with range balls is not legal, but these are since they meet all the standards set by the USGA, they have been approved and are on their "conforming list." They are marked with a unique pattern of "O rings" that show the quality of the putt. (More info: pelzgolf.com)

Full-Swing Training Aids

Training aids are created to help simplify the learning process. Unfortunately there are thousands of new golf aids available today. Many training aids might completely overwhelm junior if he is not careful. Aids should simplify the process of swinging a golf club and introduce proper feel of position and motion without too many "mechanical" thoughts. Aids should help rid a student of a state of confusion or frustration, not add to it. Repetition with many of the training aids can be a great help to a player struggling to master a certain feel or club position. It is always best that golfers of any age use aids recommended by their teaching professional. A coach will suggest drills specific to his game and particular needs.

PGA Master Professional Gary Wiren is a leading authority on training aids. In your search for the right aids for your junior, if Wiren endorses it, it is most likely an aid you can trust and will be good value for your dollar. At Golf Around the World, Wiren and his staff perform serious evaluations of every training aid available on the market. So whether the aid is simple or high-tech, Golf Around the World is a good place to start when looking for that special tool junior needs to help alleviate an annoying fault.

When it comes to training aids, it's important to know that they must be used properly and with regularity for improvement to take place. Most important, though, is choosing the proper aid for your particular problem. Like a fitted set of golf clubs, the right training aid can bring significant improvement – if it's right for you. To make sure you choose the one that's best suited to your problem, it's a good idea to consult with your pro and discuss his feelings regarding what your needs are and what aid would be most helpful. The web site golftipsmag.com is also another fun site to find the latest and great-est learning aids. Listed below you will find a few of the very good training aids available for your child:

Top Teaching Aids

- **Ground Targets** – These come in lots of shapes, sizes and colors – rubber cones, hula-hoops, plastic trashcans and ropes. Use bright colors such as yellow, orange, green or pink. Mix and match the targets and colors, and your junior is guaranteed to have loads of fun training with ground targets. Baby powder is great for making circles and shapes on and around the green or practice area as well.

- **8board** – This is a poly-carbonate board in the shape of a figure eight, about the length of a stride, that is adjustable, with swivel-ing circular footrests at its ends. A couple of tennis pros actually invented this new and different product. The 8board develops cor-rect fluidity of body movement, resulting in strokes with more power and control. Many professionals say the 8board helps teach proper stance, proper rotation and proper balance in relation to the complete swing: backswing to follow-through. It is fun and easy to use, and students get immediate feedback. It was named one of the top training aids of 2004.

- **Impact Bag** – The Impact bag, developed by Gary Wiren, is perfect for developing strength in the wrists and arms. In actuality, the "moment of truth" in the golf swing comes when the club head meets the ball. Mostly, junior's goal is to have a square clubface on line at impact. A breakdown of the wrists and arms at impact are two common problems players face, especially juniors. Using the

Impact Bag improves stability and strength, helping produce straighter and longer shots.

- **Grip Right, Swing Right and Weighted Training Irons** – The Club Pro Training Iron golf club has a form-fitted grip to help teach beginner golfers the correct hand placement with every swing. It is great for kids of all ages. Designed by PGA Professionals, the Club Pro Training Iron is the only club that teaches a grip, alignment, club positions and follow-through every time. A positioning arrow teaches the user correct alignment and club position throughout the swing, while the birdie on the toe of the club encourages a complete follow-through after each swing. It is available in four sizes. If you don't want to buy a club, formed grips are great for aiding new players or those making a slight grip adjustment. One cannot overstate the importance of a good grip. This is an essential learning aid for new players. Pre-formed grips make it easy for a beginner to pick up the club right the first time. These grips can be used by themselves or put on a club for actual practice hitting balls. They come in different sizes and are available for your left-handed junior as well.

- **CoolGrip** – This is a training device to help teach proper grip pressure. Gripping the club too tightly reduces performance in distance and direction. Too much pressure causes muscle tension in the hands, wrists, arms and shoulders. It also impedes the natural flow of the swing. Tiger Woods likes to say "Light is Right" when talking about grip pressure. CoolGrip helps develop a light and natural grip. CoolGrip emits a soft audible signal when the grip pressure gets too tight.

- **Medicus** – The dual-hinged driver is one of the best selling golf swing training aids ever. Thousands of golfers have used the Medicus driver to help with swing tempo and to teach them proper swing plane. PGA Tour champions Mark O'Meara and Davis Love endorse it, as well as Golf Magazine Top 100 instructors Hank Haney, Bruce Fleischer and Jack Lumpkin. Its patented dual hinge gives players instant feedback and helps identify critical flaws in path, grip pressure and overall tempo. It helps condition a proper takeaway, downswing and follow-through. It is available in right- and left-handed models and comes in a smaller junior model as well.

- **Momentus** – This is a fun practice club that junior can train with and use for warming up before a round. It comes in a junior version and a regular adult version in either an iron or driver. This swing trainer incorporates a patented technology, whereby the clubshaft embodies most of the weight that is evenly distributed throughout the length of the shaft. Through repetitions with the Momentus, a golfer gets the feel for swinging the club on plane.

Junior's muscles will be stretched, providing additional flexibility and strength, which are extremely beneficial to junior's overall core strength. Momentus strength trainers are great also.

- **Weighted Donut** – This is an inexpensive small weight junior can attach to the shaft of his club. An attached weight is better for proper warm-up. Some kids will swing two clubs, but a donut or a weighted sock is better than junior trying to wield two grips and two clubs heads around. It is much safer as well.

- **Weighted Sock** – This attaches easily and securely to any iron or utility wedge. It is great for warm-up and is perfect for strength and conditioning drills. An advantage the sock has over the donut is it won't slip on the shaft. The sock and the donut fit conveniently in your child's golf bag, too.

- **Swing Fans** – The PowerSwing Fan is another easy and effective product for increasing distance and control. It is easy to swing and with 20-25 swings a day, and your child will be on his way to better technique, longer drives and lower scores. It is best if a young child uses a smaller fan with a proper size grip for optimal training.

- **Speed Stik** – This tool is great for older kids. It is a training aid also empowering golfers to increase their clubhead speed. There is a speed gauge on the stick showing a player his swing speed on each and every swing. The Speed Stik comes in two different models – the blue Speed Stik is designed for golfers under 175 pounds, while the red Speed Stik is recommended for those over 175 pounds. The Speed Stik might be awkward for smaller juniors, but it is endorsed by PGA Tour great Vijay Singh.

Other helpful products include:

- Swing straps, braces and jackets
- Lasers
- Mirrors
- Balance boards
- Swing-plane regulators
- A small broom
- Medicine balls
- Beach balls
- Ping Pong paddles, tennis or racquet ball rackets
- PVC pipe
- Rope
- Foam blocks
- Video cameras and computer software

What's in a Golf Bag?

So your 11-year-old is raring to graduate from clinics and venture into the new world of junior tournament golf. Before you let your little bull loose in the china shop, teach him how to prepare his bag for actual play on the course and in competition.

A carefully stocked bag will help your kid perform his best. Here are the top essentials:

1. Fitted golf clubs.
2. Plenty of golf balls.
3. Water – Remind him to drink it often. It doesn't do any good sitting in the golf bag after the round is finished. Athletes need to stay hydrated.
4. Fuel – Energy bars, a bagel, and a banana can bring back the zip, especially when playing 18 holes. Remind him to graze every three holes or so. Often, bad decisions come from lack of fuel.
5. A golf towel – Several small towels are needed if playing in extreme heat and humidity or in rainy weather.
6. Golf umbrella (for rain or extreme heat).
7. Hat or visor.
8. Sunscreen (with an SPF of 25 or higher).
9. First aid kit – Band-Aids and tape to deal with blisters or calluses, as well as Advil, Tylenol, or Aspirin and lip balm.
10. A wind shirt, sweater or rain gear, depending on the weather.
11. Yardage books and swing notes.
12. USGA Rule Book.
13. Money and jewelry bag.
14. Mobile phone, turned off!
15. Handicap card, Junior Golf Association bag tag, bag I.D.
16. Leisure stuff – maybe an iPod or Gameboy for potential downtime.

In most junior golf events, kids have to schlep the bag themselves, so it is best to keep the bag as light as possible yet have all of the necessities. If there are blue skies and no threat of rain, remind junior to keep the umbrella, sweater and rain gear in the trunk of the car. Tour professionals have professional caddies to haul around the essentials. Every golf bag and its contents is unique, but the main thing is to simply teach your child to be prepared.

Best Buy

Know this – you can't buy your child a golf game, in spite of advertising claims by major manufacturers. Golf can be enjoyed at many levels and with many different price tags. According to the National

Golf Foundation (NGF. More info: <u>NGF.org</u>), golfers spend $22 billion-$25 billion a year on golf products. With an enormous amount of competition among advertisers, marketers and retailers, it is wise for you (the consumer) to do some bargain shopping whenever possible. However, with the vast array of choices, your kid's golf professional will be your best resource and can save you valuable time and money.

Sporting goods chain stores rarely carry the range of items you need to explore. A specialized golf store or a local golf shop is usually your best bet, more so for first-time buyers. You can find golf shops at most golf courses and resorts, often staffed by knowledgeable golf professionals. Club fitters and club makers are not as easily found, but with a little research, you can usually find a nearby expert.

Online stores are here to stay and are an awesome resource. However, the multitude and variety of goods and services can be overwhelming. The internet gives you many choices and is great for research, repeat purchases and the latest-and-greatest accessories. Many golf-only mail-order catalogs have been in business for decades. Golf Digest and Golf for Women magazines are also great resources to see "what's hot" and "what's not" in the industry. They usually do special stories or run a special issue at the beginning of the year with all the usual golf stuff, as well as interesting comparisons and commentaries on the new and innovative training aids and equipment.

Tips from the Pros

Although every major manufacturer has an official "poster player" or two, be very wary of tips from the pros in regard to equipment. Most of the time they are glamorized commercials. Touring and teaching professionals make many thousands of dollars endorsing particular brands of equipment. There are no guarantees your child will yield equivalent performance if he plays with the same brand as his favorite superstar. However, it is certainly safe to assume that if your child is confident a Titleist ball is better for him because a majority of professionals play that ball, and confidence always wins. It's interesting to keep tabs on who is wearing and wielding what, especially among the better players not being paid the big bucks.

Future Gear

It is often said the best place to look to the future is from the past. The game of golf has definitely changed over the last 20 years because of equipment. Volumes can be written about the evolution of golf equipment since the inception of the game itself. There are several excellent books on the subject of the history of golf and golf clubs.

Following is a list of some great resources available:

1. *Encyclopedia of Golf Collectibles*, John M Olman and Morton W Olman, Books Americana, Florence, Alabama, 1985. (ISBN 0-89689-050-3)
2. *Olmans' Guide to Golf Antiques*, John M Olman and Morton W Olman, Market Street Press, Cincinnati, Ohio, 1992. (ISBN 0-972117-02-6)
3. *Golf in the Making*, Ian T Henderson and David I Stirk, Sean Arnold, London, 2nd edn., 1982. (ISBN 0 9516078 0 4)
4. *Golf:the Great Club Makers*, David I Stirk, H.F.&G. Witherby Ltd, London, 1992. (ISBN 0-85493-204-6)
5. *Collecting Old Golfing Clubs*, Alick A Watt, A.A.Watt & Son, Alton, Hants, 2nd edn., 1990. (ISBN 09510923 1 6)

The game has certainly advanced from one played with simple hand made clubs and leather balls stuffed with feathers to the game we know today, based on clubs designed by computers using advanced materials such as titanium and zirconia. The history of regulations of golf equipment is quite complex. As innovations continue to be introduced, they are looked at by the world's golfing authorities – the U.S. Golf Association and the Royal and Ancient Golf Club at St Andrews – to see if they ultimately give the golfer an unfair advantage. As science and technology continue to push the limits of innovation, these governing bodies continue to rule over equipment companies with clear and defined limits, doing their best to uphold the human element. While it is clear club companies will make non-rule-conforming golf clubs for the average golfer, it is vital your child be outfitted in clubs that will make him eligible for competition.

The biggest challenge for parents and coaches raising golf kids is trying to predict the state of the game 10-15 years from now and attempting to tune training to what comes next. Legend Arnold Palmer doesn't claim to have the answers, but he does suggest that the future of the game might revolve around the golf ball. "If I were to rule the situation and had the ultimate say as to what was going to happen in the future, I would have to slow the golf ball down," says Arnold Palmer. A big part of predicting the game's evolution is to analyze where the golf ball will be years from now. "I just think that we're going to get better players. You can't stop the people from being more physical, more mentally alert, more sharp playing the game. That's going to continue, and we want it to. But if we can pull back and keep the golf courses – the old, good golf courses and the new golf courses that we're building right now – competitive with the game and the strength of the players, we must slow the ball down," he has said.

No doubt manufacturers have enhanced the possibilities of great golf with modern technology. What does it all mean? There are plenty of good reasons for junior to try the new stuff. Unfortunately, unlike Woodrow Wilson, there will be even fewer opportunities for him to blame his equipment when something goes wrong. Who knows what the future holds? One thing, though, is certain about the future. The putter won't ever putt for you, not in golf.

9
Physical Conditioning

"I know that if my body is in good shape, I'll be able to swing the club the way I want to."

Annika Sorenstam

Golf has always been viewed as a game of leisure. But today's golfer is leaner, stronger, and fitter than anytime in history. Muscle strength, range of motion, core strength and endurance were not terms familiar to golfers in the past. People didn't play golf to be fit, nor did the general population believe there was a need to be physically fit to be successful at the sport. Most looked at golf as an old man's sport, the fat man's sport, the lazy man's sport. Boy, have times changed for both the casual golfer – and especially the professional golfer. Let's face it, golf was a game that was purported to have 18 holes because that was how many holes could be played before playing partners could finish a fifth of scotch whiskey.

Walking and playing a golf course has always been a great way to keep fit, but never before has there been so much emphasis on physical fitness, or for golfers to consider themselves athletes. While Tiger Woods gets most of the credit for this new fitness phenomenon in the sport, in actuality the need for golfers to be physically fit had been preached by South African Gary Player decades before. Player is a small man in stature and was always considered to be very strong, but even with his amazing success, few took him seriously. The mindset inspired by Player started to take hold by the 1980s with the emergence of a hard-bodied Aussie athlete named Greg Norman and the fact that fitness trailers sponsored by an American hospital, Centinela, were becoming available at every tour stop. The players loved having the gym and all of its toys at their disposal every week as they soon began to see a direct correlation between strength and agility and their golf games. They noticed improvement in their stamina and overall strength immediately. Even though the workouts had become more and more prevalent in professional golf, it wasn't until Woods rocked the golf world with his phenomenal play that all golfers started paying attention to fitness regimes.

At a young age, when time is much more expendable and a variety of sports is available, participating in other physical activities can be extremely important. Kids can get strong the old fashioned way – by playing! While most adults have to work out to develop physical strength, most kids involved in sports that require running, lifting, jumping and hitting will be naturally stronger than their sedentary counterparts and will enjoy physical advantages throughout their lifetimes. Pediatricians say that from middle childhood to early adolescence is the time to acquire and develop sport-specific skills.

Participating in a variety of sports and developing an exercise routine outside of golf will help strengthen different muscle groups. Risk of overuse injuries is reduced and, in many cases, all-around conditioning improves golf performance.

Scientific studies have validated, again and again, what the Greeks taught us about the mind-body connection. Physical fitness is great for general health, but it also has a beneficial effect on academic performance.

Academic Achievement

Do you want your child to become a better reader? Insist she do some pushups every day. A statewide study conducted by the California Department of Education (CDE) matched reading and math scores with physical fitness scores of nearly a million students in grades five, seven and nine.

Announcing the results, the CDE's Delaine Eastin said, "This statewide study provides compelling evidence that the physical well-being of students has a direct impact on their ability to achieve academically." Students with high scores in fitness also scored high in reading and math. Furthermore, students who met minimum fitness levels in three or more of the six physical fitness areas showed the greatest gains in academic achievement at all three grade levels.

Reading and math levels were assessed using the Stanford Achievement Test (SAT-9), given as part of California's Standardized Testing and Reporting Program. The study used a physical fitness test known as Fitnessgram (More info: cooperinst.org) to assess health in six areas – cardiovascular endurance, percentage of body fat, abdominal strength and endurance, trunk strength and flexibility, upper-body strength and endurance and overall flexibility. A score of six indicates that a student is in the healthy fitness zone in all six performance areas and meets standards to be considered physically fit.

Golf Performance

Top golf professionals worldwide acknowledge that winning on the tour today takes much more than a great game of golf. Champions Annika Sorenstam and Tiger Woods have proven over and over again that understanding every aspect of their physical and mental being are the key factors influencing their performances. While T. Woods should be a synonym for discipline, Sorenstam didn't always have such a passion for fitness. Although she was an outstanding tennis player as a young girl, she wasn't totally committed to knowing her body and its capabilities. Her golf career shot skyward and transformed itself right before the golfing world as she dedicated herself to a rigorous, seemingly crazy workout schedule. She said, "I practice less golf, and I spend more time in the gym. But I know that if my body is in good shape, I'll be able to swing the club the way I want to."

Research scientists are not only discovering new and innovative technologies to improve equipment. There are also a whole different group of researchers studying the physical capabilities and limitations of the human body and mind as it pertains to every aspect of the golf game. Most of the findings of supreme athletes transcend golf and are basically universal, yet it is still essential that physical training be tailored for golfers. Everything Woods, Sorenstam and all other premier golfers do to stay physically fit can be learned. Fitness should be a topic addressed by your child's golf coach, and it should be closely monitored throughout her development.

While golf is definitely headed toward the elite-athlete mentality, the good news is that your child doesn't have to be 100% healthy in the eyes of the medical community to enjoy the game or to excel in the sport. There are multiple examples of golfers who have overcome physical challenges to excel at the highest levels of the game.

Michelle McGann – a repeat champion and an exempt member of the LPGA Tour – and Scott Verplank, also a distinguished champion and PGA Tour veteran, are both prime examples of determined athletes who also happen to be diabetics.

MacKinzie 'Mac' Kline, the national spokesperson for the Children's Heart Foundation (CHF) since she was 11, has a personal goal of raising $1 million to help other children born with heart defects. Kline, who despite having only a single pumping ventricle in her heart, has become one of the country's elite junior golfers. Mac uses her golf talents and her inner strength to show others that this "handicap" can be overcome, and this inspires her to attain a "scratch handicap." Her dream is to play in college, and she has already impressed a variety of golf professionals with her talent.

Who can forget Casey Martin? While most people tend to shy away from public attention toward their disabilities, Martin, the "other" famous Stanford graduate, was forced to fight for his love of the game in the public arena. Martin has a circulatory condition called Klippel-Trenaunay-Weber Syndrome, which makes it painful and dangerous for him to walk the golf course. However, he was a darned good golfer, better than most. In college, physicians told Martin he would most likely lose his leg. The NCAA granted his appeal to use a golf cart, and it was obvious that he needed a golf cart if he was going to fulfil his dream of playing on the PGA Tour.

The PGA Tour had a slew of reasons for preventing the use of golf carts, and was not about to give in to his request, forcing Martin to become the poster child for the American Disabilities Association and endure a four-year lawsuit against the esteemed PGA Tour. His case went all the way to the U.S. Supreme Court.

Martin continued to compete and enjoy some success as a professional, despite incredible legal distractions, emotional heartache and horrific pain as his case made its way to our highest court and scored a victory in May 2001. Martin was given a chance to reach his dreams as a touring professional. Healthy or not, most who try for pro status don't make it, but he was given an equal opportunity to strive for the dream. He has overcome his physical limitations and given the next person with a disability a glimmer of hope. Whether he wins at golf or not, Martin has won his most important victory – pride and belief in himself as a person with a disability, not in spite of it.

Because of his disease, his career was cut short, but his legacy will live on forever. Martin, winner of the 1998 Nike Lakeland Classic and a U.S. Open participant (a tie for 23rd was his best finish on the PGA Tour), has eloquently said, "I don't care if you're in perfect shape, it's tough out there (on tour). I knew that and was all for it. I liked the challenge. I love golf. I wanted to be great."

The key is to teach your child to become the best she can become. No one knows for sure where their limitations are, but your child won't find them as a couch potato. Instill a desire for excellence, and your child will want to train her body and mind. A little effort will go a long way and catapult your child above mediocrity. The discipline required to become physically fit will become a habit, and the benefits of a healthy lifestyle will be a gift of a lifetime, whether or not your child becomes passionate about golf.

Experts agree that physical conditioning is critical to every major contributing factor in your game, including swing mechanics, stamina, mental acuity and good judgment. Here are but a few benefits to a golfer in good physical condition:

1. Good overall health and diet, ensuring a clear mind and proper focus.
2. Balanced muscle strength for ultimate power.
3. Physical conditioning of trunk and hip joints, ensuring ultimate core strength and balance.
4. Physical strength in hands, arms and forearms, producing maximum club head speed.
5. Overall flexibility, keeping the body supple and in an injury-free state.
6. Stamina to have optimal performance for practice and play, especially in extreme weather conditions.
7. Stamina to carry one's own bag for 18 to 36 holes (six-12 miles.)

At the elite levels of the game, players are swinging the club over 100 miles per hour, making it necessary for maximum strength and flexibility. In times past, golfers interested in getting stronger would concentrate solely on weight training and build too much muscle mass, thus altering their swing mechanics. Golf fitness techniques should incorporate resistance training, strength training and a stretching regime to enhance overall range of motion and improve flexibility. Since weak muscles are tight muscles, by strengthening the muscles specific to golf, your child will have better control of her body. While all kids should be taught the importance of body balance, muscle toning, and general strength, much of this can be acquired through participating in other sports in addition to golf. Teenagers should look into golf-specific training programs since physical factors such as stamina, strength and speed will likely begin to influence a youngster's performance once she hits adolescence.

Participation in Other Sports

Perhaps the easiest way to ensure all-around conditioning is to encourage little Julie to play other sports. This is especially true for the under 14s, who may more willingly commit to participation in other sports as opposed to working out at the gym. Surfing, soccer, gymnastics, skating, baseball, football and basketball are just a few of the sports that have positive qualities in regard to strength conditioning.

Adding variety is a fun way to achieve total-body conditioning and avoid the burnout caused by golf-all-the-time syndrome. Certain sports can even help improve golf performance. Swimming and cross-country skiing are perhaps the best sports to achieve total-body conditioning. In-line skating and dancing also offer conditioning benefits.

Hockey, in both ice and field forms, is great for coordination and provides vigorous workouts. It is no wonder many good golfers excelled in other sports before taking to golf, and it is also no wonder athletes from other sports quickly become good golfers. The footwork of a downhill skier, the core balance of a surfer and the power swing of a hotshot baseball player are applicable to a good golf swing. Jack Nicklaus was dubbed "Fat Jack" when he first went out on tour, but few knew what an amazing athlete Nicklaus was. He enjoys all sports, is a strong skier and tennis player and even won a few track events in his high school days. Greg Norman is an excellent surfer and was regarded as a top rugby and Australian rules football player.

The Celebrity Tour is an organized professional golf tour for athletes and celebrities wanting to cross over into the world of professional golf. The fun thing about golf is that Super Bowl champion Jerry Rice can tee it up with baseball Hall-of-Famer Johnny Bench, and both can utilize much of what they learned in their own sporting worlds to help them become better golfers. Cross training offers benefits in the areas of conditioning, footwork and coordination – just keep an eye out for strain to the body.

Think you should start yoga or Pilates only after hitting 40? Think again. Encourage your pre-teen to hit the mat and she'll continue to thank you well beyond her 40th birthday. Yoga reduces the risk of long-term injuries by increasing flexibility and strength of the joints. It can also help sharpen focus during a match. And speaking of focus, how about Bruce Lee-style martial arts for concentration, balance and a healthy dose of assertiveness training, which is so necessary to win matches?

Not all sports complement golf, though, and a few sports can actually hurt golf development if junior plays them a lot. Contrary to a well-established rumor, baseball isn't one of them. Swimming is a wonderful sport for developing golfers – however, too much upper-pectoral development will hinder the golf swing. Too much racquetball and tennis can create a cross-the-body sensation, interfering with junior's feel of her appropriate swing plane motion. Other than injuries in more physical sports such as ice hockey, football and soccer, there are few reasons you shouldn't encourage your child to play, play, play! How about chess to improve on-course golf strategy?

Making Exercise Fun

Kids get bored when they're told to exercise as a means to an end, in this case better golf performance. Instead, consider exercise an end in itself – make it a fun activity the child looks forward to for its own sake. Double the fun by joining in.

Shoot hoops in the driveway one day, play Frisbee after a day or so and bike the next. Twirl around with a hula hoop. Looking for a fun activity that will more directly impact conditioning for golf? Skip rope. Boxers have the fastest feet in the world, and skipping is a major component of their training. It's also a great workout that demands control, endurance, speed, coordination and strength.

> **Make it a fun activity the child looks forward to for its own sake.**

Add variety by choosing a new activity for each season. Try sledding, skiing or snowboarding in the winter, swimming or in-line skating during the summer; hiking and biking in the spring and fall.

Take a routine task and make it a fun activity for parent and child – walking Fido, for instance. Develop a routine of walking the dog together. It's simple, but it works.

Where to Start

Find a trainer that specifically works with and understands the specific needs of golfers. There are many fine golf fitness instructors throughout the world to mention them all, but here are a few trusted individuals or programs that can get you started in the right direction. Susan Hill is a golf fitness expert and is the sports nutritionist and president of fitnessforgolf.com. Mike Pedersen, the author of the "Ultimate Golf Fitness Guide," is another widely acknowledged golf fitness expert in the United States. At high-performance training facilities, both Hill and Pedersen have watched, studied or trained the best players in the game. Pedersen has developed a customized online golf fitness program trademarked the "Power Performance Program," and he is also the featured golf fitness expert for Golf Magazine's web site, golfonline.com, as well as for PGA.com.

Body Balance for Performance, fitgolf.com, is another complete golf health and fitness training program. This program, started by Paul Calloway, is franchised around the U.S. and Canada. Its trained golf fitness specialists perform individual evaluations and assessments before they design comprehensive programs to help golfers improve their fitness and overall golf performance. Skip Redford has 20 years experience as a personal trainer and has used his vast knowledge as an athlete, in martial arts and as a student of sport psychology and physical education to develop a unique training model. Access to his training methods can be found at stargolffitnesstrainers.com.

The Egoscue Method athletics program, egoscue.com, is another program that is highly recommended by golfers and non-golfers alike. Elite athletes from many different sports utilize the Egoscue Method workouts. Pete Egoscue, an anatomical physiologist since 1978, is the creator of the Egoscue Method. His exercise therapy program is acclaimed worldwide, and he has been consulted by some of the biggest names in sports, including Jack Nicklaus. His programs provide personalized exercises that re-train muscles, realign posture and reduce the chance of chronic injury and pain. Egoscue has specific programs for kids as well, including after-school programs that encourage a unique combination of drills and strengthening activities. Trained to perform through optimal alignment of the human body, junior's body will reach its maximum potential without a huge risk factor. The Egoscue Method not only restores proper musculoskeletal function, but it also keeps getting in shape simple and fun.

Liba Placek, the director of athletics for Egoscue, stresses, "The most important thing is to prevent injury down the road. Yes, proper conditioning will create strength, but it is necessary to balance the body. Unilateral sports such as golf require specific exercises to counterbalance the most dominant and repetitive motions. Few people think of prevention – everyone wants to 'fix it' after the fact. Athletes do themselves a huge favor if they strengthen their bodies to support the stresses they put themselves through day after day. Learning to take proper care of the body can help athletes enhance performance, but more importantly it helps avoid aggravating and possibly career-ending injuries."

A well-designed fitness program, specific to individual needs, can catapult a golfer to the next level. It is best to let experts help you tailor a specific program for your child. Fitness experts are a big part of the future of golf. (More info: fitnessforgolf.com, stargolffitnesstrainers.com, egoscue.com, ultimategolffitnessguide.com, fitgolf.com)

Measuring Fitness

Here is a good example of some testing your child should go through as a trainer devises a personal program to develop maximum strength, agility, balance and overall health. This particular test was developed by Kent Brizendine, a physical therapist and co-owner of Nexus Physical Therapy in San Diego, California (More info: nexuspt.com):

Test No. 1: Hip Rotation Flexibility
- Sit on the front edge of a chair with your hips bent about 90 degrees (spine vertical and thigh parallel to floor).
- Cross one leg over the other, placing the ankle on the opposite knee.
- What to look for:
    - Was child able to cross leg without helping with a hand?
    - Was child able to cross leg without slouching or leaning back?
    - Can child get the shin of the crossed leg parallel to the floor?

Hip-rotation flexibility is important in the golf swing to keep the lower body stable and allow proper rotation rather than sliding during the backswing and follow-through.

Test No. 2: Hamstring Flexibility
- Lay flat on back with legs outstretched.
- Lift one leg, keeping the knee straight.
- Child lifts the leg only as far as she can with the knee straight and the opposite leg remaining flat on the floor.

- What to look for:
  - Was child able to lift leg higher than 65 degrees?

Hip-flexion flexibility, specifically hamstring length, is important in all phases of the golf swing. In address position, hamstring flexibility is required to allow proper posture for junior before she even begins the backswing. To keep a bent right knee in the backswing, she needs both hip rotation (test No. 1) and hamstring flexibility.

Test No. 3: Trunk Rotation Range of Motion

- Sit on a chair with hips bent about 90 degrees.
- Have her hold a golf club across the front of her shoulders with her hands crossed across her chest.
- Turn as far as she can to the right and then the left, making sure to stop turning when she feels her pelvis begin to move. This is to test thoracic spine rotation only so the motion should stop when the pelvis begins to move.
- What to look for:
  - Was child able to turn at least 60 degrees each direction?
  - Was the range of motion equal to left and to right?

Did she feel like she manipulated her shoulders or shoulder blades rather than turning the spine easily and fluidly?

Test No. 4: Single Limb Stance (balance)

- Stand with good posture.
- Lift one knee (bent knee) until the hip is bent 90 degrees (thigh parallel to ground).
- Try to hold balance for a minimum of 10 seconds.
- As soon as her arms start waving or she moves her foot to maintain balance, the test is over.
- If she was able to maintain balance for 10 seconds, repeat test with eyes closed. (With eyes open, lift leg and get balance, then close eyes and begin timing)
- What to look for:
  - Was child able to keep pelvis level? (Looking from the front, did the belt remain level?) If not, this may mean there is some hip and abdominal muscle (core) weakness.
  - Was balance better on one leg than the other? This may explain difficulty with weight shift during the swing, or a reverse pivot (right leg balance worse than left), or difficulty finishing on the left side (left leg balance worse than right.)

Test No. 5: Plank Position

- This test is done in pushup position on hands and toes (hands directly beneath shoulders).
- If junior can't get in pushup position on hands and toes, try it on hands and knees.
- If she's still having trouble, try on knees and elbows.
- Try to keep back straight with a straight line from heels to shoulders.
- What to look for:
    - Was child able to keep back straight without lower back dipping down (weak abdominal muscles) or upper back rounding (weak abdominal muscles and weak shoulders and triceps)?
    - Did her shoulder blades stay flat against the ribs, or did they wing away from ribs (weak scapular stabilizers)?

Weak abdominal and parascapular muscles can affect all areas of the golf swing. These areas are commonly weak in young golfers. Proximal stability/strength is necessary in order to utilize the arm and leg strength that she does have.

Core

The core is where the body's center of gravity is located and where force production begins. Most people have a very weak core, and as a result suffer chronic posture problems. Over time, this creates wear and tear on the body. A golfer with a weak core is vulnerable to injury and struggles with efficiency in her swing. How strong is junior throughout her core? It is important to find out. The golf swing relies on core strength, endurance and proper engagement in seeking elements of stabilization, control and coordination. Core conditioning is very important for a golfer because all movements in the entire body stem from the strength in this area. Strength in the trunk region or "core" area of the body produces stability and helps generate power. Wherever you find a weak core, you find a major source of energy leaks in the golfer. Junior should try this core test developed by Fitness for Golf.

- Have your child lie on her back with her knees bent.
- She should place one hand underneath her lower back, then extend her knees to 90 degrees.
- Then she should press the lower back firmly against her hand.
- Have her slowly lower her feet toward the ground by keeping the same tension on her hand.

Which one of the following best describes what happened when she performed the exercises above?

A. Her lower back lifted, and she could no longer feel any pressure on her hand.

B. Her lower back lifted, and she could feel some pressure on her hand.

C. She was able to keep the same pressure on her hand throughout the movement.

If she answered (C), congratulations! She is well on her way to developing the core strength she needs for better golf. If she answered (A) or (B), she should start with some basic exercises for engaging the core region of her body. The most important rule in a golf-conditioning program is to work to develop strength from the core region of the body outward.

Building Strength and Power

Young children don't have to take a class in strength training. Simply encourage them to play outdoors. Soon they'll be climbing trees or enjoying a swim in the backyard pool – activities that make the muscles work against resistance; they'll also be building muscle and increasing bone density.

Body-weight Exercises

Bones continue to harden during the growing years. Up until adolescence, the area at the ends of long bones consists of soft cartilage known as growth plates. Near the end of the adolescent period, the growth plate is replaced by bone.

Experts say strength-training exercises that involve light weights can be introduced around adolescence. Body-weight exercises – squats, lunges, pushups, pull-ups, crunches, resistance-band exercises, rope climbing and light weights with lots of repetitions are safe. Manual-resistance exercises use a partner to develop strength. These exercises add variety to a workout and significantly increase the number of exercises available to a young athlete. Remember, though, to stick to the light weights.

Bulking up like a weightlifter is not helpful for golf, but adding a few pounds of muscle can greatly enhance one's ability to handle stress on the body and hit more powerful shots. Combined training programs consisting of three sets of 6-8 repetitions on free-weight exercises like bench press, squat, single-arm row, lunge, shoulder press, upright row, abdominal crunch, back extension and side bends show significant changes to the body's ability to produce both club-head speed and driving distance. Workouts with weights should involve moderate weight, with medium (12-15) repetitions, and should be conducted in a time frame of 30-45 minutes. This type of weight-training program will improve strength and endurance but not build muscle.

Strength training involves body awareness, muscular control and coordination. The goal is to increase muscular and bone strength while retaining flexibility and movement. Use light dumbbells, resistance bands and other free weights with lots of repetitions. In consultation with a fitness trainer or coach, design a variety of strength-training routines, including wrist curls and sawing. The general recommendation is to introduce weight training after adolescence or during early puberty. Strength in the muscles will give junior better control of her body.

Strength comes in many forms with regard to the golf swing. Strong back muscles allow the golfer to endure the explosive movements in the swing. Combined muscle strength produces balance and coordination. Strong ligaments and tendons also prevent the joints from going beyond their range of motion. A strong trunk allows forces to be transferred effectively from the legs to the upper body. It also enables the body to withstand those forces without breakdown. Stability and balance also come in many forms for junior, including her posture, trunk and joints. A strong and stable body will allow your child to maintain a proper spine angle throughout the entire swing.

Plyometrics

"Plyometrics are exercises that enable a muscle to reach maximum strength within a short time," says Dr. Donald Chu, a leading authority on power training and author of more than half a dozen books on plyometrics, including "Plyo Play for Kids."

Plyometrics can best be described as "explosive-reactive" power training. The most common human movement, running, is completely a plyometric event. Swinging a golf club is also a plyometric event. Every day we participate in random plyometrics, but specific plyometric training will enhance a kid's ability to increase speed of movement and improve power production. The exercises start with a rapid stretch of a muscle followed by a rapid shortening of the same muscle. There are many injury-proof plyometric drills designed for kids using soft cones, medicine balls and other accessories. Common games that kids play, such as skipping, hopscotch, leapfrog, jumping jacks, bunny hops and certain moves in aerobic dance are all forms of plyometrics.

Golf-specific plyometric exercises such as seated horizontal twists, standing horizontals twists, standing back extensions and golf swings performed with medicine balls – consisting of three sets of six repetitions performed at least twice a week – will increase junior's club-head speed and driving distance.

Flexibility Training

Flexibility is the single most important physical characteristic likely to influence your golf swing. Flexibility refers to the range of motion in a joint and its related muscle groups. Flexibility training increases the length and elasticity of muscles, reducing the risk of pulling a muscle when unleashing that explosive hip turn. A tight body creates restricted motion in the swing and produces injuries as a form of compensation. It is important junior be as supple as possible, so tight muscles never become a limiting factor in performance. Proper strength training will improve flexibility.

Though most kids are naturally flexible, a regimen of stretching for five or ten minutes before and after golf goes a long way in preventing injuries. More important, forming a habit of stretching will pay dividends as they grow older and their bodies become less flexible.

It's not uncommon for eager kids to rush into a full golf swing and top speed as soon as they're dropped off for practice. If the coach is not including a warm-up routine at the start of every practice, it is the parent's responsibility to arrive five or ten minutes early and go through a warm-up routine with the child. A cool-down stretch after practice is also important.

Use "funny talk" to get kids motivated. For instance, stretching the quadriceps muscles in the front of the thigh is a core component of any warm-up program. This involves raising one foot behind you and bringing your heel to your butt. Naming this routine "The Stork" is a fun way to help kids remember it.

Depending upon your child's situation, it may be wise to enroll in a flexibility training class such as yoga or Pilates. Flexibility aside, these programs improve agility, increase strength without bulking up and work on the mind-body connection. There are lots of great videos and books on stretching, yoga, as well as Pilates produced by specialists. Educate yourself, and be sure to consult with your child's pediatrician before starting any physical training program.

Balance

Does junior have proper balance? Does she know what good balance feels like? Can junior maintain balance and produce proper weight shifts? Junior needs to learn to increase body movements and club-head speeds without wasting energy or improper balance. Is her golf swing motion efficient? Smooth? While performing, good balance can often make up for poor swing mechanics.

Endurance

Performing a physical activity for a long time without getting breathless requires good aerobic capacity. Aerobic capacity and endurance are important for your junior golfer. Does your child have what it takes to last through a solid 18 holes? Keep in mind that the teen years are the most important time to develop aerobic capacity.

Stamina is clearly the most underestimated aspect of the game. Golfers tend to ignore the cardiovascular component of golf. However, most junior golfers are required to walk the golf course, and golfers can cover an approximate walking distance of five-six miles each round. Even golfers who ride in carts put in their fair share of walking depending on local cart rules or weather conditions and while following errant shots. Poor cardiovascular conditioning can certainly have a negative impact on your game. According to Tiger Woods, "Fatigue can affect your focus and cause you to make a bad decision. I never want to lose a tournament because of a bad decision precipitated by my being out of shape."

Although over 70 percent of a golf match consists of short bursts of intense activity, aerobic capacity is still important for golf players. Short bursts of intense activity produce lactic acid that is associated with premature fatigue. Experts suggest sufficient aerobic capacity is needed to remove the lactic acid buildup, thereby emphasizing the need for increased endurance.

Swimming laps, doing step aerobics and jogging are all activities that will improve aerobic capacity. For golf-specific training, instead of long runs, focus on interval training. Alternate between reaching maximum speed and reverting to a normal pace.

Interval Training

It may surprise you to know that a fit tennis player who can breeze though a vigorus tennis match lasting many hours, won't last through a marathon. Golf, like a marathon, will require energy over a longer period of time, rather than repetitive bursts of intense energy workouts. Slow distance workouts alternated with longer duration of normal activity, provide good training. Any form of cardio training to build stamina is good for overall health at any age. Slow, deep breathing is a consistent and essential part of training as well, because golfers do not want their heart rates to spike or to stay high during the round.

During short bursts of activity, the body uses energy stored in the muscles – glycogen and ATP. The byproduct is lactic acid, which is responsible for the burning sensation we feel in our muscles during strenuous workouts. During periods of normal activity, the heart and lungs work together to break down any lactic acid buildup. In this phase, oxygen is used to convert stored carbohydrates into energy.

Training for this form of repetitive activity, called interval training, leads to the adaptation response. Muscles develop a higher tolerance to the buildup of lactic acid. The body begins to build new capillaries and is better able to take in and deliver oxygen to the working muscles, thus strengthening the heart muscle. These changes result in improved performance.

Playing Frisbee in the park is as good as any interval training involving running sprints. Use intervals for walking, running, cycling or in-line skating. Your kid doesn't like watching the clock? Encourage her to walk faster at the mall or speed up between streetlights. Walking faster between shots is great for junior's body, and it will also encourage a good pace of play. Basketball, baseball, ice hockey and even fly-fishing closely approximate some golf movements. A season enjoying any of these sports is a natural way to improve ability. Interval training and plyometric exercises that involve sideways and forward-backward movements are also good for improvement.

Whew, that's a lot of information! Just know that many golf coaches incorporate such training for kids to keep things fun and interesting while trying to keep them in good shape as well.

Good Eats and Body Composition

You are not only what you eat, but also how much you eat. Most parents and coaches have become very aware of the importance of a well-balanced diet with healthful portions of proteins, fats, and carbohydrates.

Competition demands even more attention to good nutrition. Eating right the night before a tournament, two to three hours before tee time and throughout the round will keep your child's energy high on the golf course. Eat small amounts of energy foods rich in carbohydrates are solid fuels – brown bread, potatoes and pasta, pancakes, bagels, raisins and bananas. Refuel with similar high-carb foods one to two hours after the match. Never forget the importance of regular hydration. Choose sports beverages or plain old water. Junior should avoid caffeine and alcohol.

Supplements

The scientific community has finally proved the efficacy of vitamin supplements. A multivitamin, antioxidants and mineral complexes are now an athlete's essentials.

Teenagers develop special nutrient needs as they experience tremendous growth spurts and hormonal changes. Individual likes and dislikes, as well as peer pressure, can contribute to poor diets. Because of their eating habits and special nutrient needs, certain food supplements may be useful.

Avoid supplements formulated to optimize hormone levels, including testosterone and growth hormones, because they may interfere with natural growth patterns. Meal-replacement shakes and powders may sometimes be the only hope for a rushed teenager, but limit their use and seek medical advice before using these products.

Body Composition Tests

There are two simple tests available to determine body composition – Skinfold and Body-Mass Index. Golfers need not know exact body composition, but should a kid want to know if all her healthy eating and exercise is paying off, a parent or fitness trainer can perform these tests. The results provide an estimate of a child's percentage of body fat when compared to body mass composed of muscles, bones and organs:

- **Skinfold Test:** Using a basic device called a skinfold caliper, measure the thickness of the skin fold on the back of the upper arm. Use this measurement with the Skinfold chart to obtain body fat percentage (More info: cooperinst.org).

- **Body Mass Index:** Based on height and weight measurements, a BMI table will provide an index number. The index will tell you if the child's weight can be considered healthy, overweight or obese (More info: cooperinst.org).

Injuries

"No pain, no gain." While this can be true at times, it can also be a dangerous motto. Kids need to realize that they should never play if they are experiencing chronic pain. A little discomfort is part of any sports and fitness routine. For a muscle to become stronger, it must experience a higher than normal load. This slight overload is perceived as "the burn" and is the "good pain" necessary for improved performance. Onset of fatigue is another sign that activity is pushing the limits.

Good Pain, Bad Pain

The discomfort associated with "good pain" is short-lived; it should not persist for hours or days. With rest, the slight fatigue should also go away.

Certain pain, though, lasts long after exercise. It affects sports performance as well as functions outside sports like walking, sleeping, shaking hands or getting dressed, and does not go away after rest. These are examples of the "bad pain" one should always be concerned about. Discourage your child from playing through pain. Seek medical evaluation right away if pain persists.

Sometimes kids are less than honest about disclosing the real nature of their pain, either because they want to compete in an important tournament, attain a certain ranking or make a team. The best antidote for this behavior is talking to the child about pain and injuries before they occur. Explain how to distinguish good pain from bad pain. Tell them why they need to be honest with you and with themselves about the "bad pain." Make them understand how timely care of pain and injuries will enable them to enjoy the sport for a lifetime.

Common Pains

Pains associated with shoulders, elbows, wrists, hips, knees and the back are most common to golf. These common problem areas used to be accepted and dealt with simply by taking a couple more pain relievers. However, it is not good practice to teach your child to ignore such symptoms. Prevention is the best remedy, and with more and more education about fitness, some of these ailments can be completely eliminated.

Short and tight hip flexors are a known source of lower back pain in which the low back muscles tighten while hamstring and abdominal muscles lengthen. Everything has a cause and an effect within the body. Tight hip flexors limit a golfer's body in trunk rotation, which ultimately leads to compensations at the shoulders, elbows and wrists. It is important to clearly understand where the chain broke down in the first place so corrective action can be taken. The parent, coach, and player should all keep an eye out for this kind of "bad pain." At the first sign, seek medical advice.

Golf elbow is an injury associated with pain on the outer side of the elbow. Any combination of repetitive rotation of the wrist and forearm while using force can cause golf elbow. Making simple adjustments can help avoid golf elbow. Adjustments that reduce stress on the forearms will help. Shoulder ailments are also common among golfers, especially elite golfers. Often a rotator cuff impingement is the culprit. Problems with shoulders can also be helped with specific therapy, exercises and strength conditioning.

The most common causes of injury are:	
Improper grip size	Violent repetitive motions
Clubs being too heavy	Lack of appropriate conditioning
Shafts being too stiff	Lack of warm-up
Bad swing mechanics	Continual unilateral motion

Healthful Habits

The problem with most sports injuries is that athletes don't know they have them until joints become tender and they start to feel pain. Rehabilitation usually requires extensive treatment and rest. Once again, it is important to educate your child on good pain versus bad pain. Help him understand the importance of practicing good habits that will help prevent injuries that can appear, without notice, years later. Here are some helpful tips:

- Overall fitness is the best way to avoid injuries. Pay special attention to the demands of golf and those parts of the anatomy that are not worked as much by golf alone – strengthening the legs, forearms, shoulders and abdominals.
- A cardio routine followed by stretches before any workout and another few minutes of cool-down stretches afterward is essential.
- Always wear proper golf shoes.
- Have clubs fitted yearly (more often if a child is growing more rapidly)
- Never play through pain. Seek medical attention right away and follow a doctor's orders. If rest is necessary to attain health, don't risk further injury – rest as many weeks or months as the doctor advises.
- Make drinking plenty of water a habit on the course and during workouts.
- Have an annual extensive physical examination by a doctor.
- Play with proper balance and proper mechanics.
- Rest. Take timeouts from vigorous physical activity of any kind from time to time.

The National Youth Sports Safety Foundation (More info: nyssf.org) and the sports medicine section of the National Federation of State High School Associations (More info: nfhs.org) are two sources of current information regarding safety issues in sports.

Conditioning Roadmap

You can find loads of scientific research, books, videos and television programs that discuss the nuts and bolts of physical conditioning. It's easy to get carried away. Educate yourself and keep current, but remember to avoid too much structure at a young age. Keep conditioning simple and balanced. Above all, make physical conditioning enjoyable for its own sake. Jogging along a beautiful trail beats the treadmill hands down. When looking to set fitness goals, begin with weaknesses, not strengths.

A balanced conditioning program will include training for flexibility, strength, power, speed, agility, quickness and cardio. Incorporating all these elements into routines appropriate for your golf kid can be challenging. Table 9.1 provides a general roadmap that can help. Personalize the roadmap depending upon your child's physical growth and level of golf intensity.

Consult your child's doctor and a certified trainer before starting any physical training regimen. Complete physical examinations by a doctor once or twice a year are a must. Whoever you choose to work with your child, they should have baseline tests to evaluate a starting point and be able to measure improvement in targeted areas. Assessment tests should definitely cover flexibility, strength and power, body composition, speed and agility and aerobic capacity. Obtaining a current fitness profile every three months or so helps the player train more efficiently and design a custom fitness program that not only improves golf performance but will reduce the risk of injuries.

Table 9.1

Age	Physical Conditioning Program
Under 13	Make a habit of doing warm-ups before golf. Start with cardio and follow with stretches. After golf, perform a cool down routine, including stretching again. Incorporate age-appropriate conditioning drills during golf lessons. Drills that focus on speed, agility and quickness are best. Plyometric exercises are great. Participate in a variety of sports in addition to golf. Achieve beginner-level proficiency in at least one sport in each group: • Swimming, skiing, snowboarding and dancing for all-around conditioning. • Ice hockey, field hockey, basketball, baseball, softball or soccer. Allow time for unstructured outdoor activities.
14-15	Add light structured training, selecting at least one from each group: • Yoga, martial arts and other flexibility and mind-body workouts. • Body-weight exercises, plyometrics, interval training, light weights and resistance bands are good for strength and power.
16-plus	Hire a fitness expert and develop an individualized conditioning program.

Most schools have physical education classes. In California, students in grades seven through 12 must participate in more than three hours of physical exercise each week. Factor in such hours of exercise when designing a program for your child. You can find after-school sports and fitness classes at health clubs, YMCAs, junior camps and community centers.

Do you have to be fit to play good golf? You may be surprised, but it isn't necessary to enjoy the game at a basic level. However, if your child wants to be able to place at the top of the leaderboard on a consistent basis from tournament to tournament, then the answer changes to absolutely "YES."

10
The Mental Game

••

"The mindset you bring to the game determines not only the enjoyment you derive from golf but also the level of proficiency you will achieve."

Jim Flick, professional golf instructor

••

While it can be argued that golf greats of the past didn't rely on sports psychologists, Ben Hogan once confided in Dr. Bob Rotella, "Valerie was my sports psychologist. I would have quit a long time ago if she hadn't believed in me. I was absolutely mortified that I wasn't making enough money to support this woman in the way that I wanted to take care of my wife. I tried to quit many, many times. And every time I tried to quit, she would tell me, 'No way.'

"I think she knew I would never be a happy, content man if I quit before I achieved my dream. But I don't know if I would have gotten there without her. I needed that." The same could probably be said of Winnie Palmer and Barbara Nicklaus. Raymond Floyd has often publicly attributed his success to his wife, Maria. Players may still depend on their spouses or family members for encouragement or that kick in the butt, but many modern golfers are employing sports psychologists to help them with the frailties of the game. With the emergence of Tiger Woods in the late 1990s, a new industry within the golf world grew exponentially. The golf psychologist is here to stay.

"Golf is 90 percent mental. The other half is physical." Yogi Berra's infamous quote adequately adapted to golf describes what most good athletes already know – there is much more than physical supremacy to achieving success in sport. Success in golf requires more mental aptitude than even the toughest of sports. The nature of many other sports might limit the level of excellence your child can attain simply due to the physical traits required to excel. In golf there are fewer physical demands, but if success in golf could be boiled down to simply mastering the golf swing, many avid golfers would realize their dreams. Golf legend Sam Snead aptly illustrated the importance of the mental game with his quote years before it was in vogue to discuss mental frailties: "Golf is a game played on a six-inch course – the space between your ears!" In fact, golf requires more mental discipline than one wants to admit. In a game that routinely takes four hours to play, a player's mental approach and attitude can make a significant difference in his results on the course.

In no uncertain terms, sports psychology has been around a long time, but the scientific study of athletes and how they perform started to take root in the United States after a noticed mental toughness in Olympic athletes from behind the iron curtain. After 25 years of study and relationship to performance, psychologists were developing strong theories about superior athletes and their ability to perform. Just before the new millennium, a revolution took place in the golfing world, and something other than traditional swing development became available to help golfers. Players started to seek help with "mental" development to help deal with their emotions. Through the research available, players and teachers became more aware that the "mental" aspects of the game were just as important as the "physical" aspects of the game, if one expected to stay off golf's emotional rollercoaster. One of the biggest changes that took place in the game is that players were more willing to share experiences and open up about their raw emotions. While players are still hesitant to talk to one another about some of the subtle mental aspects of the game, they are realizing they need to become familiar with relaxation techniques, positive self-talk and strong visualization. Some of history's greatest athletes were naturally strong mentally, but many golfers have come to realize that one can train the mind to acquire mental strength.

Mental conditioning can be an emotional boot camp, but it doesn't have to be. When incorporated into routines like golf practice at an early age and fostered gently, mental conditioning can become a tool to develop not only a better golfer but also a better person.

Mental fitness includes three key components: mental attitude, emotional toughness and mind-body coordination. Mental attitude can be nurtured on course by the coach and off course by the parent. Emotional toughness and mind-body coordination develop naturally with golf training, but if you want to up the ante, consider training in martial arts or yoga.

Parent as Mental Coach

Parents are coaches – they are life coaches! Healthy mental outlooks on life are rooted in early development. Success in relationships, education and sports is indirectly related to parental involvement or an enriching environment.

There are several key areas in which parents can be instrumental in assuring success. Early on, active participation with your child is helpful - ongoing encouragement and edification, being a good listener and becoming an active observer, having a positive attitude and insisting on good diet and physical conditioning habits are all important.

Teaching your child about discipline and hard work and setting goals are things that are better "caught" than "taught," but kids need to realize early that success often comes with sacrifice. Children learn best when lessons are consistent and part of family culture. Spiritual guidance and financial support are two other areas in which your children need to know your expectations and boundaries.

Mental coaching does not have to be complicated or time consuming. A simple insistence that the child smile and shake hands after a golf match sends a number of positive attitudinal messages. This behavior helps the child learn relaxed play and to de-emphasize wins and losses, a critical component of the development phase. Many times, just playing the game instills a winning attitude. Also, it is simply good etiquette, certainly a positive side effect of learning golf and one that will carry over into other aspects of life. The handshake means the player is thanking the competitor for allowing him to give his best effort. The focus of competition is shifted away from beating the other player to challenging the child's own potential, and reinforces the desire for continued improvement. It also allows a player to put the round, whether good or bad, in the past and let his mind focus on something else until the next time he reaches the first tee. The finest athletes in the world are great at "letting it go."

Choosing an appropriate time to teach your kid mental aspects of the game is important. Just as you always want to be a skilled listener, you want to make sure he's an effective listener as well. He will "hear" you better if you are consistent with your attitude and your actions. He won't "hear" you if you just "talk the talk," but don't actually "walk the walk." Your attitude is just as important, if not more so, than his. If his mind is pre-occupied, you'll get an impatient nod or an "I know, I know." Talk to him during non-golf activities. A good time might be during exercise or while walking the dog.

Reinforce those discussions with gentle reminders as you drive your kid to the golf course or the driving range. "Tyler, remember the other day when we talked about how to stay focused on the shot? Today, work on that a bit. Don't hit a shot without a clear purpose. Identify things that make your mind wander. Establish a routine and stick with it. Practice the imagery techniques that you and coach worked on during Saturday's lesson." Ideas stay fresh in his mind, and the kid can implement them and see how they work for him.

Here are a few questions to stimulate a lively discussion with your child. Just laying it out there will often work wonders with mental attitude and preparation. It will be your job to put on your psychologist's cap and become a mental coach at every stage of your child's development. It is best if the questions below are introduced casually, consistently, yet sporadically (not the main topic every night at the dinner table), and slowly integrated over time:

- What is the true nature of competition?
- Is competition a threat or a challenge?
- Can competition help improve your game?
- How can competition help you become a better person?
- How is amateur competition different from professional competition?
- Are you afraid of competition?
- How do you feel when you compete?
- Do you like competing?
- Do you feel any pressure from us (parents or coaches) to perform?
- Do you enjoy the challenge?
- Challenges and competition – are they the same to you?
- How are you going to stay motivated to keep improving and challenging yourself?
- How are you dealing with the natural pressure that comes with competition?
- How do you relax?
- How do you feel when competing against good friends? Are you distracted? Confused? Emotional?
- How do you prepare to face the challenges of maintaining friendship and doing your best, regardless of outcome?
- You will face off against your best friend, Tom, in the next match. How will you handle the desire to win? Against your best friend?
- Are you worried about your friend's feelings? Can you reconcile this dichotomy and approach the match prepared to win?
- You beat your friend by seven strokes – how do you feel?
- Your friend beats you by several strokes – how does this make you
- Do you feel like a winner even when you aren't the best?
- Can you see your improvements objectively?
- What do you think about yourself when you perform poorly?
- Do you always find redeemable qualities in your performance and truly feel like a winner at whatever level you find yourself?
- At what stage of golf development are skill development and effort more important than the result of the match?
- Do you compete to please yourself, your parents and coach, or both? Why is playing for your own enjoyment important?

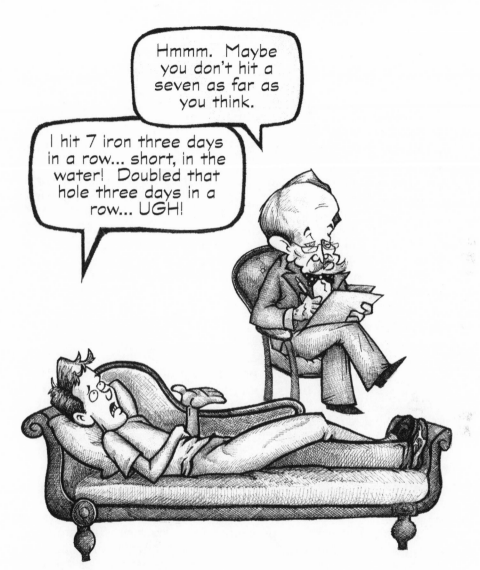

On-course Mental Conditioning

At one time or another, most players have been victims of nervousness, choking or even tanking during a match. These difficulties are all symptomatic of other underlying causes. For example, nervousness and choking may be the result of worrying too much about the end result of the match.

"You're not thinking about the fairway if you're thinking about the rough," says Dr. Deborah Graham, a leading sports psychologist who works with players on the PGA Tour and other tours.

Another common problem is negative thinking. A player who worries about missed putts or poor drives is less likely to be successful than the one who burns in his memory the great shots he has made in the past. Noted sports psychologist Dr. Bob Rotella likes to tell a story about a speech Jack Nicklaus made in which he professed to have never three-putted or missed a putt inside five feet on the last hole of a tournament. This, of course, is not true, but Nicklaus' selective memory allowed him to forget the bad putts and remember the good ones. It's a special trick that lent him confidence and helped make him one of the best golfers in the world.

Learning to focus on each shot and being in the "here and now" is a major part of on-course mental training. What about the time between shots? The mind has to be trained to utilize this free time positively. The late Bruce Edwards, Tom Watson's caddy of 27 years – and when Watson wasn't playing, one of the most sought-after caddies in the history of the game – eloquently simplified this important concept by saying, "If you have a bad hole, forget it. Go to the next tee and do better."

Awareness

Forget the previous shot. It sounds cliché, but it's oh so true. The here and now is where your child's mind must be to play his best golf. There's a lot happening in the present that demands junior's attention – the wind, the lie of the ball, the length and type of the upcoming shot as well as attention to water hazards, bunkers or rough that should be avoided. Whether it is playing golf or taking a math test, learning to be focused on details of the moment are critical for success. "Awareness is everything," says Phil Jackson, world-champion professional basketball coach. Learning, playing and overall enjoyment all greatly improve when the mind is taught to stay interested in the here and now.

Peace of mind is critical. As soon as doubts or uncertainties creep into the shot process, the percentages for success will diminish. Sometimes it is a fine line that separates the tournament champion from the rest of the field, whether you are a junior golfer or a professional. When junior removes doubts, he is able to be more patient with himself. It is confidence and a clear mind that will allow him to achieve a state of being, in which nothing bothers or upsets him. He can then truly play shot after shot in the present, not concerned with the shots he has already played or those that may be ahead of him.

The challenge for a coach is how to teach kids to be more aware. Once kids learn the physical basics of the game, they need to learn that their mental approach is paramount to their future success.

Mental fitness skills are not easily imparted by just talking to kids. Merely lecturing them to stay focused and aware will not work. The skills must be woven into drills and activities.

One good way to habituate kids is via Timothy Gallwey's awareness drills. First presented in his seminal "Inner Game" classic, the drills and modern-day variations have become part of the standard repertoire for teaching golf. Here are a few other common drills:

1. **Mark the Spot** – Most kids are so caught up in the right technique they forget about the end result. Where do they want the ball to go? This drill simply asks the young player to focus on hitting a series of shots to pre-determined lengths. Rather than swinging for the fences or going for the farthest flag at the driving range, a player may be asked to use his 3-wood or an iron to reach a closer flag. The effectiveness of the shot will be determined by how close to the target the shot lands.

2. **Height Drill** – This is similar to Mark the Spot. In the Height Drill, the player is asked to hit a number of balls to the same target but with different trajectories. He might be required to hit a high sand wedge while envisioning stopping the ball near the hole, or might pretend he is playing the same shot from behind a tree with low branches and thus hits a lower-lofted club to the green.

3. **Eyes Closed Drills** – Putt, chip and hit full shots with eyes closed. Junior can do these alone to work on feel and awareness, or he can have someone there to watch the results. Your child will tell his partner whether the ball went toward his intended target, left, right, long or short. He may also describe whether he hit the ball on the toe or heel or hit it on the sweet spot! This is a great drill for awareness and mental imagery.

4. **One-handed Drills** – Practice all aspects of the game with one hand and then the other. In addition to heightened awareness, this drill is great for strength conditioning.

5. **Visualization and Imagery** – Pretend! Encourage your child to play mental golf, hitting every shot just the way he wants to, making every putt. No limitations – what fun.

Sighting the Ball

For golfers, sighting the ball means understanding each shot and how it moves, or anticipating the trajectory and shape of the shot. Not every shot is straight. As a player becomes more advanced, he will begin to understand how to hit fade (left to right) and draw (right to left) shots to work to his advantage depending on the design of a specific hole or a particular pin placement. Different players will use a variety of variables to change ball flight. Players tend to have a natural ball flight. Personal preference will dictate how he chooses to manipulate his shot making. The key is that he understands ball flight in relationship to variables such as aim, alignment and swing path.

Teaching professionals agree that there are two ways to effectively teach players to "work the ball." The first is simply to instruct the player before each shot on the range to hit a fade or a draw. The success of the shot will be determined not only by whether it reaches its target location and distance, but most importantly by the route it travels to get there – would the shot have negotiated the dogleg to the fairway, or would it have ended up in the trees?

The second method is more advanced and truly tests the player's understanding of and ability to hit different shots. The type of shot is not called out until the player has started his backswing. This gives the player almost no time to think about the shot before hitting the ball, but a player who has effectively mastered the fade and draw will be able to adjust on the fly and make the shot work under the fabricated conditions.

Staying Focused

Watch Phil Mickelson as he walks down the fairway from shot to shot. Once burdened with the label "The best golfer never to win a major," Mickelson has always had a casual way about him, but he acquired a little more bounce in his step sometime around the time he won the Masters in 2004. He smiles much more as he walks the course now – he remains focused but relaxed. He has fun! Mickelson has won dozens of events and seemed to always be apologizing for not reaching his potential (which goes to show you how brutal the media can be). With his first major finally on the record books, he could relax more – no need to press. After 12 years of "trying to win" a major, his mind was free at last to simply "do it" – it's no wonder his second and third majors came back to back with victories in the PGA Championship in 2005 and the 2006 Masters.

During a typical four-hour round of golf, the amount of time a player spends actually striking the ball is shockingly short. Most of the time is spent between shots – walking to the ball, setting up the shot and taking a few practice swings. With all this extra time, it's easy to let the mind wander and get all wound up in the score, the trouble you're having with your long irons, or even the ecstatic, "My gosh, I can't believe I'm so far ahead of this great player!" The more distractions, the more difficult it becomes to recover focus when play resumes.

Like many golf psychologists, Dr. Graham has worked with athletes in a wide variety of sports, but believes golf is the most demanding mentally. "There are many reasons for this, one of which involves the regulation of thoughts and focus for four-plus consecutive hours," he said. Individual sports are unique in that your child is on his own and doesn't have a team member to bail him out when he has on off day.

One strategy for maintaining focus on the golf course is to focus only when it's important. In other words, your child shouldn't try to focus intensely for the entire timeframe of his round. A golfer might allow part of his mind to consider the next shot, but the sharp focus required to execute his shot should last only about 10 seconds. During the rest of the time, he can relax, smile and take in the surroundings of the golf course. This will allow him to stay fresh and be sharp when he addresses the ball for his next shot.

Another way your child can choose to look at it is "he is controlling only what he can control." Just as it isn't prudent in life to dwell in the past or to worry too much about the future, a golfer must realize that nothing is going to change that muffed approach shot on the second hole or that bogey on the easy par-3 11th hole. The key to a good drive on the difficult 12th tee is a clear mind and a commitment to personal routines and preferences. Trying to make up for poor play or looking too far forward to take advantage of a round that is starting well can only take focus away from the task at hand – hitting the next shot as well as possible. Too many rounds have been ruined by mentally calculating a final score. "If I shoot such and such, I will have my best round ever." Whether it is starting off hot with three birdies and "trying to keep it going," or starting off poorly and "trying to get something going," this sort of "scorecard" mentality will not yield favorable results very often.

Volumes of books have now been written on the mental aspects of golf, and there are scores of professionals specializing in helping golfers enhance their performance by analyzing their mental habits. Yet with so many more resources available and with research showing that mental toughness, fitness and mastery are the keys to sustained extraordinary peak performance, why do so few bother to work seriously on their mental game? Any player can learn and apply the techniques used for mental mastery. Success is only limited by how open-minded an athlete can become. Golf psychologists, mental-golf experts, inner-game coaches and personal-development trainers come with a myriad of different credentials. Check out their resumes carefully and do your homework when considering an expert.

Dr. Jay Brunza, a clinical psychologist, taught Tiger Woods skills early on in his junior career that helped him concentrate better, which naturally enhanced his performance. Brunza even taught young Tiger to hypnotize himself to ensure that Zen-like state of mind.

Dr. Debra Crews, an assistant Research Professor at Arizona State University, an advisor to ASU's men's and women's golf teams and an expert instructor for the LPGA National Education Program Series, verifies clinical hypotheses with actual physical studies of the brain as it pertains to performance. She stresses that children are not simply miniature adults.

"There are several differences in working with top-level kids compared to adult top-level amateurs or professionals," she said. "However, in sport, kids can be much more advanced than their age in regard to cognitive development. They process information slower than adults and they will see objects as a whole – they are not good with specific details yet." She has hundreds of clinical studies on behavior modification and is an expert in directing golfers toward the goal of automatic responses.

Dr. Crews has seen patterns that show how kids are wired differently. "Children need help to group and label information," she said. "A coach that uses irrelevant cues can interfere with performance. Really young children need information given to them in small pieces and related to them in 'their language.' Concepts need to be presented as a whole and repeated over and over. They do not need specific details, and learn well when a coach is animated. A five-to-nine-year-old benefits from verbal labels and needs to keep instructions in order if he is to recall them. Children need to understand a start and finish, understand target and use imagery."

Research shows that kids that are five years old process information differently than seven-year-olds do. Even 11-year-olds process info differently than 15-year-olds do. Twelve- to fourteen-year-olds are often in that fearless state of mind; a good thing for sports, a tough thing for parents. "Realistically, a kid's 'hardware' isn't even complete until they hit 15 or so," Crews said. "Puberty hits, and the mind gets mucked up for a while, and by 17 kids are much more analytical. A great age range for working on swing mechanics is between 15 and 18. Unfortunately at 19 or so, they get stuck in a new stage of trying to be perfect." Crews is a great resource for understanding the mental development as it relates to the physical development of your child. She can be contacted through the university at crewsd@asu.edu.

Jeff Troesch is an internationally recognized expert in the field of mental skills training and performance enhancement who has been involved in training top-notch athletes for almost two decades. Troesch describes why he and other mental training gurus are so important for serious golfers.

According to Troesch, it is important to:
1. Understand how to deal with lapses in concentration.
2. Deal with situations of accumulating frustration.
3. Develop coping strategies to deal with increasing anxiety.
4. Improve decreasing motivation.
5. Examine and reinforce slipping confidence.
6. Develop strategies to reduce breakdowns under pressure.
7. Create procedures and routines necessary to increase consistency of preparation and play.

8. Assess procedures and routines currently being used.
9. Give players the tools and skill set to use in practice and competition.
10. Personalize instruction specific to the individual player, including follow-up adjustments.

For more information on Jeff Troesch see fitnessforgolf.com. For other nationally recognized mental game gurus, check out golfdigest.com.

Reference: Instructional Books on the Mental Side of Golf

1. *GolfIs Not A Game Of Perfect* by Dr. Bob Rotell. This is his diamond, but any of Rotella's books will give your child some insight into what it takes to play with more confidence and achieve better performance. *The Golfer's Mind: Play to Play Great, Golf Is A Game Of Confidence*, and *The Golf of Your Dreams* are all gems.

2. *The Eight Traits Of Champion Golfers: How To Develop The Mental Game Of A Pro* by Dr. Deborah Graham and Jon Stabler. This book pretty much tells you all you need to know about your personality traits and those of the greatest players in the game. It describes how these traits can affect your game.

3. *The Simple Mental Secrets of Golf: How to Make Them Work for You* by Stan Luker. "Simple" and "straightforward" are the key words for this book. There is no psychobabble, and it gives common sense approaches to golf's mental challenges.

4. *Golf's Mental Hazards: Overcome Them and Put an End to the Self-Destructive Round* by Dr. Alan Shapiro. This book examines how increased self-awareness can positively affect golf scores and put an end to self-destructive rounds.

5. *The Golf Magazine Mental Golf Handbook* by Dr. Gary Wiren This is a top teaching pro's straightforward discussion of the benefits of taking the right mental approach.

6. *The Inner Game of Golf* by W. Timothy Gallwey. A classic. Topics include: trying mode, relaxed concentration, natural learning process and awareness instructions, plus a whole lot more.

7. *Zen Golf: Mastering the Mental Game* by Joseph Parent. This volume provides an Eastern perspective and a different approach to unconditional confidence, swing routines and expansive awareness.

8. *Tiger Woods: How I Play Golf* by Tiger Woods and Editors from Golf Digest Magazine. This book gives an intimate view of both his game – mental and physical – and his unique personality on and off the course.

9. *Every Shot Must Have a Purpose: How GOLF54 Can Make You a Better Player* by Pia Nilsson, Lynn Marriott, Ron Sirak. This offers cutting-edge techniques for integrating the physical, technical, mental, emotional and social parts of a player's game. This book is written to change your mind.

10. *Fearless Golf: Conquering the Mental* Game by Dr GioValiante. This one offers a detailed plan for conquering the fear that sabotages swings and ruins psyches. Techniques are shared that have benefited Davis Love III, Justin Leonard and numerous other world-class golfers.

The Other Parent

You can teach your kid all you want, but you have to take into account the effect of his "other parent" – the television. Say you just talked to your kid about how effort is more important than winning during the development phase. He then watches a certain television show where Thomas is the toast of the town because he won the Little League championship for the home team. Maybe the show portrayed Thomas working hard, and that's good. However, the reality that everyone on the show is completely focused on winning at all costs is sending a detrimental message to your child – and this is not good.

Whether it's a fictional television program or an ESPN special, winners make for exciting television, but this can possibly send the wrong message to junior – one opposite to what you want to teach.

Media so saturates our lives that it isn't possible to protect kids from every message that runs counter to those of well-meaning parents. Whether the television message is appropriate or inappropriate, morally right or wrong, if not monitored carefully it undoubtedly plays a role in the development of your child's mental attitudes.

Setting good television habits can help. For instance, teach your young child to ask permission to watch television. Take advantage of the new gizmos that let you record the programs you're comfortable allowing your child to watch. Share television shows with positive messages with your child. Always be aware, for better or worse, that your messages compete with those of some ill-bred advertising executive heralded heralded by Madison Avenue for your child's attention.

Professional athletes in all arenas of sport also have a major influence on your child. Their lives are often played out on the world's stage for all to see – thus, it is wise to discuss the positive and negative choices these "superstars" make.

Redefine "Making It"

Okay, Mr. Jones, please lay down on the couch and let's talk.

In our hearts, we parents and coaches are conditioned to define "making it" in the world of golf as winning a major or taking home the big check at a PGA Tour event. For a moment, think about how many times Tom Kite, Corey Pavin, Davis Love III or Phil Mickelson was asked in the pressroom during a major championship if they "could actually consider themselves to have had successful careers if they never won a major." Lucky for these gentlemen, they will never have to answer that silly question again. Unfortunately, the question will always be posed to the next rising superstar by some unknowing reporter. Historically, how will a great player like European sensation Colin Montgomerie go down in the record books? Who defines these boundaries of success? So how is success judged best? Do the consistent stream of titles that Montgomerie has won count for nothing if he never manages to land a major? Simply consider how crazy that is considering his amazing resume.

At other levels, a player may think of success in golf as achieving a lifelong goal of attending a major Division I university on a golf scholarship. It is important to remember that success is different for everyone. Sure, players like Tiger Woods (Stanford) and Phil Mickelson (Arizona State) and Annika Sorenstam (University of Arizona) played at Pac-10 colleges and went on to success on tour, but there are also examples of players who attended lesser-known schools and have entrenched themselves as solid pros. Kenny Perry, for instance, played at Western Kentucky University. Perry is now a nine-time winner as a professional and has played on the U.S. Ryder Cup and President's Cup teams.

We visualize success in golf as a pyramid and subconsciously prod our kids and ourselves toward what we believe is the "pinnacle." Instead of the pyramid, imagine the landscape as a beautiful valley of flowers. Surrounding the valley are gorgeous mountains. You and your kid are enjoying a beautiful hike up the side of one of these mountains. First you conquer one mountain, then another. Any time you choose you can have a picnic on a rock or in the valley of flowers. Each mountain presents different challenges. If one is the tallest, the other has the highest rock face; yet another tests navigational skills. In other words, there is no one Mt. Everest in this valley. You can enjoy an "ultimate" challenge by scaling each of them. Or you can choose to simply enjoy the beauty of the trek.

"Okay, okay, Dr. Filbur, I think I've got the imagery – not a pyramid, but a valley of flowers and mountains and all that. Now you expect me to read this passage to my 10-year-old? You must be kidding, right?"

Actually you don't have to say a word. Just believe in it and live it in your everyday words and actions. Trust me, the kid will soon learn to discover a Mt. Everest in every mountain he climbs. More important, whether you and your kid are climbing the mountains or relaxing in the valley of flowers, you will both learn to enjoy today's challenges and rewards.

You may get off the couch now. That will be $125, Mr. Jones. Thank you.

Drug Abuse

Professional golfers are not tested for drugs like players in Major League Baseball, the National Football League and the National Basketball Association. That's because those sports are mostly concerned with the use of strength-building steroids, and in the past golf has not been considered a game that relies on power. Hopefully golf will stay clean and professional golf will never have to deal with the scandals that have plagued other major sports.

The PGA Tour has, however, put out a statement on the dangers of alcohol and recreational drugs. Whereas these might have at one time been accepted by some in the sport, the prevailing thinking now is that alcohol and drug abuse can only hurt a player's game. A late night of partying between rounds of a tournament certainly won't benefit a player's swing or his focus the next day. Teenagers need to understand clearly that alcohol and illegal drugs are addictive and should be avoided in order to reach full potential and the realization of one's dreams. Give your kid as many incentives as possible to avoid the pitfalls that come with drug use. Be armed and ready during the junior and senior high school years – remember you will be fighting pop culture on this one. There are no guarantees, but in general, kids involved in sports are much more likely to stay clean.

Avoiding Burnout

This could be the No. 1 concern of a parent with a highly successful young golfer. Balancing all areas of life is essential to enjoying the journey, whatever journey your child chooses to travel. Be in tune with your child's emotional, social, spiritual, physical and intellectual embodiment. It is paramount to manage a reasonable practice regimen, as well as the type and number of tournaments he plays on a yearly basis.

During the development phase of a young player, rewarding effort and de-emphasizing tournament results is certainly necessary. Unfortunately, it takes an extraordinary player to hang tough during awkward developmental stages or difficult periods of high scoring and undesirable results. At times, no amount of mental coaching can help a player maintain his psyche when he is constantly last on the leaderboard. Most likely, before long, he will lose confidence and quit the sport. Conversely, too much winning may lead to boredom. A top-ranked teenager can become emotionally spent trying to stay on top, tournament after tournament. To keep a player interested while also ensuring that he builds confidence and continues to enjoy golf, it is important to ensure the level of competition is appropriate. Self-expectations, your expectations and coaches' expectations have to be discussed openly and honestly. Effective goal setting is critical to avoiding burnout in this game.

Manage Tournament Play

While golf is a unique sport in that a player's performance is measured against oneself and the golf course, young players will surely compare their progress to that of their peers. Parents, you too must avoid the compare snare! A parent should consider adjusting the level of competition so that the child is playing well enough that he feels successful. If he is constantly dominating the field, you need to look for other tournament opportunities to challenge him. In some parts of the country, it might be necessary to move him up an age group or two or enter him in higher-level tournaments. If the child is struggling, focus more on skill development and enter lower-level tournaments. With hundreds of regional tournament opportunities for various ages and levels, managing development this way shouldn't be difficult.

Other Passions

Develop a passion for other activities – a hobby, musical interests or other sports. In your golfer's competitive slow season, encourage him to participate in a different sport for recreation. Playing a variety of sports also exercises muscles differently, and chronic injuries are less likely to occur. However, do not overlap too many sports seasons and stretch your child too thin.

"Children should play more than one sport, but they should also cultivate other interests such as computers, music or the arts so they don't always focus on that next tournament," says Michelle Klein, executive director of the National Youth Sports Safety Foundation in Boston.

In our go-go-go culture, it is wise to take a break from all organized sports for two or three weeks a year. Simply taking time out, going on vacation or attending a special family function will replenish the mind and body. This also helps to encompass people outside of golf in a young player's life in order to take the focus off the game and its demands. Watching a movie or diving into a good book can sometimes be just the right strategy for a momentary escape from the game during a particularly stressful time.

Have a Higher Goal

Spiritual awareness is the most probable area where a major revival or transformation of study will be centered next. "New Age" golf will be next. Locker room prayers have been long-held traditions in team sports, but athletes in all sports are using their very public stage to share their personal beliefs in record numbers. Those athletes grounded in strong religious beliefs or commitments to faith are making headlines.

The late Payne Stewart and major champions Bernhard Langer, Scott Simpson, Paul Azinger, Larry Mize, Corey Pavin and Larry Nelson are but a few professional golfers who profess their religion as the cornerstone of their lives. Says Langer, "I was ranked No. 1 in the world. I had a beautiful wife and had achieved everything I could have dreamed of. But something was missing. My priorities were golf, golf and more golf, then myself, and finally a little time with my wife. Every now and then I prayed or went to church. But if my golf game was not good, my whole life was miserable, and I made everyone around me miserable. I believe that when your priorities are in the right place, everything is managed better."

Tiger Woods' father, Earl, has been given much of the praise publicly for his phenomenal success. However, Tiger himself often praises his mother and credits the discipline of Buddhist teachings she instilled in him as a source of his inner strength. "I like Buddhism because it's a whole way of being and living," Woods says in a Sports Illustrated article about him. "It's based on discipline and respect and personal responsibility." Personally, he admits he has to continue to work most on his stubbornness and impatience. "I used to want things to be perfect right away," he has said. As both Tiger and Langer allude, religion, dedication to family, community service and involvement in public causes can help keep golf in perspective.

Helping your child realize priorities will ease needless pressure and may actually benefit your child's game by allowing him to stay relaxed. Once again, these important life lessons are often caught rather than taught. So, be a good example and keep your priorities in check; your child will hear you better when you explain that schoolwork comes first, and then sports.

Detecting Early Signs of Burnout

You have taken all steps necessary to avoid burnout in your young golfer – managed his tournament play, ensured his participation in other activities and encouraged him to develop goals beyond golf. How do you know if these are working?

Burnout often kicks in when kids reach their teens. When they're young, they generally go along with whatever their parents have planned for them. Meanwhile, years of junior competition and over-scheduling may have taken a secret toll – physically and emotionally. Around adolescence, kids begin to assert themselves more and express their true feelings. Unfortunately, if you have a compliant kid, "symptoms" of rebellion may surface in his first two years of college.

For girls, anorexia and bulimia are eating disorders that can surface as a means of personal control. Due to the physical body types required for top gymnasts, ice skaters, runners and swimmers to compete, they were the population that most often fell victim to this terrible malady. However, with more and more parents pushing their children in sports, athletes in other individual sports such as tennis and golf are succumbing to this disease. Through dieting, a young athlete gets a sense of empowerment, achievement and control. It becomes a wicked cycle of "The less I eat, the more control or power I feel."

For boys and girls, a change in attitude, inexplicable rebellion or sudden behavior change would be more common signs that something is going on. If sleeping patterns, eating habits, school grades or friends start to radically change, there is probably a problem on the horizon – quite possibly burnout.

Detect burnout early and make needed changes. According to experts, a child who asks to miss practice or complains about his coach or his lesson is really telling you there's a problem. Often a child suffering from burnout will show signs of sleep disturbance, headache and muscular rigidity. He may also show signs of depression, such as sadness and lack of energy.

As soon as you are reasonably sure that the problem is burnout, cut back on golf and extra-curricular activities. If he has been exclusively focused on golf, encourage participation in another activity. Make that new activity, rather than golf, the focus of dinner conversation.

11
Pushing: How much is too much?

....

**"I believe you should push your child. Not
only is it okay, it is your right, responsibility
and your absolute moral imperative as a parent."**

Dr. Jim Taylor, Positive Pushing

....

Parents want the best for their children. It sounds so simple. Goals usually center around helping the child to be confident, happy, and of good character. Why is it then that children, especially adolescents, resist well-intentioned efforts to help? Why is it that loving parents sometimes feel the need to push – to direct the child to do something she doesn't want to do? These paradoxes are often most apparent in cases of sports parents.

Parental Goals

Sports psychologists trace many parent-child conflicts to parental goals that are outcome-based and confuse the child's goals with their own. Setting outcome-based goals is tempting and deceptively easy. "I want to do everything I can to help my 10-year old become the next Michelle Wie," a parent might think. Achieving this so-called "parental" goal is dependent on four actions:

1. The child has to take up golf, not as a sport but as a career.
2. The child has to put in the necessary practice hours.
3. The parent is able to provide the financial support necessary to reach the goal.
4. The parent is able to provide the time and emotional support necessary to reach the goal.

Clearly, fifty-percent of the actions required to accomplish this goal successfully are dependent upon the child. If the child wholeheartedly embraces her end of the deal, then everything should be fine. However, there will be trouble in paradise when an adolescent decides to change course to pursue other goals or to divvy up his limited time engaging in other activities. The outcome-based parental goal is suddenly no longer achievable, leaving the parent bewildered and frustrated.

Instead, revise the parental goal to something more specific and directly controllable. For instance, "I will provide the financial help to pursue serious golf development." Certainly setting such a goal does not preclude a parent from trying to pique the child's interest in golf or actively encouraging her to take up serious golf development. The process-based parental goal simply clarifies that the adolescent is the one in the driver's seat, while the parent plays a supportive role as far as golf development is concerned.

Process-based goals that a golf parent can set for himself include:

1. Highlight the value of golf as a lifetime sport for fun, fitness, and skill development.
2. Provide necessary time and financial and emotional support.
3. Use golf as a vehicle to teach good attitude, teamwork, discipline and character.

Choose a parental goal that will offer you a sense of accomplishment, whether your child ultimately decides to pursue a career in golf, baseball, law, medicine, music or poetry. Knowing your child well – her personality, strengths and weaknesses – will make it easier to lead your child to fields of interest. Once she discovers her talents and begins to use them, it is her responsibility to meet her own self-developed goals. No matter her field of choice, you may guide your child, but you must do so through process-based goals.

Why do Parents get Pushy?

After years of financially supporting a child's golf development and carting her to lessons and tournaments, even the most patient parent can be ready to explode. "Jill, win this match or else..." There is no excuse for actually saying such a thing, but it illustrates how parental pressure can fester. Parents feel that because they're contributing time and money, they're also justified in demanding a result – winning.

Measuring Results by Wins

Parents are perfectly justified in demanding results. At the very least, it helps them decide whether their time and money has been well spent. However, the trick is to measure results not by a young child's wins, but by the development of good attitudes and improvements in golf skill. Parents who measure results this way are less likely to push unjustifiably.

Winning is nice, but winning is only a desirable outcome. The purpose of sport for a child is to create an opportunity for fun and growth. Parents of especially gifted athletes get lost right there. Are you still with us? The triumphs and heartaches inherent in sport can provide a child with the learning experiences and life lessons that help pave the road to adulthood.

Ask yourself – Is Jill regularly picking up on important life lessons on the course? Is the game emotionally healthy for her? Has it made her more mature and better prepared for life? If the answer to these questions is yes, your time and money have been well spent, regardless of the outcome of a match.

After a few years of golf, you can add a second component to monitoring progress – improvements in golf skills. Sports psychologists say that emphasis on sports mastery demonstrates a focus on performance, whereas emphasis on sports competence is used to describe focus on winning or losing.

Under-emphasis on mastery and over-emphasis on sports competence account for many children appearing to fall short of parental expectations. When that happens, parents intuitively begin to push harder. Instead, measure the results as improvements in skill mastery – better strokes, strategy, physical ability and mental toughness.

Life lessons and improvements in golf skills are the yardsticks parents should use to measure results. Chances are you'll notice your kid has made great progress in vital areas, in spite of playing poorly in her match, making all your efforts worthwhile.

Early Parental Goal

Another reason parents are driven to push is that they decide very early on that they are going to raise the child to be a professional golfer. First, a parent is making a crucial life choice for the child – a choice that may not survive her adolescent years. Next, the pressure to constantly practice and perform takes the "sport" out of the game. Instead, it becomes "work" for the child. As a result, the parent has to push even harder to get the child to practice. A lot has been said about Earl Woods and his involvement in Tiger's development. However, it is apparent that the desire to become the world's greatest golfer was Tiger's goal, not simply that of his father. Earl fueled Tiger's dreams and aspirations in a very disciplined and healthy manner.

Of all the young players out there, a very small percentage will earn college golf scholarships. Each year, there are 1,970 NCAA Division I men's players on scholarship and 1,788 women's scholarship players at that level. Those numbers are cut in half at Division II schools, and less than two percent of these college players become professionals. Notwithstanding the statistical long shot, what golf parents wouldn't want their child to be the next Phil Mickelson or Paula Creamer? Any parent would be ecstatic to see their kid reach the pinnacle of the game. By all means, dream big for your child, hope for the best, afford her opportunity, but always remember that any actualization of your dreams can not be realized by your child. She can only realize her own dreams.

Success at the professional level is more dependent on ability than on effort, though there is also a significant psychological component that differentiates pros that are all at about the same skill level. Undoubtedly, it takes tremendous effort, ability and mental strength to keep an LPGA or PGA Tour card and climb to the top of the money list.

The decision whether to turn professional should really be made based on a scientific method rather than at the emotional level. Realistic goals need to be set so that the young player first is focused on becoming a good high school golfer, then moves on to developing her skills at the college level, and finally, considering a pro career. Placing too heavy an emphasis on a professional career too early can get in the way of achievement at each level along the way. Understanding that the choice to become a professional should be made much later in a child's golf development and that it is a team decision (child, parent, coach) based on specific criteria will help parents look at short-term goals more objectively. Hence, a parent will be less pushy.

The trick is to keep the dream of becoming a professional player in perspective; look at it as just one of many equally challenging and ambitious aspirations you have for her. Perhaps, as a parent, you also have hopes that she will one day graduate from an Ivy League college, become a life-saving doctor, a public service lawyer, or head up a volunteer organization that gives back to the community.

Just in case you skipped a paragraph or two, it bears repeating – always distinguish between your dreams and those of your child. Separate your dreams from your parental goals. You must remember – you have little control over whether your adolescent child aligns her dreams and goals with yours. It's best to avoid verbalizing your dreams to the child, or, as the British would say, "Keep mum." Instead, keep working toward your parental goals.

That the journey is the reward might be a cliché; nevertheless, it is so true. Steven Tyler of the rock group Aerosmith sang a memorable lyric that said, "Life's a journey, not a destination," a phrase that can be applied to many exciting pursuits, no less golf. If your child competes for any length of time and winning is one of her "goals," she will quickly learn that even "winning is a journey, not a destination." Best-selling author and founder of the American Wellness Project Greg Anderson wrote: "Joy is found not in finishing an activity but in doing it." Repeat this to yourself and you'll find less reason to push.

Sacrifices - Too Many, Too Soon

"You have to understand that nobody in skating realizes, starting out, just how expensive it's going to get," advised world-champion figure skater Kristi Yamaguchi's father, Jim, in the San Jose Mercury News. "It sort of creeps up on you, because as Kristi got better, she began to have more needs, so we got in deeper and deeper." This is a universal truth applicable to most individual sports and the arts.

Commitment to golf is no different, and possibly even more expensive. A golf career will require that the family make choices, compromises and a whole lot of sacrifices. Depending on your economic position, some will be more costly than others will. If financial sacrifices are not required, then maybe you will be required to relinquish your time. It is not unusual for athletes and their families to miss important social gatherings such as weddings, anniversaries or special activities with family and friends. Educational and career plans may get postponed or family vacations altered. In rare instances, families may move to accommodate necessary coaching, a better practice environment or competitive opportunities.

Reasonable compromises are okay, but only after a decision has been made to take up golf as a career. Parents need to be careful to make sure their young golfer doesn't become overwhelmed with the pressure that she has to achieve great things because her family has rearranged its life around her golf career. "If a child's worth is being based on being successful in sports," former world-record holding runner Jim Ryun told USA Today, "boy, there's going to be a tremendous disappointment, because at some point in life you have to lose."

Sometimes parents make too many sacrifices very early on. When your child has just started playing golf simply for recreation and there is no evidence yet of consistent performance or ability – and, most important, before she has developed the maturity to weigh in on where golf fits into her future, you must proceed down the road slowly. Hard sacrifices, especially financial ones, made too early in a child's golf development add an unnecessary mental burden on your child. Juniors confess to having to work hard to block out thoughts of their family's financial and lifestyle sacrifices during tournament play. At some level, golf development suffers.

However, there is something to be learned from a biblical verse that reads, "To whom much is given, much is required." Support should not be unconditional, but it also should not be tied to success or failure. Once families invest so much of themselves in a child's golf game, it clouds decision-making. Children find it harder to quit if they want to. Read what you wrote on your second-grade assignment when the teacher asked, "What do you want to be when you grow up?" If you are what you said you would be, you are in rare company. If you are not, when did you acquire the freedom to change your mind? Third grade? Tenth grade? Graduate school? Gifted athletes and gifted people are often caught up in the "please everyone else" game of life. Competition and talent sometimes will weed out those who are stuck in that vicious cycle, but sometimes it doesn't, and a kid doesn't feel like she can change the course of her life if she chooses. Often women will use marriage and children to bail out graciously.

We like to believe that anything is possible, but parents ought to look ahead to the financial demands of competitive sport. This doesn't mean you can't help your child succeed even if income is limited. A little planning goes a long way. Trade off a few private lessons for self-practice; search for sales when buying equipment, redeem travel bonus miles and stay at less expensive hotels. Plan your travel itinerary well so you aren't crossing the country two and three times a year. If possible, be selective when planning your competitive schedule.

Planning ahead for the financial commitments will ease pressure on the parent. A parent not consumed with money worries is less likely to be pushy, thus creating a healthier and more relaxed environment for the child's golf development.

This doesn't preclude parents without swelling bank accounts from seeing their children develop into professional golfers, though. One example of a player who has achieved success on the PGA Tour without a privileged country club upbringing is Notah Begay, a four-time winner since joining the Tour in the mid-1990s.

Begay is the most successful Native American golfer in history. He grew up in Albuquerque, New Mexico, where as a child he would sneak through a hole in the fence by the 14th hole at the public golf course near his home to watch players coming through hit their approach shots to the green. He later begged his way into a job at the course, where he worked in exchange for playing privileges. Begay would show up to junior tournaments wearing hand-me-down clothes, and sometimes traveled to national tournaments via bus because that was the only method of travel his family could afford.

Begay didn't learn some of the finer points of the game until arriving at Stanford on a golf scholarship, having taken a different route than most of his teammates to arrive there. Begay, like others before him, didn't let excuses get in the way of his dreams or his success.

Playing Up

Opting to "play up" – the practice of competing in an older age division – can be quite an ego trip for the parent. The decision to play up a mature and competitive kid who is consistently trouncing his peers is not always cut and dried. Is your 11-year-old ready to stroll the fairways with a more savvy 17-year-old? Competition in the various age groups is random in certain parts of the country. If you see your child needs to move up an age group to keep her challenged and interested, then by all means have her compete in an older age division. In less populated regions, you may have to move her a couple of age groups to find some competition. Seek out tournaments with stronger fields with kids closer to her age group, though, whenever possible.

In the case of a younger child, the decision needs more careful consideration. A nine-year-old may be consistently outplaying his peers, but you have to consider that he's also having a lot of fun practicing with them. Maybe the kids have formed an adventure club and play together regularly after golf practice. Moving the kid to an older age group could be great for his golf, but may not appeal to him socially.

Another pitfall to watch out for is when a young child who is playing up begins to develop a convenient excuse for playing poorly. Parents may also have a tendency to convince themselves their child isn't playing well because his competitors are older. Such rationalizations become habitual and can prevent kids from developing mental discipline. Move her back to her peer group if you see this happening.

Jack Nicklaus resoundingly believes that "Winning breeds winning." Who can argue that? Especially for younger players, success generally breeds confidence and can help maintain interest. Some teaching professionals argue that young golfers shouldn't play up until they are in their early teenage years, and then only if they are experienced players who get paired with beginners. Every situation comes with its own unique circumstances. If 12-year-old Sally is ready to play up and finishes strongly against a field of talented teenagers, this should inspire her and give her a lot of confidence that she can compete with the best. However before she ever considers playing up, Nicklaus' theory would suggest that little Sally should have several wins to her name. She must experience winning first!

Another great example of playing up and gaining valuable experience is when juniors or top college players qualify or are invited to play in a tour event. That is the ultimate in playing up. Of course no one expects them to win or even compete really, but history shows that kids do the darndest things! Phil Mickelson won the PGA Tour's Northern Telecom Open in Tucson, Arizona while he was still playing college golf. Sergio Garcia turned pro only after playing in 28 professional events as an amateur. High school sensations Michelle Wie and Morgan Pressel have been atop the leaderboard on many occasions and in many prestigious events in their young careers. Only a select few have been able to boast such accomplishments at such a young age. These players would all agree that they gained valuable experience each time they teed it up with the best players the game has to offer, regardless of their finish in the event.

Experts suggest that the best way to take advantage of the benefits of playing up, while avoiding the drawbacks, is to "mix it up." For younger children who are consistently out-performing their age group, start by phasing in practice sessions with the next older group. A kid practicing three times a week can be allowed to practice with older kids once a week while continuing to practice with his peers.

A few more things about playing up: a wise coach will try to avoid creating the impression that one particular kid is being handpicked for promotion. Also consider that in some cases, kids who are playing up may need to return to their own age group. They may not enjoy the new challenge, or perhaps the coach or parents will decide junior is not quite ready for the next level of competition after all. Try to avoid this scenario by carefully considering playing up in the first place, because this can feel like a demotion to the child. Never mention playing up to your little phenom until it is about to take place so she doesn't get haughty or have a holier-than-thou attitude with her peers. If playing up is essential, consider it part of the regular program and do it without a lot of hoopla.

Only after your child develops consistency in an older age group and is able to win or compete at the top of the field at the local level should she advance to older age groups at the national level. In most cases, age appropriate groups will be right where your child should be competing. Evaluate her goals and desires year to year to make sure you haven't pushed her farther up the competitive ladder than she wants to go. New, stronger competition is good for her, so look for tournaments in a different region to see how she competes with kids her age from a different geographical location. Very rare is the case in which kids need to or should play up more than a single age group.

Some believe kids develop faster when they play with older children. It really depends on the child, her unique personality and her psychological makeup. Playing up may be necessary to keep proficient kids engaged, but it is still best to mix in play in their age group so they continue to have fun and develop a social network for practice and tournaments.

Burnout

More and more attention is being given to the term "burnout" and its relationship to overzealous parenting. Let's face it – there has always been that one extremely pushy parent, the nightmare parent, the one the rest of the parents would laugh at as they saw him hanging from a tree trying to get a good vantage point in order to view every shot junior made that day. Parents don't need to hide anymore. They are allowed to walk every step of the way; they get a bird's eye view of junior's great shots and his not so hot ones too. For many parents, this means they now have the opportunity to rehash every shot played and discuss each decision made that day, for better or worse. It is a never-ending situation, and unfortunately the overly obsessed parent is becoming the norm. Scolding in the clubhouse, demeaning remarks at the scoreboard and sadly enough, physical abuse in the parking lot, are becoming way too commonplace in the world of junior golf. It's not new, but it's no wonder we are discussing burnout more often than ever before.

Earl Woods and his military style tactics have created a generation of copycat parents. Unfortunately parents are copying the wrong things. His unconditional love and ability to encourage his child is what they should be studying. He has written a couple of books on the subject – more parents need to read them and heed his advice.

World renowned teaching professional Peter Kostis wrote an enlightening article about the Woods' unique parent-child relationship and burnout in a 2005 Golf Magazine article. He quickly acknowledges how most touring professionals were introduced to the game by parents for all the right reasons – fun, camaraderie or as an exciting family activity. He goes on to add that traditionally kids were allowed to learn, play and develop at their own pace, for the joys of the game. Sadly, he adds that youngsters are now being "specifically groomed for a professional career from the time they're in kindergarten." He continues, "This intense immersion strategy has not groomed a crop of great champions, and in some cases, the parents have pushed their kids into a world that they might not want to be in." He also gives an example of a young PGA Tour rookie who had to cut off all ties with his father after his dad's pushing became abusive. While he admits this is rare, it is becoming less and less rare. Parents with well-meaning efforts spin into out-of-control behavior.

Less than a decade after Tiger hit the tour, professionals around the country debated the decision of 15 year-old Michelle Wie to turn professional. Wie had 10 million great reasons to support her decision. Even if most agree that she is obviously one of those unique talents with the skill set and ability to compete at the highest level, the debate will last for years to come. Psychologists will spend the next couple of decades documenting her every move and trying to prove one way or another whether this was in her best interests. However, what many teaching professionals fear is that her unprecedented success will add fuel to the pushy parent syndrome that is already burning out of control. Pushy parents used to give their kids some time, but now golf coaches are worried that parents will start demanding more of their kids at an earlier age. This is recognizable as the trend that has plagued professional tennis for years, one that leads to kids burning out.

Where does it end? This question is best answered by posing a different question: Where does it all start? As scary as this is, it's not an isolated incident. An official of the American Junior Golf Association recalls the parents of an 18-month-old boy asking about golf lessons for their baby. Many experts will argue that the sooner kids start, the sooner they'll quit. On day one, examine your motives, and continually check your motives as your kid grows up. Don't end up like the frustrated dad who throws his hands up in disgust as his daughter informs him that she is never playing golf again. Dad has given up promotions at work, has shuttled her to and from practice, spent thousands of dollars on top-notch instruction and sacrificed all his free time to accompany her at tournaments around the country. He can't understand it – she has a national ranking, but now at age 13 she wants to be "normal." Her nerve!

These two tales are definitely isolated incidents, yet are just a couple of dramatic cases depicting the woes of parental psychosis. Kids quit golf for lots of reasons. Some kids lose the sense of play and view the energy required for holding a ranking as "work." Here's a tip – kids aren't really fond of work and really like to play. In some instances, a kid who may have enjoyed early success and trounced her competitors in the younger divisions is now noticing that as an older kid, her peers are catching up. This plays havoc with junior's confidence, and if not dealt with gingerly, she will quit.

Prevention

Dr. Shane Murphy, a sports psychologist at Western Connecticut State University in Danbury and author of "The Cheers and Tears: A Healthy Alternative to the Dark Side of Youth Sports Today" says the best thing you can do is recognize "The Parent Trap." Murphy adds, "Unfortunately, parents get caught in this trap all the time." He warns that the trap shows itself in the following ways:

1. **Over-identification** – You naturally identify with your child, but over-identification may lead you to ignore your child's feelings and focus instead on your own.
2. **Selfish dreaming** – It is normal, as a parent, to dream of your child's future, but sometimes parents get so attached to their own dreams that they lose sight of what the child wants.
3. **Confusing investment with sacrifice** – As a parent, you love your children so much that you are willing to make tremendous sacrifices on their behalf, spending money to support the child's sport and taking the time to be there for the child. But parents may come to see these sacrifices as investments and then expect that the investments will pay off and yield tangible benefits.
4. **Competing with other parents** – You want your child to excel, but it easy to get caught up in competing with other parents, pushing your child to succeed and hoping that the other children will fail, giving your child a chance to shine.

The "How To" of Prevention

Specific strategies can be employed by parents and coaches to help prevent the "I want to quit" syndrome before the fact:

1. Keep a healthy perspective. More than a few parents have believed they have the next Tiger Woods or Michelle Wie in the family.

2. Avoid pushing young kids into a high degree of specialization in a single sport. Becoming too specialized often leads to burnout. Many parents encourage or even force their children to play just one sport on the assumption that it will allow them to develop more competitive skills in that sport. There is little or no evidence to support that theory. Randy Hill, a research assistant for the United States Olympic Committee, says that the one common denominator shared by most elite athletes is multi-sport participation during the developmental years. Cathy Sellers, a USA Track and Field official, encourages athletes not to specialize in a sport until the ages of 12 to 14. Coaches of elite teams often require their athletes to participate in a second sport.

Many parents believe coaching their child strains the parent-child relationship. Leave the coaching to a professional. Make sure the coach doesn't have his own agenda. Kids quit because of a bad coach. A kid with a pro who is consumed with winning at all costs is destined for burnout. It isn't uncommon for a child who has a bad experience with a coach to get turned off altogether. The quality of the coach is essential.

Emphasize sports mastery over individual results. Teach kids to enjoy the process of developing proficiency. Help them measure accomplishments by improvement in various skills rather than by who they beat or lost to. "I beat my scoring average by three strokes today" is a better yardstick for junior competitors than "Today, I beat Sara." Parents make mistakes by emphasizing short-term results instead of enjoyment.

Enter tournaments that allow the child to score well and continue to reduce her scoring average. Kids begin to compare themselves to a more select group of athletes, and then they become increasingly aware of their own abilities and interests. They will start to evaluate their situations and make decisions about how far they can go. As a group, kids are a lot more perceptive about understanding their talent level than we give them credit for. Some of them may assess the situation and decide to direct some of that time and energy to other endeavors. Let them!

Be prepared to lessen the degree of parental involvement in decision-making as the child grows older. Earl Woods was a master at this. Most parents become more of a servant as their child progresses, fueling the prima donna-like attitudes. They run around doing everything for their child, thinking they are helping her. In reality, an opposite marvel should be in the making. The better a player becomes, the more personal responsibility she should be accountable for. She needs to make more decisions. Get out of the way and let her.

Warning Signs

If your antennas are up and you are in tune with your kid, you should be able to recognize some early signs of burnout. Simply recognizing the signs and addressing the issues early on can prevent major rebellion and the abandoning of the sport altogether. Some of the signs include:

● She doesn't want to practice
● She suddenly doesn't want to compete
● She complains about her coach or complains about everything
● Constant negative self talk
● She doesn't care about goals and doesn't want to talk about them
● Falling grades
● Chronic fatigue and lack of energy
● Lack of joy – nothing makes her happy
● More injuries and illness – even faked or psychosomatic illnesses and injuries.
● Major changes in overall personality

Now What?

A parent has done all the right things, yet sometimes the kid is ready to quit anyway. Sports psychologists say that up to ages 10 to 12, a child will probably go along with what Dad and Mom suggest. Over the next couple of years, though, the child wants to begin making her own decisions, including those related to sports participation. By adolescence, the influence of peers is replacing that of parents.

Leaving golf behind might be the kid's way of asserting independence. "Mom and Dad want me to play, so I won't." Or maybe it's time to face the fact that she really doesn't like the game. Whatever the reason, parents ought to prepare for the day when their child announces, "I want to quit golf. I don't want to play golf in college. I need time to study, I want to be a veterinarian." Whether that day actually arrives or not is irrelevant.

Remember that the choice to play should always be your child's. All you can do is gently nudge her in the direction that you believe is best for her. Let's say your young child has expressed some interest in golf. You think she might enjoy it, and let her sign up for golf lessons. Three weeks into the lessons, she hates them. "All I do is hit the ball on the ground," she complains.

At that point, the best choice is to make her stick with it. Often, after a few lessons, the child becomes more proficient and may want to continue. Younger children may be confused about the rules of the game. Explain the rules or practice with them so they feel more comfortable. In any case, she only has a few weeks to go, and she'll probably learn a valuable lesson by following through on something she started but now doesn't enjoy. Be sympathetic, but firm. Don't force her to sign up for the next program, but make her finish this one.

Older children may have more complex reasons for wanting to quit. Help your child articulate those reasons. Talk to her coach. Study her performance at practice sessions and tournaments. Think about whether one or more of the following come into play:

- **Golf isn't fun anymore:** Make sure the coach is compatible with your child. Tread carefully, but don't be afraid to try a new coach. Maybe your child has been played up too quickly and is unable to keep up, preventing her from having fun. Reduce competitions; instead, focus on casual practice with family and friends. Rekindle interest by taking her to watch a professional or regional tournament. Sometimes simply taking a complete break from golf for two to three weeks can help the child return with enthusiasm.

- **Too much pressure:** A kid can experience pressure from a parent, coach or teammates. Maybe it's time for the parent to get out of the advice business and leave the training to the coach. Praise effort, skills and technique rather than focusing on the numbers on the scorecard. Maybe the school team needs opportunities to bond and relax outside of golf. Find time to play golf with the family. Replace a weekly hour of golf with another hobby – music, photography or anything else you know interests your child.

- **Not enough time:** Experts recommend focusing on one extracurricular activity at a time. Help your child prioritize. Instead of doing both soccer and golf each week, suggest she select one sport and put off learning the other until there's an opportunity to attend a related sports camp. Of course, as a loyal golf parent, you will instinctively guide her toward golf as a first choice, won't you? Don't worry; these things have a way of sorting themselves out.

- **Mismatched skill level:** Again, this means the child has either been played up too quickly or placed in an inappropriate class in which her skill level doesn't match that of others in her group. Perhaps not enough attention has been paid to learning the basics. Go back to the drawing board. A few months of private lessons and a different class level may be just what the doctor ordered.

Sometimes, though, even these methods don't work. It's not uncommon for children between the ages of 12 and 14 to lose interest in a sport. Rick Wolff, a well-known sports psychologist, says this is not always due to burnout. The child may simply have more of an affinity for another activity and wants to budget precious hours towards that activity. While it is okay to stop pursuing a sport, ensure that the child puts time and energy into another productive outlet.

If every golf lesson counts as a life lesson, then nothing has been lost. Remember that. Once you've exhausted all strategies and your child comes to you to announce, once and for all, that she's joining the band instead of her high school golf team, train yourself to respond appropriately, "Do your best kid, and have fun."

Key Parental Roles

Few players have reached their potential without support from their families. This support can be expressed in many ways – love, money, guidance, motivation, coaching, time and travel assistance. There are other parental roles that may not be as obvious but, nonetheless, determine whether a child becomes not just a golfer, but a healthy young adult.

Parental Involvement: Finding a balance

Study the success stories of famous parents like Earl Woods who make major contributions to their children's development by staying involved, but keep your story unique to you and your child. If your focus is on the end result rather than the process, you have missed the point. Generally, a parent's involvement ought to focus on financial and emotional support, character development and education.

Having carefully chosen a coach, a parent can have input, but should ultimately let the coach and junior decide on lessons, practice, and competition schedule. Periodic conferences with the coach and child will help communicate parental goals, assess progress and synchronize tournament travel with family plans. In the six to 12 age group, the time when experts suggest it's okay for a trained golf-proficient parent to coach, one consideration ought to dominate everything else, and that's keeping the game fun.

Sometimes parents get over involved, scrutinizing every practice and agonizing over each loss. The trick is keeping the outcome in perspective. When the primary reason for parental involvement in a child's golf is to teach goal setting, discipline and increasing self-esteem, a parent can't go wrong.

Physical Fitness

Physical conditioning is too often an afterthought, even though any professional will tell you how important proper conditioning is to golf development. As the coach essentially works on the kid's golf, it's up to the parent to help carry out conditioning routines.

Parental support can be a determining factor in whether a golf kid stays healthy, fit and injury-free. Parents have to insist on proper warm-up and stretches, before and after practice. They may have to arrive a little early for a lesson so the kid can get in an effective warm-up.

The weekly workout doesn't have to be "work," a thought process to keep in mind especially for children who resist working out because they feel their parents are always nagging them about it. Fun routines such as medicine balls, hula hoops, skipping rope, playing basketball in the driveway or walking the dog are creative ways to get the child conditioned, often without her even realizing it. It helps when parents lead active lifestyles, too. Remember, leading a healthy lifestyle, like everything else, is best learned by modeled behavior. What did we say before? "Caught, not taught."

Encourage Your Child to Dream

Goal setting is about keeping feet planted firmly on the ground and choosing goals over which one has a reasonable degree of control. Children, however, are natural dreamers. The movie October Sky is the triumphant true story of Homer Hickam, Jr., a high school student in 1950s rural West Virginia who refuses to give up his dream, regardless of how unrealistic it seems to the adults in his life.

Too small to earn a football scholarship, Homer is destined to follow in his father's footsteps and become a coal miner – until the Soviets challenge America with the successful launch of the Sputnik satellite, that is. With the help of his loyal band of friends, Homer embarks on a mission to build and launch his own homemade rocket.

Despite repeated setbacks and early failures that nearly get them shut down, the group of friends stick with it and do the impossible, successfully launching a functional rocket and winning prestigious college scholarships in the process. Their success inspires the whole town to believe miracles can happen, even in Coalwood, and that there's nothing wrong with shooting for the stars.

Children's dreams are the stuff of creativity; they are the fuel that motivates them to try the impossible. Dr. Alan Goldberg, a nationally known expert in sports psychology, advises parents to encourage children to dream. Inspire them. Tell them stories of all the "impossible" things that have been accomplished by people following their dreams.

Help the child understand the difference between goal setting and dreaming. For instance, making the high school golf team might be an ambitious goal for a golfer new to the sport, but if she practices hard and smart and focuses on learning the essential skills of the game, there is a good chance of accomplishing it. On the other hand, beating the No.1 ranked player in the world might be considered a dream because it presents too many variables outside one's control. For instance, one can't control how hard the No. 1 player practices.

By all means, encourage your child to dream big and chase her dreams, to set big goals and go after them. But also teach your child to measure success by goals accomplished rather than dreams realized.

Let your child enjoy the fact that she made the high school golf team, or that she won the section championship, without always harping on the next goal of attaining a college scholarship or playing on tour. This is the practical way she can learn to relish the process and lead a successful life, even though not all dreams come true. By all means don't shrink her dreams or let anyone else steal her dreams. The facts don't count when you are a kid. It is your job to be her No. 1 cheerleader.

Keep 'em Playing

Watching a group of kids play golf and grow together over the years is a fascinating study in physical and psychological development. One day you see them as eight-year-olds, playing and behaving similarly. Come back after the holiday season and at least one of the boys has probably shot up in height. His golf ability is now likely to be above everyone else in the class, too.

Give it a season or two; a couple of the girls have not only caught up with the boy in height, but some will be starting to overtake him. Their golf ability may well follow. A child's golf development occurs in sporadic spurts, even past the adolescent stage.

The key is to keep children interested in golf whether you think they have the ability needed for the sport at that time or not. More importantly, even if the child feels she lacks natural talent, encourage her to persist. When she catches the next growth spurt, she is bound to do better, and her interest level will bounce back.

Basketball legend Michael Jordan did not make his high school team, even as a sophomore, because he just wasn't good enough at the time. A kid who is so-so at 10 years old may be a kid who is great at 16, and vice versa. It's a shame for a kid to drop out before he can find out how good he can be. Conversely, a kid used to dominating at an early age may drop out at 16 because he can no longer do so.

The best thing a parent and coach can do is to encourage golf mastery over winning or losing. Competing with one's own ability naturally discourages unnecessary comparison with other kids during the growth phase. Physical changes, especially in girls, can lead to uneven performance on some days. Gently nudge kids through the ups and downs of golf. With the growth spurts, one never knows who'll turn out to be the super player.

The Reserve Parachute

Life has a perverse way of throwing curveballs – injury, burnout, an unexpected move, financial fallout. Some parents feel they ought to help develop another talent, in case the child is unable to pursue his interest in golf, or at least pursue it as seriously as he wants to. Like a skydiver using dual parachutes, a child should be encouraged early on to pursue other interests, not as much for backup as for a more-rounded childhood development.

All golf all the time can become exhausting. A second passion offers an outlet to break away from the intensity of golf for a while and return rejuvenated. While golf offers the longest career span of any major professional sport, there are many examples of players who move on to successful careers in other arenas once their playing days are over. Jim Colbert, for instance, won multiple events on the PGA Tour in the 1970s and 80s, then ran a golf-course management company and was involved in broadcasting before joining the Champions Tour. As a youth, he also played football, well enough to earn a scholarship to play at Kansas State.

Positive Pushing

The argument for pushing is really simple. Kids love any activity they're good at. Becoming good requires practice. As long as practice is fun, kids will do it. This is the "high" of the sport. Sometimes, though, they may need to practice skills that are a little hard to learn. A young golfer who has become adept at chipping may need a gentle push to sustain an effort to learn how to hit out of the sand. It's during these times – the "lows" of golf – that a parent has to push.

The bottom line is, for healthy development of a golf kid, the highs have to outweigh the lows. When it becomes necessary to push a child through the lows, the parent or coach has to do so in a way that is deliberate and vigorous, but always with a positive message that reaffirms unconditional love and helps build self esteem.

Dr. Jim Taylor is a psychologist who lived the life of a young achiever. A top-ranked skier, certified tennis coach, black belt in karate, marathon runner and an Ironman triathlete, he has developed five tips for "positive pushing":

1. Set expectations that emphasize healthy values that will help your child become successful and happy. For example, focus on hard work, responsibility, cooperation, patience and persistence, rather than expectations that stress grades, results and other outcomes.

2. Allow your child to experience all emotions – don't assuage, placate or distract them from their feelings. Help them to identify, understand and express their emotions in a healthy way.

3. Actively manage the child's environment and activities – peer interactions, achievement activities, cultural experiences, leisure pursuits – in ways that reflect the values, attitudes and behaviors you want the child to adopt.

4. Create options from which a child can choose a direction. Stress that doing nothing is not an option.

5. Help your child find something she loves and is passionate about in her efforts. She will be successful and happy.

Achieving success in almost anything requires a sustained effort that will always have its highs (the fun parts) and lows (the parts one doesn't like). The trick is to maximize the highs and ride out the lows through positive pushing. Many champions are made simply by the fact that they were willing to do what nobody else was willing to. When your kids are tired, the weather is atrocious or they just don't want to practice, tenderly remind them this is when they must muster up the guts to go give it their all. Praise their efforts. Win or lose, the way one handles adversity defines a champion.

12
Money Wise

Contrary to popular belief, the cost of raising a child who plays golf doesn't have to be prohibitive. Sure, getting junior a membership at an exclusive country club, providing him with the very best equipment and flying him all over the country can run up some pretty big bills, but there are also more cost-effective ways to keep your kid involved in the game. In fact, with younger golfers, the expenses are often minimal, and getting your child started can be as simple as picking up a few clubs and paying for range balls.

The Cost of Raising a Golf Kid

As a child begins to show serious interest in developing his game, a little initial budgeting goes a long way. Of course, like with just about anything, as your child gets older and begins to be more involved in the game, costs will rise. This is especially true in the case of teenage players competing at the regional and national levels. Some parents estimate they have dished out $20,000-$25,000 per year to develop the careers of their competitive junior golfers, depending on the level of play and the extent of time spent with private coaches. Many of these parents believe the investment becomes worth it when their child receives a college golf scholarship. However, there are no guarantees in life, and parents should also be prepared for the possibility that their child does not get his college education paid for in full.

A Sample Estimate

At the higher echelons of junior competition, the real kicker is tournament expense. That includes travel for the player and his entourage – a parent or coach – and accommodations. Private lessons, group clinics, and camps are a close second expense wise.

Table 12.1 gives a sample estimate of costs to train a junior player over an eight-year period. Year 1 is when the junior decides to move from recreational play to serious golf development. Estimates for Years 5, 6, 7 and 8 include costs associated with high-performance training and national and international travel outside of collegiate golf. If your child is a collegiate athlete or a highly ranked amateur, equipment costs should be significantly lower in these later years as well. Coaching costs could also be a lot less in years 7 and 8 depending on the coaching situation and the arrangement made over the years. A good coach should be teaching junior to be less dependent as he matures as a golfer, not more. Hopefully coach and junior have developed a good working relationship. The costs indicated below might be as such for a new coach or for one who travels to a couple of tournaments during the season.

Table 12.1

Year	Level	Equipment[1]	Coaching[2]	Competition[3]	Total
1	Novice	$185	$835		$1,020
2	Regular	$260	$995	$320	$1,575
3	Regular	$275	$995	$450	$1,720
4	Sectional	$275	$1,220	$540	$2,035
5	Regional	$825	$3,060	$2,460	$6,345
6	Regional	$825	$3,060	$2,460	$6,345
7	National	$825	$7,280	$8,650	$16,755
8	National	$825	$9,280	$9,350	$19,455

1. Includes clubs, shoes, balls and attire.
2. Includes lessons, tournament training and camps.
3. Includes travel, hotel and entry fees.

Instead of hassling with the logistical details of travel and coaching, some parents choose to enroll the child in a golf academy. In addition to golf instruction and tournament travel, an elite golf academy takes care of physical and mental conditioning, high-performance coaching, room and board and a regular academic education. An all-inclusive package can run close to $40,000 per year.

The Good News

If your jaw is beginning to drop, lock it back into place – there's good news. The USGA, in its efforts to develop the game of golf and foster participation by people in all walks of life, offers grants for player development and fellowships to build the infrastructure that is the business of golf. These programs, along with the efforts of a number of other organizations, can help cut the cost of developing a young golfer.

Individual and corporate entities may play a big part in developing players by offering scholarships and sponsorships; although most company support and private sponsorships aren't usually offered to juniors. It will be up to you to actively seek available financial assistance. When you pursue financial aid, it is vital that you are aware of amateur status rules and player eligibility rules set forth by the NCAA. Many local teaching professionals, bless their hearts, subsidize their fees on a case-by-case basis for promising juniors who cannot otherwise afford the lessons.

Golf equipment manufacturers like Titleist, Callaway, Nike and Ping make a significant contribution to player development by offering free golf clubs, balls and other support to top-ranked juniors who are competing at the sectional and national levels, as well as to junior programs for beginning golfers around the country.

In the early years of golf development, the costs are more or less the same as they are in other sports. However, as the player gets into serious golf competition at the regional and national levels, the bucks can add up fast. So it is gratifying to know there are many individuals and organizations willing to chip in at that level of competition. Local clubs and organizations are proud to help and be associated with a top competitor, so don't be shy about sharing needs for financial assistance if it is necessary for your child's future development. Combine this with some smart planning and savvy saving tips and any parents should be able to see their golf kid through serious competition.

On the Cheap

The wholesale shipment of sporting goods tops $50 billion annually, according to the Sporting Goods Manufacturers Association. That includes sports and fitness equipment, athletic footwear and sports apparel. It's not hard to find the reason for this astonishing sales total. Just check out the price tag on the latest Nike Tiger Woods attire your son wants so badly.

If you don't have money to burn on the extras – designer attire, expensive equipment, brand name lessons and costly accommodations – take heart. With a little creativity, you can limit the costs and stay within your means. Being money wise can also teach your child an important life lesson.

Golf Clubs

Whatever else you skimp on, experts will tell you not to skimp on golf clubs. An ill-suited set of clubs – ones that are too short or too long -- can wreak havoc with a young player's developing swing, but you don't have to splurge on high-ticket equipment either.

Quality models are available in the mid-price range. They don't break the bank and are perfect for a child's growing years, when children might go through a set of clubs every year or two. If you know what you are looking for, you can often find great buys at general merchandise stores and used sports equipment stores like Play It Again Sports. Keep your eye out for specialty clubs such as lob wedges, sand wedges, putters and perhaps a driver when bargain hunting in discount stores. A worn out Scotty Cameron putter can be sent off to the Scotty Cameron Putter Restoration Studio and be customized to feel like new at half the cost of purchasing a new model. However, it is always best that your junior is with you for the purchase of any clubs, and most important, do not buy clubs just because they are a good deal! Misfit clubs are never a good deal!

Local pro shops and online golf stores sell closeout models and blemished or slightly used demo clubs at bargain prices. They're worth checking out. You can also visit online auction sites, especially if you know the specific model of clubs and the specifications (length, loft and lie) you want to buy.

Another smart way to save is to turn necessities into presents. Buy your aspiring Sergio Garcia a new sand wedge for his birthday. That Scotty Cameron putter he has had his eye on would be the perfect present under the Christmas tree. Tell relatives he would love a new golf glove or gift certificate to his favorite golf course. Re-grip his clubs as a reward for that awesome report card. If you time it right, he will need those clubs re-gripped just about every grading period. Incorporate his love of the game into all gift giving.

Consider donating golf clubs he has outgrown to a grassroots junior golf organization or to another youngster learning the game. Besides warming your heart, your donations may help you save some on your taxes.

Balls

As surprising as it might seem, golf balls can be among the biggest budget drainers. A few dollars for a bucket of range balls might seem like a good deal, but for a young golfer who spends countless hours at the driving range, the expense can add up quickly. Teaching professionals estimate parents of a serious young golfer can expect to dish out at least $75 per month on range balls.

Many golf facilities offer special discount range cards for juniors. For example, JC Resorts in San Diego, California offers a card good for $100 worth of range balls for $40. Other discounts might include a frequent buyer benefit such as buy nine buckets and receive your 10th bucket free, or half-priced buckets for juniors. Always encourage your child to practice, and also encourage him to be inquisitive about savings programs designed for juniors.

Of course, a supply of golf balls will also be needed for days spent off the range and on the golf course. Just like with golf clubs, there are plenty of different brands and types of balls. Think of all the golf ball manufacturers you can name off the top of your head – Titleist, Callaway, Slazenger, Wilson, Top Flite and Pinnacle all quickly come to mind. Each of these companies produces a variety of products. Titleist, for instance, makes a ball designed for distance, one for improved control on iron shots, another for low spin and yet another that is advertised to offer "responsive, soft feel and consistent playability." Much of this won't matter to your young golfer, though, until he gets older and begins to get a better feel for the game and his strengths and weaknesses on the course. For beginning golfers, just about any ball will do. Relatives are always looking for gift ideas for those special occasions. Grandma may love to have his name imprinted on golf balls as an extra-special treat. For the golfer, golf balls are the perfect gift. Reward your youngster whenever you can with some new balls (they don't have to be expensive), because there is something special about watching your little guy's face as he opens his own "brand new" box of golf balls.

While Titleist's top of the line golf balls can sell for $58 a dozen (that's almost $5 a ball!), the company also sells a more basic ball for $28 a dozen (a little more than $2 per ball). During the holidays, stores such as Costco may have a special deal on the top brands. If you come across a bargain, purchase more than you need and hide them away for the next special occasion. An excellent option for golfers new to the game is to purchase used, or "X-out" balls, which are basically manufacturer's defects (the term "X-out" is derived from the "XXXXX" that's usually stamped over the brand name). Used or "X-out" balls are often available at golf pro shops or golf retail stores for $1 or less per ball.

Buying used balls also provides a way to save on practice time. Rather than spending a few dollars per bucket at the range, fill up a shag bag with 50-100 balls and use them to chip with in your yard. Most local parks prohibit golf practice, but if you live in a more rural area and your child has access to an open field or grassy area, he can spend hours there getting a feel for the game. You should also invest in a hitting net for the yard, patio or garage. These are great when junior just wants to swing for a few minutes in between homework assignments or when you don't have enough time to take him to and from the course. An initial investment in one of these items might save you a bucket of money in the long run.

Once players get older and become more and more involved in high-level tournament play, golf ball expenditure is the one expense that is minimized. Organizations like the American Junior Golfers Association (AJGA) generally provide free golf balls for their players. Collegiate programs also provide plenty of golf balls for their team players. The only drawback is if your child prefers a different golf ball than that which is offered.

Greens Fees

Greens fees can add up quickly if you pay a daily fee at a public golf course each time you or your child plays. One way to limit this cost – as long as you're sure your junior player is committed to playing regularly – is to join a private country club. The most exclusive clubs have steep membership fees and annual dues that will make you take three steps back, but there are others that come with a more reasonable price tag. If there are a few avid golfers in your household, membership to a club may be worth looking into.

A club with a golf course good enough to help your child develop his game but not so challenging or aesthetically pleasing to woo the big-money players could offer a rate of $8,000-$12,000 for an annual membership. Some private clubs will offer a special junior membership to aspiring young players who do not have any other golfers in the family. These severely discounted junior memberships are limited and are often restrictive, but can offer golf-course access to kids who wouldn't otherwise be allowed to play. Usually a membership at a private course also entitles the member to access to the driving range, short-game practice area and putting greens or at least offers some kind of discounted fees for practice. Acquiring one of these discounted memberships for junior is certainly one of the benefits of getting your child started early.

Somewhere in the middle of the public golf course-private country club divide is the semi-private club. These golf courses are often more challenging and better-maintained facilities than public courses. They are often resort courses and are open to the public in conjunction with a hotel stay or timeshare agreement. They may also offer public play on certain days of the week, but they are available for play through the purchase of special memberships, usually at a lower rate than memberships charged at a fully private club.

Lessons

Golf lessons are expensive, but no more than art, music, academic tutoring, other sports or any other type of private instruction. There are a variety of ways to help cut lesson costs over the career of your junior.

Use clinics and group lessons to your benefit whenever possible, but always consult with your child's instructor. Cut lesson cost in half by signing up for semi-private lessons instead of private ones. By pairing with another student in a semi-private setting, you not only save money, but the child is likely to have more fun when he has another kid his age to learn and practice with. Besides, a full hour of one-on-one learning may be too much for a young child to handle. If your child is currently doing half-hour private lessons, consider switching to a one-hour, semi-private format that includes another child.

Also, most instructors have price breaks for juniors, and their series rate is set up for savings. For example, with a series of golf lessons purchased, it may be you purchase five and get the sixth free. This often drops the hourly rate significantly. Some instructors will offer a monthly or yearly rate for their more serious juniors. Be upfront and discuss lesson fees, budgeting and how financial implications might affect your decision making. Ask your child's coach if long-term arrangements are available. Most decent golf instructors will do what they can to assist you and your junior if they see dedication on your part.

Golf professionals may barter as well. If you have a service or product you can barter with your child's instructor, ask if the professional is interested in trading services. For example, maybe you are a dentist. A deal could be made for trading out services. Another example might be if you might own a furniture store. You never know if your child's golf instructor might need a living room setup for his new home. The key is that you never know unless you ask.

Tournament Travel

Take advantage of the hotel discount deals most tournaments offer. Tournaments may also offer private housing. Staying with a local family is a big cost-cutter in tournament travel. Host families are generally carefully screened, but it's always a good idea to verify this with the tournament director.

Parents often develop friendships with parents of junior golfers from other cities and host each other's kids. Join the frequent-flier and frequent-traveler programs offered by airlines and hotels. Tournament travel is an easy way to rack up additional points. Cash in the earned points for free hotel stays, air travel and upgrades.

Another way to reduce the costs involved with tournament travel is to pair up. Find another golfer your child is friendly with and arrange to share some of the expenses to travel to faraway tournaments. This might mean sharing a hotel room or a rental car. One other benefit of pairing up is that it can ease the burden on parents with already overtaxed schedules. If your child and his friend play in six tournaments a year that require travel, you can split the chaperoning duties with the friend's parents.

Lastly, kids that have parents in the travel or hotel industry really make out when it comes to tournament travel schedules and expenses. If you or a spouse must take on a second job to help support your junior golfer, look for a job at one of the main hotel chains or airline companies. The benefits and discounts offered would be worth more than any of the salary you will bring in!

Savings on Stuff

Shoe companies like FootJoy, Adidas, Nike and Reebok offer deep discounts on shoes and attire for school and recreational teams. Most golf companies include a free annual supply of balls, shoes, clubs and attire to top-ranked juniors and collegiate programs in their promotional budgets.

Check with your child's high school golf coach before purchasing those trendy new spikes. Coaches can often get shoes that retail at $90 for $40 by buying directly through the manufacturer.

The Lemonade Stand

Sidewalk lemonade stands are a cherished memory of childhood. This American rite of passage embodies hard work, dedication and reward. Once upon a time, the only regulation for lemonade stands was that you had to be home for dinner by six.

Today, baby boomers may lament the fact that this simple childhood enterprise now seems to require licenses, liability insurance and permission from three different government agencies. That doesn't mean that your child can't find a way to earn some money while also learning valuable lessons about work ethic.

It is not uncommon for young golfers to work part time in the golf shop or at the driving range at a course in exchange for playing privileges. A youngster might be in charge of washing golf carts and manning the cart barn, or of cleaning players' clubs. Other duties could include collecting and bagging range balls or stocking merchandise in the golf shop. Most facilities won't hire your child for a golf cart job unless he has his driver's license, for liability reasons. However, most golf professionals encouraging young golf enthusiasts will find something for junior to do to "earn his keep" once they know your child needs to help support his "golf habit."

The important thing to remember in this situation is that, if your child really wants to develop his game, the job should truly be part time. It won't do the child any good to work 30 hours a week at an after-school job and not have any time left in the day to play golf.

Grants and Scholarships

There are a number of golf organizations out there that offer grants and scholarships to help develop junior golf programs and assist college-bound golfers in furthering their education. These can help make enjoying the game of golf affordable for those who might not otherwise be able to participate.

Many professional golfers have set up foundations with the purpose of supporting golf at the grassroots level. For instance, the Tiger Woods Foundation provides financial support for educational programs, mentoring and tutoring programs and programs based in urban areas. Caddy Steve Williams supports youth programs in his native New Zealand.

USGA Grants

The USGA made a commitment in 1997 to expand its grant program, and the idea seems to have worked. In its first year, the program offered 66 grants totaling $3.7 million to various organizations. By 2005, those numbers had increased to 182 grants worth $4.7 million. Fifty-nine percent of those grants went to junior golf programs, 16 percent went to developing affordable and accessible golf facilities, and 12 percent was earmarked to help sustain programs for disabled golfers. The rest of the money supported school-operated programs and caddie/occupational programs.

Golf programs or facilities interested in applying for a grant from the USGA can do so at the USGA's website (More info: .usga.org).

AJGA Grants

The American Junior Golf Association (AJGA) offers grants to players who have the ability, but not the financial resources, to participate in its programs. Dedicated to the development of young golfers who aspire to earn college golf scholarships through playing competitive junior golf, the AJGA developed its "Achieving Competitive Excellence" (ACE) program in 2003.

The ACE program provided financial assistance to 12 junior golfers in 2003, allowing them to participate in tournaments they might not have been able to play. That number jumped to 51 in 2004 and should continue to grow as more families become aware of its existence. Independent donors and a partnership with Rolex fund this program. Parents can apply for ACE grants through the AJGA's website (More info: ajga.org).

The AJGA also makes financial contributions to golf programs across the country. In 2005, its contributions to junior programs and schools totaled $240,000.

PGA of America Scholarships

Through its PGA Foundation, the PGA of America offers partial scholarships for college-bound golfers. The foundation provides college scholarships for those planning to study golf journalism or professional golf management. It also gives scholarships to caddies going on to college, supports the children and grandchildren of PGA Professionals in attaining their college goals, and targets minority golfers for scholarships.

Other Grants and Scholarships

While these grants and scholarships are not easy to obtain, there are plenty of organizations offering financial assistance. The LPGA, First Tee and Pro Kids Golf are just a few of these. Sometimes the men's or women's club at your local golf course or country club will give help financially, paying for one or two of their local junior golfers to participate in a top-level junior tournament.

These grants and scholarships are all allowed under the USGA's rules of amateurship, which state that an amateur golfer may accept expenses from golf clubs or associations or from a family member. These rules have been loosened by the USGA in recent years, presumably to continue to allow the development of young golfers without subjecting them to overwhelmingly strict and unrealistic regulations.

Finding Sponsorships

You, the consumer, watch a television commercial touting the superiority of Titleist golf balls. There's a fair chance the next time you purchase a sleeve of golf balls, it will be from Titleist. Now you watch the television coverage of a prestigious PGA Tour tournament. The Titliest logo prominently placed on club covers, golf bags and a caddy's hat are hard to miss. Seventy-five percent of the field on the LPGA Tour is teeing it up with a Titleist. If eight of ten players on the leaderboard are playing a Titleist, the odds that your next golf ball purchase will be Titleist are now even greater. This is the basic premise for corporate sponsorships.

Corporate Sponsorships

Almost all sporting goods manufacturers, and many other companies, allocate marketing dollars for athlete sponsorships. While the big bucks go to one or two famous athletes, a good portion of the budget is allocated for distribution among a number of up-and-coming professionals and hotshot juniors.

A top junior golfer is no match for Phil Mickelson on the fame index, but there are good reasons why Callaway or Ping would want to sponsor a young, relatively unknown player:

- Parents and players hoping to defray training costs are attracted to a sport that offers corporate sponsorships. A sport's popularity moves the company's products.
- Junior tournaments are great testing grounds for consumer opinion.
- By supporting a particular junior, the company is essentially betting he will emerge as a top professional player and become famous. The company wants to earn the goodwill of and develop a relationship with that junior and his parents. It is also betting on product-player loyalty.

Private Sponsorships

Support from a grandparent, another extended family member or a community group is a quick way to cover a large, one-time expense such as travel to an important international tournament. If the financial support comes from family members, it's probably best to keep the amounts reasonable so you and your child don't end up feeling uncomfortable about accepting help.

Some companies have a special fund for community outreach programs and may be willing to use some of that to help out employees and their children. There's no guarantee that a company will contribute, but a parent shouldn't automatically assume it won't either. It never hurts to ask.

Individual sponsors, sports marketing companies, player agents and some golf academies occasionally scout prestigious tournaments looking to find top talent for sponsorship deals, but for the most part the top players and personalities are identifiable by their performances.

Levels of Sponsorship

The different ways in which a sponsor can support a promising junior are narrowly defined and limited to underwriting a portion of the training, travel and living expenses. These types of support allow a player to maintain amateur status, making him eligible to apply for college golf scholarships. Later, should he choose to turn professional, the sponsorship deals can include salaries and signing bonuses.

In general terms, a top player can expect sponsor participation to keep pace with the level of golf development, but there are still no absolutes or guarantees of financial assistance for players at any level.

Table 12.2

Level	Type of Sponsorship and Support	Status
Sectional ranking	Discounts on equipment and apparel.	Amateur
Top sectional ranking	Free equipment and apparel; USGA section-level grants for training and travel; college athletic scholarship.	Amateur
Top national ranking	Free equipment and apparel; USGA national-level grants for training and travel; college athletic scholarship. National Team Play.	Amateur
New professional ranking	Free equipment and apparel; support for training and travel; bonuses and contingencies.	Professional
Top professional ranking	Free equipment and apparel; endorsement contracts including salaries, bonuses and contingencies.	Professional

It is always important to keep in mind the level of golf development and whether or not maintaining amateur status is important when tailoring a sponsorship proposal.

Amateur Status and Athletic Scholarships

Generally speaking, to maintain amateur status, sponsorship money or support should directly underwrite an athlete's training and travel expenses, there being no out of the ordinary quid pro quo agreement. For example, an agreement that purports to fund a player's training for two years but expects the player to do a photo shoot for the company may be jeopardizing the player's amateur status.

If the player is banking on a college athletic scholarship, it is prudent to check with the NCAA (More info: ncaa.org) before accepting sponsorship support. Generally speaking, an amateur player can receive support from sponsors until the first day of class his freshman year in college. Anything he receives after that day that does not come from the school could jeopardize his amateur status and his ability to compete on the college level. The NCAA is extremely strict in these cases with athletes in all sports. So much so that in 2004, it ruled that Colorado wide receiver Jeremy Bloom was ineligible to play football for the Buffaloes because he was also a top-ranked freestyle skier and was accepting skiing-related sponsorships during college to finance his skiing career.

It is important to note that a junior also jeopardizes his amateur status and both high school and college eligibility if he plays in fun "skins" games or the like at his local golf course. For example, in Ohio, if a junior is caught playing in the Men's Club's Friday Skins Game, he may find himself ineligible for high school golf. Playing an organized "money" game is usually not a good idea and could cost your kid much more than it is worth. (More info: Check with your specific State's High School Athletic Association for standards and rules of conduct for competition and eligibility.)

Of course, amateur status is not necessarily the Holy Grail. When sponsorship money is lucrative and the player doesn't need the scholarship, he can accept sponsorships – effectively turning professional. Michelle Wie became the highest paid female golfer in the world just before her 16th birthday. Her unprecedented endorsement contracts with Nike and Sony were estimated at around $10 million a year. By comparison, the world's number one ranked player, Annika Sorenstam, was earning around $6 million a year from endorsements at the time of Wie's professional debut.

Developing a Sponsorship Proposal

Unless your child is on the radar, meaning he is listed on one of the national junior rankings, chances are you will be footing the bill for his golf development. Various sponsorship opportunities may be available if junior earns a high ranking. For example, at the basic level, sporting goods manufacturers often send out free or discounted equipment offers to the top 100 or so ranked players in various youth categories each year. The number of offers varies based upon the region, or what the manufacturers refer to as the "golf market."

If your junior has not been contacted, either because he's a beginner or his performance has not yet been noticed, take heart. There's nothing in the Constitution that says you can't contact potential sponsors yourself. Many manufacturers will reserve the right to offer support on an as-needed basis.

Before contacting a company, sporting goods manufacturer or other private sponsor, develop a sponsorship proposal. Put yourself in the shoes of the company you are soliciting. Why should they support your child? What benefit is it to them? Remember to highlight the player's record and tournament schedule. Always include answers to the following information:

- Why do you need a sponsor? Of course you need financial and equipment support. Explain why you are interested in their company or product and how their support is going to make a difference in training, development and performance.
- How long will you require sponsorship? Is this is a one-time deal or are you looking for a long-term relationship?
- How much do you need? Be honest about your needs – coaching, equipment and apparel, pre-competition training, travel and entry fees.
- What do you have to offer a sponsor? Some individual sponsors are altruistic and expect nothing in return. The sporting goods manufacturers that offer free or discounted equipment do it to generate goodwill and don't expect a quid pro quo. But most private sponsors will expect something in return and want to know from your proposal how their sponsorship of your junior will contribute to the company's goals. Be sure you are not violating amateur status rules and regulations if your child expects to continue to play amateur golf.

In many companies, the marketing or promotions department is the contact for sponsorship proposals. Your child's coach may also be able to identify the local representative of a potential golf equipment manufacturer who will be receptive to your proposal.

Due Diligence

It's exciting to earn a sponsorship. Even what might appear to be a routine offer for a grant, free or discounted equipment or clothing should be carefully considered. You, the parent, should carefully scrutinize the deal and get expert advice from the USGA, the NCAA

(More info: ncaa.org) and an attorney in order to evaluate the sponsorship. You'll want to know the following:

- The background of the individual sponsor or agent and his reliability going forward.
- The effect of the agreement on planned college scholarships and junior competition.
- What the sponsor will expect from the player.
- The importance of contingency clauses and other fine print.

Before signing on the dotted line, consider the player's needs and capabilities and reconfirm that the sponsorship deal helps to meet them.

Internship or Golf-related Work

Phil de Piccioto, current president of the leading sports marketing company, Octagon, was once an intern at the company. If you're thinking that this dream career path of intern to company president is rare, think again. Alastair Johnston, head of the golf division at the world's largest sports marketing organization, IMG, and the person credited with the financial success of Tiger Woods, also got his start as an intern at IMG.

Most sports business internships pay less than a summer job, and some just cover out-of-pocket expenses. But landing an internship at a top sports company can be key for a young golfer and will help him appreciate the business side of the sports world while gaining valuable work experience for future career options.

Many of the large corporations advertise internship opportunities, but most smaller companies don't, simply because no one has asked them for a position. Put them on your call list; they may be thrilled to offer a position. There are all kinds of sports-related internships out there. Here are a just few examples:

- Sports marketing: IMG (More info: imgworld.com), Octagon (More info: octagon.com)
- Sports media: CNN (More info: cnn.com).
- Endorsement businesses: Burns Sports Celebrity Service (More info: burnssports.com).
- Sports related non-profits: Women's Sports Foundation (More info: womenssportsfoundation.org).
- Golf organizations: USGA (More info: usga.org), AJGA (More info: ajga.org), IJGT (More info: ijgt.com), also other junior golf information at juniorlinks.com.
- Summer camps: Start with online directories and local community centers such as the YMCA.
- Teaching professionals: Contact a local PGA or LPGA golf professional to find out about assistantship opportunities.

Large corporations generally seek out applicants at colleges. The ratio of open positions to applicants can be as high as 1:20 or higher. Local and smaller-sized businesses, camps, community centers and local teaching professionals are the best bet for high school students. There are also options for golfers who simply want to work to earn money for greens fees or range balls. Many golf shops, cart barns and bag rooms hire part-time employees on summer break from high school or college. And who's to say that summer gig won't turn into a high-flying career?

Publicity for Your Junior

Who wouldn't enjoy reading glowing newspaper articles about themselves? Media coverage that highlights a young player's efforts and accomplishments can be exciting. As long as the coverage doesn't turn the kid into a prima donna, publicity can provide healthy motivation, attract potential sponsors and inspire other kids.

Make it Unique

Media experts advise potential publicity seekers to look for something unique in their story. There are probably lots of young, aspiring athletes in many different sports in your area. What's special about your youngster's story?

A newspaper or magazine article or TV news feature is often more engaging to readers or viewers if they can get a view inside the life of the subject. When pitching your kid's story to local or national media, don't forget to include what makes him different. Does he come from an interesting background that differs from other kids he plays with? Or does he have a unique hobby he uses to distract his mind from the rigors of high-level golf? Maybe he has tracked the career of Tiger Woods from his early days, much like Woods did with Jack Nicklaus' career. Each of these things could separate your child from all the other young golf prodigies and attract the attention of the media, who are always looking for new and different stories.

Earl Woods and the Wies discovered early on how to promote their gifted children. Tiger Woods at age 2 made a now-famous appearance putting with Bob Hope on The Mike Douglas Show. Michelle Wie made appearances on The Tonight Show and The David Letterman Show before she was a teenager. With the cameras on them constantly, these kids became comfortable with fame and popularity at an early age. Even so, no one could have predicted how these two superstars would have impacted the sport. It becomes a precarious position when your child is faced with living up to his press clippings. From start to finish, these two young prodigies have had the press clamoring after them for a newsworthy tale to tell. Great golf fuels the frenzy, but unfortunately now every area of their lives is game for front-page headlines. This is exactly what makes them sports-marketing dream machines!

A parent who knows how the publicity machine works can also help grease the wheels for media exposure. Bugging the local newspaper every time your eight-year-old son finishes in the top 10 in your club juniors championship might make the sports editor dread your every phone call. Your child will also sense when he is being promoted beyond his talent level and may negatively respond to the pressure. Living up to personal expectations is hard enough without a constant added pressure of living up to the expectations of a growing fan base. Some kids start to play below their potential because they do not like the media attention. Flattery and microscopic reporting can do more harm than good, but well-timed communication with the newspaper and other media outlets when he does something truly outstanding can go a long way.

Tools of the Trade

Establish direct contact with journalists. Before that, assemble the communication tools you will need:

- **Targeted media list** – Names, email addresses, phone and fax numbers of reporters who cover sports and youth-related stories. Newspapers, magazines, television, radio stations and web sites are the media outlets you should consider contacting. Most, if not all, of these have web sites that should include contact information.

- **Prepare a media kit** – Information about the player's record and planned activities; points you would like highlighted, photographs, and third-party quotes.

- **Identify a spokesperson** – Designate a parent, coach or relative as the exclusive contact for the media.

- **Prepare your child to handle media questions** – Show him how the professionals answer similar questions. Remind him that his behavior is always free game for a reporter and that post-play interview etiquette is critical to an image that will be portrayed to the public.

- **Remind your child to speak clearly** – Make eye contact and always treat people with respect.

Create your own buzz – Develop interesting story angles and pitch them to the media on an ongoing basis.

Homeschooling

This may remind you of your ACT and SAT tests. Homeschooling means:

A. Postponing school until after the golf years.

B. More time for your kid to practice golf.

C. Freedom from math and science.

D. None of the above.

If you selected D, then you're on the right track if you decide to homeschool your golf kid. For a variety of reasons, the homeschool movement is growing in the United States. The only golf-related reason that should compel a parent to decide to homeschool is to achieve the scheduling flexibility that serious pursuit of golf often requires. Olympians were the first athletes to choose homeschooling specifically to allow a more flexible training schedule, but the concept has become common across many athletic disciplines. As more and more parents are seriously considering the possibility of their children becoming top-level golfers and pursuing golf careers from a young age, they have moved more and more toward the option of homeschooling these kids in order to accommodate their unique lifestyles.

Many parents and children have made it work for them. Homeschooling can provide an excellent education, and it can open opportunities for young golfers that they might not have attending a public or private school. And don't worry about them missing out on the traditional experience of playing on a high school team. There are options for that, too – in 2006, the first annual National Homeschool Golf Championship was held in Fort Worth, Texas.

Is Homeschooling Right for You?

Homeschooling is not a euphemism for dropping out. Neither should it mean reducing school hours and substituting more golf. And don't try to rationalize. "Golf teaches life skills, doesn't it? Besides, last summer after the tournament in Washington DC, Duncan and I visited the Smithsonian. Duncan learned a lot about history, didn't he?" Well, this doesn't cut it – and it's not homeschooling.

Good homeschooling means the parent has chosen to be a teacher, administrator and parent all rolled into one. The parent has to maintain the same number of hours for academic teaching as a public or private school would. For the kid, homeschooling means increased self-discipline and adjusting to a different schedule for socialization. When you and your child understand these basic tenets and can make the necessary adjustments, then and only then consider homeschooling.

The National Home Education Network (More info: nhen.org) is a good place to get a comprehensive understanding of what it takes to homeschool a child. There are hundreds of books to help navigate the world of homeschooling. Read a few so you can make an informed choice. "The First Year of Homeschooling Your Child" by Linda Dobson; "What about College?" by Cafi Cohen and Patrick Farenga; and the "Homeschooling Almanac" by Mary and Michael Leppert are some of the best-selling books on this subject.

Having decided to homeschool your kid, it's good to know you don't have to have mastery of every subject. There are all sorts of wonderful resources to help you – homeschool suppliers, web sites and academic tutors. There are also support organizations that will guide you in helping your kid develop socialization skills and tutors to teach subjects that may be hard for some parents. The resources are endless, and so are the curriculums you and your child can enjoy together. There are even helpers who will organize proms for home-schoolers.

Homeschooling is a legal education option in every state in the United States. While some colleges are more homeschool-friendly than others are, homeschoolers routinely earn college scholarships and obtain admission to Ivy League schools like Harvard and Yale. Understanding state homeschooling laws, diligent record keeping and taking the standardized tests are keys to homeschooling success. The parents' organization and dedication to education is paramount.

Steps to Successful Homeschooling

It's not uncommon for kids to homeschool during the middle-school years with the goal of jumpstarting their golf careers. After a year or two of exclusive focus on golf, they return to their regular public or private high school.

One can argue that the ideal years to begin homeschooling for golf reasons are between grades nine and 12. During younger years the intensity of the game is low and scheduling time for golf is generally not a problem. It is during the high school years that a flexible schooling schedule can help the golf kid train better. A high school freshman will also have sufficient golf experience to decide whether he wants to pursue the development of his game seriously. Usually by ninth grade, you will have a good idea of your child's academic needs as well. Some kids need to be pushed and prodded through school while others are self-starters. Carefully consider your child's personality before attempting a homeschool arrangement.

Before allowing a kid to pull out of public or private school, there is groundwork to be laid:

1. **Know the state law** – Become familiar with and ensure you are meeting all the requirements of your state's homeschooling laws

(More info: unschooling.com). Georgia law requires that a parent possess minimum teaching credentials, maintain adequate home-schooling records and teach a curriculum "equivalent" to that of the public schools. Call your state legislature to obtain current information.

2. **NCAA and school requirements** – The NCAA has specific core course guidelines for homeschooling. If your kid is aiming for a general or athletic college scholarship, ascertain the latest require-ments from the NCAA (More info: ncaa.org). It may be a good idea to contact the admissions offices of select schools for information about their homeschooling policies.

3. **Develop a support network** – Homeschooling families in your area, Scouts, 4-H, YMCA, YWCA and volunteer organizations are some ways your kid can receive the social benefits of homeschooling. Bring together homeschooling kids in your area who may be inter-ested in golf for group lessons. Join or form a local golf team with kids from homeschools and public schools to encourage interaction.

4. **Preparing to teach** – Chart the required academic courses and identify subjects you are already qualified to teach. Learn about topics not familiar to you by taking courses at a community col-lege or through computer-based or video-based training packages. Enlist the aid of tutors to teach subjects that are hard for you. If eli-gible and it works in your schedule, enroll junior in a night class at the local junior college.

5. **Standardized testing** – The SAT (More info: collegeboard.com) and ACT (More info: act.org) tests not only help a homeschooler get into college, but the test scores can be used to measure general educa-tional development. During the freshman year, prepare a schedule of all the standardized tests your homeschooler will want to take over the next two to three years. Preparation and testing occur during the sophomore and junior years, in time for college admissions.

Ultimately, homeschooling goes beyond education – it's a lifestyle choice. Sometimes homeschooled kids complain about feeling lonely. Other times a parent's circumstances may change, making it impossi-ble to dedicate the time necessary for homeschooling. Realize that it's okay to return to public school if things don't work out.

Homeschooling is more mainstream than ever before, and it may very well work for your family. If you choose to homeschool, know that you're in illustrious company. Thomas Edison; famous photogra-pher Ansel Adams; Frances Collins, leader of the Human Genome project; astronaut Sally Ride and Supreme Court Justice Sandra Day O'Connor, as well as 2005 LPGA rookie Brittany Lincicome are just a few of the many famous homeschoolers.

College Golf Scholarships

Top advice for golf scholarship applicants? Keep your grades up! Remembering that grades count is probably the most important lesson for parents and children hoping to attain a college scholarship.

Your kid doesn't have to be a star player to earn a golf scholarship. Good grades, a reasonable player record and good sportsmanship may well land him a free ride through college, particularly if he keeps his options open – another state, a Division II college, partial scholarships and so on.

Even if the kid has other plans and isn't remotely interested in college, encourage him to go through the college admission and scholarship processes. You never know – when the mailman delivers the actual offer to the door, the kid may just decide it's one he can't refuse.

True Cost of College

According to the College Board, the average cost of tuition and room and board at four-year public schools is a little more than $12,000 per year. Private schools run up to four times as much (More info: collegeboard.com).

Fortunately, Uncle Sam, community organizations and private enterprises are all on your side when it comes to paying for college. Few students pay the "sticker price," and it's not uncommon for 60 to 75 percent of students to receive some sort of financial aid.

For starters, there are attractive federal tax breaks for saving for college. On average, $6,000 in financial aid is disbursed annually to every college student, totaling about $129 billion. Your tax dollars make up a large percentage of this amount. It makes sense that you'd want to get some of it back as financial aid for your child.

The Numbers

There are over 225,000 kids playing golf at the high school level, with more than 8,000 schools offering girls' golf and more than 13,000 offering boys' golf, according to a recent study by the National Federation of State High School Associations. Several thousands of these are high school seniors looking forward to participating in college golf.

More than 10,000 athletes play golf at 1,200 colleges. If we assume an annual graduation rate of 25 to 30 percent, this means over 2,500 freshman men and women are needed each year for college golf teams.

The good news is that most golfers benefit from some form of financial aid. For example, NCAA (Divisions I, II and III) schools alone have some 3,000 scholarships for men and almost 2,800 for women. Say we have 300 boys and 300 girls qualifying for a national ranking. Estimating two-thirds are age appropriate and ready for college, only 400 nationally ranked players are thus available for recruiting by college coaches dangling scholarships. There are also almost 300 universities and colleges comprised in the NAIA division, many of which also have fine golf programs and offer some sort of scholarship money.

As promising as those numbers appear, it will take a ranking in the top three percent of players to assure your child a full scholarship at his school of choice. A decent ranking in the AJGA will allow a player to pick and choose from the best college programs. The scales tip further in favor of a strong player when he is considering a Division II or III program. However, also consider the college of your child's dreams may not offer golf scholarships, or worse yet, may not even have a golf program.

The Road to College

Taking the necessary steps early will offer your child the greatest number of options and help him make sound decisions. No later than freshman year of high school is the time when parent, child and coach should obtain information and begin to develop a roadmap. The idea that starting early is critical cannot be stressed enough. Too often parents wait until their child gets to his junior or senior year to really start looking at the college recruiting process, and by then it is almost always too late. Most often it is during the beginning of the senior year when your child will make his final decision. In the interim, the parent and coach need to offer plenty of help to a kid on the road to college.

Getting into the college of choice is not a foregone conclusion. Stay on top of things and do the following:

1. **Collect information** – In the first year of high school, you and your child should absorb as much information as possible about the college admission and financial aid processes. Keep your options open and contact all major college associations – NCAA (More info: ncaa.org), NAIA (More info: naia.org), and NJCAA (More info: njcaa.org).

2. **Compile lists** – The NCAA and NAIA require certain core courses. Make a list of the nearly 15 or so core courses and be sure they are completed during high school. Consult a high school counselor and compile a list of at least 50 colleges from among the NCAA, NAIA, and NJCAA members that interest you. Contact the admissions office of these colleges to discuss any special needs – home-school policies and so on.

3. **Preliminary tests** – Be sure the child takes the PSAT/NMSQT (More info: collegeboard.org) tests during the freshman and sophomore years. Use the reports to analyze your child's strengths and weaknesses and to prepare for the SAT. As a bonus, the PSAT results also automatically put your child in the running for the merit scholarships and corporate scholarships awarded by the National Merit Scholarship Corporation (More info: nationalmerit.org). Also remember during this time to keep grades up, because falling behind early can make catching up difficult.

4. **The All-important junior year** – The child should now take the SAT (More info: collegeboard.com) and ACT (More info: act.org) tests. Report scores to the NCAA Clearinghouse. Register with the NCAA Clearinghouse at the end of the junior year (More info: ncaa.org). Arrange recruiting visits to the colleges. Monitor core course selections. Your child should also be registered on all junior golf-related web sites and in the national database for junior golfers.

5. **Apply** – During the child's senior year, finalize the college list and apply. If highly recruited and your child has been offered a scholarship, the college coach may also help with the application. Find out about private and local scholarships and apply for them. Include in your child's portfolio the following:

   - The player's record. Generally coaches value results in AJGA tournaments more than high school golf results. However, state championships carry some weight.

   - Newspaper clippings and other media coverage.

   - Letters of recommendation from both past and present coaches.

   - Letters of recommendation from prominent citizens or strong alumni.

   - Details of sponsorship by golf club and apparel manufacturers and so on.

   - Video presentation of golf swing.

   - A letter from your child telling why he wants to attend the particular institution and specifically why he wants to be a part of its golf program.

6. **Meet the coach** – Arrange recruiting visits to the colleges and get to know the coaches. While the NCAA allows only five official visits to schools, unofficial visits can be made as long as the recruit doesn't accept anything (i.e. a free lunch) from the coach or the school. These can be made when you are in the area for a junior tournament or a family vacation. Show the coach your interest is genuine by contacting the school several times. Too many kids assume a coach just isn't interested in them, when, in reality the

coach may be questioning the kid's interest because there has been insufficient follow-up.

7. **Final selection** – You may receive a National Letter of Intent from an NCAA-affiliated office or an offer letter directly from the school. Experts advise selecting a college based first on academic strength, then on the size and location of the school, the quality of the coach and team, graduation rate and, finally, the scholarship money available. Don't let the best financial aid package unduly influence your decision. Scholarships are awarded on a year-by-year basis. Even if there is little or no money available for your child's freshman year, that doesn't mean there will be no money for subsequent years. Coaches are good at explaining the details of what financial support is available from their programs.

8. **After the high school graduation party** – Have the high school counselor mail final transcripts to the NCAA Clearinghouse and NAIA/ NJCAA colleges.

A lot of students have to work or take out student loans to pay for college, but with reasonable grades, a decent golf record and an organized plan of action, your golf kid can play his way through college.

13
Careers in Golf

A kid may excel at golf. This does not automatically mean he has to take up golf as a career. He may not even want to. A good golfer can choose to become a scientist, entrepreneur, police officer or musician. Who's to say a top junior won't turn his golf excellence into an Ivy League scholarship, major in business and become a wildly successful entrepreneur? He might even surpass the fame and fortune of a world No. 1 golfer.

That said, realize that golf can play a major role in achieving success in any field. The self-discipline, focus, organizational skills, strategic thinking and, most important, friendships developed playing golf are all invaluable, no matter what career path one ultimately follows.

Defining Career Success

Career counselors will tell you that kids who develop early career plans are most likely to succeed. Most kids start to weigh career options during their high school years. Support from the parent, coach and career counselor can come in the form of helping the golf kid develop a plan that includes at least four or five career options. Parents need to consider the financial implications of each choice – what it will take, financially, to prepare for and achieve each career option.

A chosen career path can affect just about everything: how much time you're willing to devote to a specific activity; what you read; what your hobbies and interests are; the people to whom you're attracted. Career-planning experts advise their clients to think big and be prepared to adjust their plans as they move forward.

Any career plan should include a definition of success. That definition might include money and fame. Hall of Fame basketball coach and recognized "life coach" John Wooden eloquently defines success as, "Peace of mind, which is a direct result of self-satisfaction in knowing you did your best to become the best that you are capable of becoming." Whatever you choose to include in your personal definition, don't forget to add a healthy dose of personal happiness and community service to your own definition of career success.

Teaching Professional

A player with even a modest playing record can aspire to be a great teaching professional. In fact, some of the most groundbreaking and respected coaches like Butch Harmon, David Leadbetter, Dave Pelz and Jim McLean had less than modest playing records.

To be successful, a golf pro must possess qualities more critical than a top playing record: keen observation and deduction skills, knowledge and love of the game, patience, the ability to motivate and a capacity to focus on a single individual, even in a group setting. For teaching young children, one quality stands above all others – the ability to make lessons fun while recognizing special "teachable moments".

There are a number of different organizations offering certification as a golf professional, but the only two that carry much clout in the golf world are those offered by the PGA of America and the LPGA Teaching and Club Professional Division. PGA Professionals are not to be confused with players on the PGA Tour. The PGA Tour is the association of touring professional players like Tiger Woods and Phil Mickelson, while PGA Professionals are those individuals certified by the PGA to be teachers or run golf shops. Chances are the head professional at your local club is a PGA Professional.

Certification by the PGA of America

Aspiring teaching professionals seeking certification as a PGA Professional must go through one of the PGA's Professional Golf Management (PGM) programs. These programs can be taken as a regular course of study at any one of 17 universities, where the PGM major is treated like any other major but takes 4½ years to complete.

The PGA also offers accelerated PGM programs for those who have already graduated college with a different major. The accelerated programs include none of the general education requirements that college students in the PGM programs must complete to receive undergraduate degrees from their schools, but instead focus solely on golf.

Professional Golf Management Programs

Seventeen schools currently offer undergraduate-level PGM programs accredited by the PGA: Arizona State, Campbell University, Clemson, Coastal Carolina, Colorado (Colorado Springs), Ferris State, Florida Gulf Coast University, Florida State, Idaho, Methodist, Mississippi State, Nebraska, UNLV, New Mexico State, North Carolina State, Penn State and Sam Houston State. New schools continue to express interest in the PGM programs, so research if there are new opportunities in your area.

The programs require classroom study, on-course work experience and the passing of a playing ability test (PAT) to qualify for graduation. The PAT is designed to ensure all prospective teaching professionals meet a certain standard in their own games, and passing it is difficult. In fact, according to the PGA, only about 20 percent of players pass the PAT on their first try.

Most schools with PGM programs offer assistance in finding graduates placement at local golf courses or teaching facilities, and the networking opportunities allowed by the required internship experience often helps graduates find their way in the profession.

Other Certifying Organizations

While obtaining certification as a PGA Professional is the best path for prospective teachers to learn the craft, there are also a handful of other organizations that offer certifications in teaching golf. These certifications are not nearly as demanding of their students, nor are they as prestigious. Teachers going this route aren't required to put in the same time commitment and effort to achieve certification.

The Professional Golf Teachers' Association of America (PGTAA, More info: pgtaa.com) and the United States Golf Teachers' Federation (USGTF. More info: usgtf.com) each offer programs that certify its students as Master Teaching Professionals (MTPs). The MTP programs generally cost $1,000-$2,000 and include one-week courses followed by a written exam and a playing ability test.

More Avenues within PGM

Not everybody who graduates with a PGM degree ends up being strictly a teaching professional. In fact, there are about as many different career paths within the realm of professional golf management as there are majors at any college or university. PGM graduates can choose from career opportunities that include but are not limited to: golf professional, golf instruction and player development, executive management, association management, marketing and promotions, consulting, sales, research and technology, merchandising, broadcasting and journalism, tournament director or manager, golf course development, golf course management, club fitting and repair, and golf retail.

PGM graduates have so many different opportunities in the golf industry because the programs cover all aspects of the industry. The course description includes required classes in PGA constitution and bylaws, the rules of golf, golf car fleet management, tournament operations, golfer development programs, career enhancement, introduction to teaching, golf club design and repair, business communication, turfgrass management, analysis of the swing, business planning and operations, customer relations, food and beverage control, supervising and delegating, swing concepts of teaching, and merchandising and inventory management.

PGM programs also offer electives in golf course design, golf facility design, golf range management and caddie management. Learning about the business side of golf makes a PGM graduate better prepared to assume the duties of teaching professional, tournament director, golf shop operator, greenskeeper or golf industry executive. A PGM degree is also useful if you want to start your own business, such as owning or leasing a golf club, becoming a supplier of golf goods or a developer of golf courses.

The PGA offers extensive information about its PGM program on a link from its website (More info: careernet.pgalinks.com).

Golf Course Superintendent

Along with the teaching professional and golf shop manager, among the most visible jobs at any golf course is that of the golf course superintendent. This person is in charge of all the maintenance on the course, with his main responsibility being to keep the greens and fairways in good, playable condition.

A superintendent (or greens keeper, as they are often called) manages a staff of employees whose basic duties are to cut and water the grass and maintain every other natural element of the golf course. There is much more science to it, though, than the average person who keeps up his yard at home might think. Greens, fairways, tee boxes and rough are cut to specifically desired lengths and watered on a precise schedule. Superintendents are trained and accredited professionals who have studied how to combat various diseases, insects and other animals that regularly conspire to keep healthy grass from growing.

Superintendents and their crews keep their golf courses in playable condition by staying one step ahead of the golfers who play the course. Even if you go off on the first hole with the earliest tee time on a Saturday morning, you can guarantee the greens crew arrived an hour or two earlier, most likely starting before sunup mowing greens and smoothing out sand traps.

School Sports Management

College and high school athletics represent a huge segment of the sports industry. Almost every academic institution has an athletic program. The NCAA (More info: ncaa.org), NAIA (More info: naia.org), and NJCAA (More info: njcaa.org) together have nearly 2,000 member colleges, and nearly half of them offer golf programs.

According to the National Federation of State High School Associations (More info: nfhs.org), 161,284 boys played high school golf during the 2005-06 school year, and 64,195 players participated in girls' high school golf programs. Most jobs in high school sports management are far from glamorous, but high school sports attract more fans than do their collegiate and professional counterparts. High schools spend about six times as much on sports programs as does the NCAA.

Many sports industry executives began their careers in school athletics. Coaching a golf team is just one of the many exciting opportunities available. Most athletic departments have a variety of staff positions, including athletic director, sports information director, facilities manager, tickets director, marketing director, fund raising manager, student-athlete affairs, academic advisor, to name just a few.

Most jobs in this field require a degree in liberal arts, education, kinesiology, sports administration or business management. Again, volunteering or interning with an athletic department can open the door to these positions.

Sports Marketing

Love of sports is just one of the qualifications needed to succeed in sports marketing. A bachelor's degree in law, business management, communications, public relations, or advertising, combined with solid experience and good communication skills, is key to doing well in a sports marketing career.

Some of the larger sports marketing companies that have an active involvement in golf include IMG (More info: imgworld.com), Octagon (More info: octagon.com), and SFX Sports Group (More info: sfxsports.com). Sports marketing firms usually focus on some or all of three functions: athlete representation, corporate marketing and event marketing. Companies like IMG have a fourth component – managing sports events.

Athlete Representation

Aside from hard-nosed contract negotiations on behalf of a professional athlete, representation for financial counsel, endorsement marketing and public relations are becoming more prevalent. A representative may do all of these things for a client or choose to specialize in one aspect.

Between state requirements and fierce competition, breaking in as an independent player agent can be daunting. Fortunately, there are hundreds of medium-to-large sports marketing companies hungry for quality recruits.

Corporate Marketing

An agency's work consists of developing and executing a marketing program that utilizes sports and sports personalities to market a company or product. A sports marketing program can include a variety of components, from simple projects such as designing and manufacturing sports giveaways or distributing match schedules to much grander undertakings like developing a sports-related advertising campaign, naming a stadium or garnering a celebrity endorsement for the company's products.

Working for a college athletic department or local sports team will provide invaluable experience for almost any sports marketing career. Find out what you're good at, and what you enjoy most, by exploring various departments, from operations to creative design to management. Understand the game, not just the statistics. Know the players and the sports media; stay on the cutting edge; be informed about current industry trends and where they might lead in the future.

Event Management and Marketing

Managing and marketing major tournaments like those on the PGA Tour and LPGA Tour require considerable experience and expertise. Millions of dollars are spent on these events, and a large team is required to manage them. A typical event team includes the event director, marketing director, sales director, director of operations, and client services coordinator.

The event director oversees the entire event, works to secure major sponsorship from corporations and signs up star players. The sales manager sells advertising space and coordinates promotional campaigns and ticket sales. The client services coordinator is responsible for responding to the needs of sponsors, advertising clients and players and also oversees corporate ticket sales. The marketing director coordinates advertising and promotion in advance of the event.

Along with event staff, many hundreds of volunteers are needed to make any such tournament a success. Volunteering is a great way to build a resume and will give you an up-close-and-personal view of event management and marketing. It can also lead to a wealth of industry contacts. Junior golfers can volunteer to help at their local professional event. It is a great opportunity to learn about a professional golf event from inside the ropes.

Golf Officiating

Some might say that the official Rules of Golf include too many silly and inconsequential rules. Tell that to the golf officials working at any tournament who are required to know the rule book inside and out!

Golf officiating can be a very easy job if there are no questionable rulings during a round. But it can also become quite difficult because there are so many possibilities for different circumstances in a playing field as large and with as much varied terrain as a golf course.

The game of golf is unique among sports in that players are, for the most part, responsible for policing themselves. You could watch a thousand baseball games and never see a batter admit that a ball he hit was foul, not fair, but the onus is on a golfer to point out if she hits a ball out of bounds. Golf officials are intended to serve as independent arbiters, essentially to rule on difficult decisions and to know the rules that a player might not. Generally, there may be two or three officials who roam the course and are ultimately responsible for final rulings during a tournament. There are also unofficial markers that usually accompany each group during a tournament.

A prospective rules official must attend a three-day seminar put on by the USGA and score at least 85 percent on an open-book exam. The exam must be re-taken every four years to retain status as a certified rules official. Of course, only the best and most experienced rules officials get to rule on free drops at the majors. Like everything else, to get to the top, you have to put in your time and prove you can do the job well.

Athletic Trainer

The trainer's goal is to keep the player in top physical condition, prevent injuries, and provide care for the injured athlete. If a player does sustain an injury, it's the trainer's job to design treatment programs and oversee rehab. The athletic trainer is closely associated with other sport professionals such as personal fitness trainers and strength and conditioning coaches.

The American Medical Association recognizes trainers as allied health professionals. The National Athletic Trainer's Association (NATA. More info: nata.org) primarily certifies trainers. The minimum educational requirement is a bachelor's degree, with the completion of a program in athletic training. NATA also requires passing a multi-part examination and hundreds of hours of supervised experience, usually working with head trainers at their colleges. Many states require trainers to be registered or licensed.

Most jobs are in college and high school sports. Health clubs, large corporations and golf organizations like the PGA Tour and LPGA Tour also hire athletic trainers. Once again, a great way to get started is by volunteering or working part-time while in school.

The best-paying jobs are held by those who work with professional players. As you might expect, these positions are also the toughest to find.

Sports Entrepreneur

Charles Hoeveler came to the Stanford Business School on an NCAA postgraduate scholarship, the result of academic and athletic achievement at Dartmouth College, where he was Eastern Intercollegiate tennis champion. A 1969 graduate, Hoeveler has not only kept his competitive spirit alive by winning national father-son titles with Charles Jr., but Hoeveler Sr. has also turned his passion for tennis into a thriving enterprise.

Back in the 1970s and 80s, sports camps were mom-and-pop shows. Organizers relied on flyers and faxes to get the word out about an upcoming camp. Enrollment was basically local.

Charles Hoeveler changed all that, bringing together multi-sport and multi-city camps under the umbrella of a single company – US Sports & Specialty Camps. Instead of flyers and faxes, Hoeveler relies on a top-notch web site for registration and camp administration, along with professionally designed brochures. A sponsorship arrangement allows him to use the world-class Nike brand name for his camps.

Today, US Sports & Specialty Camps pulls in nearly $17 million in annual revenue, offering 26 different sports and specialty programs serving tens of thousands of campers each year. Charles Hoeveler's entrepreneurial spirit has enabled him to create the world's largest sports camp operation.

Professional Player

Players seeking to test their readiness for the PGA Tour can attempt to work their way in each week through Monday qualifying, or they can try to earn a Tour card for a year by playing their way on through the Qualifying School process.

Players who perform well enough on the Tour each year retain their Tour card for the next year, but every season, there are 30 spots that come open and are filled through the "Q School" process. "Q School" is actually a bit of a misnomer – there are no classes or books involved, but rather a series of three tournaments in which a large national field gets pared down to 30 players.

The first stage is held in October at 14 sites across the country, is open to all players with a pre-determined handicap, and generally takes the top 19 or 20 players from each field of 78. The second stage comes in November, when the top players from each of the regional fields are joined by players who have earned exempt status through the PGA Tour, the Nationwide Tour or one of the international tours. The top players move on to the final stage in late November, where they compete against more players with exemptions.

Once the final stage is completed, the top 30 players earn their Tour cards, while the next 50 earn membership on the Nationwide Tour. Every other player who advances to the final stage earns a conditional exemption on the Nationwide Tour.

The entire two-month process whittles a field of more than 1,000 hopefuls down to 30. The percentages are not good, but that doesn't keep some players from coming back to Q School year after year. It is not cheap, either – the entry fee for the first stage is $4,500, followed by $4,000 for the second stage and $3,500 for the third stage.

PGA Tour and LPGA

This is the real deal for an aspiring professional player – the PGA Tour (More info: pgatour.com) for the young man, and LPGA (More info: lpga.com) for the young woman.

The PGA Tour operates tournaments nearly every week from January through early December, with purses ranging from $3,000,000-$8,000,000. The four events that stand out above the rest are the majors, though they are not all directly affiliated with the PGA Tour: the Masters Tournament, the U.S. Open, the British Open and the PGA Championship. Aside from its traditional stroke-play tournaments, the PGA Tour also works with the International Federation of PGA Tours each year to put on the World Golf Championships, a series of four tournaments that bring U.S. and international players together to compete in match-play, team and stroke-play events. In addition, the PGA Tour runs the Champions Tour, for players over 50, and the Nationwide Tour, essentially golf's minor league.

The LPGA runs tournaments from February through December, though the total prize money, which ranges from a low of $1 million to a high of $2.2 million, is significantly lower than that on the PGA Tour. The four women's majors are the Kraft Nabisco Championship, the McDonald's LPGA Championship, the U.S. Women's Open and the Weetabix Women's British Open. Also under the umbrella of the LPGA are the Women's Legends of Golf Tour (seniors) and the Futures Tour.

Life on the Tour

The travel opportunities, earnings, friendship, and media attention are all worth soaking up, but turn pro on the basis of clinical assessment rather than emotion. Have a sound financial plan to support the initial learning curve. These things are key to making the player's professional years some of the best years of his life.

Caddy

Being a professional caddy on the PGA Tour is one of the more unique jobs in sports. While it doesn't require a high degree of specialization (or any sort of college degree or accreditation, for that matter), the job does require extreme precision and attention to detail.

A caddy for a professional player is basically that player's confidant. He not only carries the player's golf bag, but is responsible for providing yardages, knowing the course inside and out and providing moral support during a round.

Caddies are essentially independent contractors. They can be hired or fired at any time, and their income is generally based on a percentage of their player's winnings. Because of that, it is in the caddy's best interest for his player to perform well. Most caddies will arrive with his player at each tournament a day or two early to study the golf course meticulously, making notes in a yardage book on everything from the speed and difficulty of the greens to the distance from tee boxes to fairway bunkers.

Outside of the professional ranks, where caddies can earn six figures, caddying is often a means young golfers employ to earn money for equipment or greens fees. Many public and private clubs offers caddies to their players for a round. Depending on the club, a caddy can make anywhere from $20-100 for 18 holes, and the job description is quite a bit simpler. Caddies hired for the day are simply expected to carry the bag, provide yardages (which can often be paced off from the nearest sprinkler head) and help read putts.

Sports Media

Once limited to the sports page of the local newspaper and a few radio and television reports, sports media now includes glossy magazines, entire television networks and the internet. Sports Illustrated, Golf magazine, CNNSI.com, ESPN, IMG, and the ubiquitous sports talk radio shows are all examples of how wide the reach of sports media has become.

A print and online media team is typically comprised of sports editors, writers, photographers, advertising salespeople and graphic artists. For radio and television shows, there's the show host, the producer, and the engineering and camera support staff.

Most specialized jobs require a degree in journalism or a number of years of experience in the field working at publications or stations with smaller audiences. Popular players often find their way into broadcasting because of their celebrity and knowledge of the game. PGA Tour Hall-of-Famer Johnny Miller may be the most well-known of this group. The former U.S. Open and British Open champion retired from the Tour following the 1994 season, and quickly settled into his new role as NBC's lead golf commentator. Miller has become known for his quick wit and willingness to express his opinions on the air – traits he developed as a youngster through his association with a rough-and-tumble group of golfers in San Francisco.

"They were the most opinionated people you ever met," Miller told Golf Digest in its October, 2003 edition. "To survive, you had to be quick and give the needle back. That's where it came from."

14
College Golf

"The right decision will make your college career successful and enjoyable. You will develop your game, enhance your skills, further your education and build valuable friendships and relationships, so make sure you consider all the important factors in your decision."

Greg Priest, Baylor University men's golf coach

For many young golfers and their parents, the ultimate goal of the time they put into developing their golf game is to earn a college scholarship. The chance to have your child's education paid for, as well as the prestige that comes with playing for a well-known institution, is enough to push parents and their aspiring golfers through years of hard work, tournament play and hectic travel schedules. Some see it as a relationship in which the effort put in during the years leading up to college equals the daily 9-to-5, and the scholarship is the paycheck, paid in one lump sum at the end.

While it should be noted that there are plenty of other benefits to a youngster playing golf – the game is a great social and networking tool and something that a young player can learn to love for life – if the true goal is to use the sport as a road to college, there is plenty to learn before the first day of freshman year.

The process of preparing a young golfer for college is complicated, and there are more options out there than the average player or parent might think. Realize not every young golfer will end up starring at USC or Ohio State, but with the proper perspective, almost anybody with a solid golf resume can find the right fit and continue his career on the course after high school.

Weighing the Value

How much will it cost to raise a child to play golf at a high level? How much will it cost to send him to the college of his choice? These are just some of the questions parents need to ask as they consider embarking on a journey with their children into the world of golf.

At the most basic level, it might be best to think of the relationship in terms of a seesaw. On one side, picture a stack of money that represents the cost of a college education. On the other side, picture another stack that represents all the money you'll spend developing your child as a golfer – greens fees, club costs, travel, coaching and more. While these numbers won't be able to be calculated exactly, they can be approximated for your purposes.

If the side of the seesaw with the cost of college is far heavier than the other side, then perhaps it makes sense to put a bunch of money into developing junior's golf game with the hopes that it results in a free education. Of course, if parents think of this like any other investment, they'll realize there is some risk involved. There are no guarantees – that college scholarship might not materialize.

In other words, don't bank on your kid getting a scholarship unless you've got enough in the bank to pay for college on the chance his career is derailed by a snowboarding accident or he suddenly takes an interest in playing the tuba and puts aside the golf clubs.

If the side of the seesaw with the stack of money for developing his game weighs heavier than the cost of the four-year education, realize that it's not an equal relationship and that it may not make sense financially to push your child at every turn to earn a college scholarship.

Instead, maybe you decide to foster in him an interest in the game with the goal of competing on his high school team and enjoying golf as a lifetime hobby and social activity, rather than banking on your "investment" of money and time to pay off with a full ride.

College Costs

To really get an idea of whether it is smart to invest all your time and money into trying to earn junior a college golf scholarship, you'll need to get an accurate assessment of what it will take to get him there and how much you would pay if he were to go to college on your dime.

Estimating the cost of college is the easier part. A 2006 report by the College Board found that the average cost for one year at a private university (including tuition and fees only, but not room and board) during the 2006-07 school year is $22,218. With room and board it may cost over $30,000. At public universities, the costs were significantly lower – about a quarter of the costs of the private institutions – averaged $5,836. Tutition and fees tend to be a little less in the western United States.

Private schools are generally thought to offer the better education, but that isn't always the case. For example, many of the schools in the University of California system have excellent reputations – Cal is number 20 and UCLA number 25 on U.S. News and World Report's 2006 America's Best Colleges list.

A web site that is helpful for calculating the potential cost of college is lunch-money.com. The site allows you to input the current cost for one year at a specific college or university, the number of years until your child will enroll in college and the number of years he plans to attend. Using the rate of inflation in college costs per year, it then calculates the estimated cost for each year in school.

The numbers may look astronomical, especially for parents with young children still years away from starting the admissions process, but the figures don't always reflect what students actually pay to go to college. The same report showed that 25 percent of students at public schools and 60 percent at private schools received some grant money, which is money received from the school and is not expected to be repaid. Grants are usually need based, though the College Board report showed that more and more, schools are giving grants on the basis of academic merit rather than financial need.

Many students or their parents also take out college loans, generally low-interest-rate loans that can be paid back over time after the student graduates and begins earning money from a full-time job.

Golf Costs

Some parents have estimated they have spent $20.000-$25,000 or more a year on developing their child's golf game. As detailed in chapter 12, these costs can include everything from equipment to clothing to greens fees and private coaching. Top-level tournament play later in a child's golf career can drain the budget with travel costs and tournament entrance fees.

The numbers can creep even higher when specialized recruiting services are enlisted in order to secure that college scholarship you and junior have worked so hard and so long for. The amount you'll pay to develop your child's budding golf career shouldn't simply be guessed at. Rather, smart parents weighing the merits of helping their children become high-level golfers will forecast these costs as best they can, continually adjusting them from year to year as they learn more about the process. Talking to parents of older children in a similar situation can help.

One other thing for parents to consider is the possibility of paying for both golf development and college. It may seem like a paradox to pay for college after you've put so much into trying to get junior a scholarship, but often it can become reality. If you have the money, it may be worth it to you and your kid to develop an interest in golf even if that interest isn't so keen as to lead him toward playing the sport in college.

Opportunity Costs

In economics circles, opportunity cost is defined as what you give up to earn something else. For example, your child going to college not only includes the real cost of $100,000 for four years, but also the opportunity cost, which might be the money he could earn working full-time during those four years.

Opportunity costs are not all measured in dollar signs, though. The opportunity cost of attending college for four years might be that Jimmy missed out on traveling Europe or working in the Peace Corps like some of his friends from high school.

In terms of raising a child to play golf, opportunity costs should be considered. If your child starts spending all his time on the golf course or range at age 10, that decision could keep him from playing Little League baseball or Pop Warner football, or simply keep him from spending much time goofing around with his friends in an unstructured environment. If as parents, you feel this is a healthy situation for your child, then by all means, go for it. But if junior starts on this path and it becomes evident that the opportunity costs are too steep, then it might be time to consider re-directing your priorities.

Assessing the Options

Until recently, it used to be that every household in the United States paid its monthly phone bill to the telephone company, the one and only entity providing phone service in the United States. With the advent of de-regulation in the 1980s, the monopoly was broken up, and now people have so many choices for phone service it's almost head spinning, and the change has generally been considered a positive thing. The point of this brief history lesson is that parents of prospective golfers might not realize just how many choices are available to them. Whereas many probably think of their youngster's potential college golf career in terms of well-known Division I colleges from the major athletic conferences, they should know that there are just as many – if not more – opportunities at smaller Division I schools and other schools in Divisions II and III, in the NAIA and at the junior college level.

For every Arizona State out there, there is a Southern Methodist. For every Florida, there is a Valdosta (Georgia) State or an Alleghany (Pennsylvania). Each of these schools finished in the top 15 in either the NCAA Division I, II or III men's golf championship tournament in 2001.

And plenty of PGA Tour players attended colleges that might not jump to mind as athletic powerhouses. You don't have to go far down the Tour's list of career money leaders to find the names of Kenny Perry, who played collegiate golf at Western Kentucky University, or Brad Faxon, a graduate of Furman University.

The PING Guide

There are literally hundreds of choices available for the potential college golfer. At the NCAA Division I level alone, there are approximately 289 schools offering men's golf, and 217 offering women's golf, all with scholarships available. Scholarships are also offered at the NCAA Division II level, where there are about 186 men's teams and 90 women's teams. Since golf coaches can share allocation of scholarship money between several players, many more players have a chance to play and be part of collegiate golf program.

There are also hundreds of Division III golf programs (without scholarships) and NAIA golf programs. And there are plenty of junior colleges, where players not quite ready – either academically, athletically or financially – for a four-year school can go for two years before transferring to a college or university for the last two.

With all these varied options, this is where the PING Guide can be extremely helpful to an aspiring college golfer and his parents. Officially called the "PING American College Golf Guide," it is a comprehensive resource published each year by the golf club manufacturer that provides tons of useful information about the process of getting into college to play golf. It is a publication that should be on every young golfer's bookshelf.

The PING Guide can be purchased for $14.95 through the web site collegegolf.com, and it is well worth the cost. It includes everything from a comprehensive list of contacts for every college coach in the country to a calendar of important dates for the college-bound golfer. For a young golfer intent on playing at the college level or his parents, the guide can essentially walk you through the process of selecting a college, contacting the coach, applying and preparing for all the steps along the way.

The book is published each summer, after the NCAA championships are concluded, and contains the most up-to-date information available. Some of the most important information for prospective college golfers trying to find their best fit is contained in the PING Guide: the varying academic requirements at each level, along with type of play that can be expected at each level.

To compete at a Division I college, students must meet certain standards based on their grade-point average, SAT scores and ACT scores. The PING Guide lists a chart of the exact requirements – for example, a student with a 2.5 GPA or higher must also achieve a combined SAT score of at least 820 and a total ACT score of at least 68. The lower the GPA, the higher the SAT and ACT scores must be. A student with a 2.0 GPA needs a 1010 SAT score and an 86 on the ACTs.

For Division II schools, the qualifications are more straightforward: a prospective student-athlete needs a GPA of 2.0 or higher and test scores of at least 820 (SAT) and 68 (ACT).

To be eligible to compete for an NAIA school, an athlete must satisfy two of the following three requirements: 1) Achieve a 2.0 GPA or higher; 2) Graduate in the top half of his class; 3) Score at least 860 on the SAT or 16 on the ACT.

The qualifications for competing at a junior college are almost non-existent. A golfer must only have graduated from high school or have received a GED. Certain schools and their conferences do maintain stricter standards, however, and athletes at these schools must abide by them.

Athletes are eligible to compete at a junior college for two years only, and may not compete if they have already used up two or more years of athletic eligibility at a four-year school. Some athletes will use a year or two at junior college as a stopping-off point between four-year schools, though. A golfer might compete at a Division I college and decide after his first season to transfer, but because he would by rule have to sit out a year by going directly to another D-I college, might choose to compete at a JC for a year before moving to another four-year school the following season. This information just touches on what you'll need to know, but all the details can be found in the PING Guide.

NCAA.ORG

In addition to the valuable Ping Guide, most juniors and their parents should be become familiar with the information on the NCAA (More info: ncaa.org). Andrea Gaston, the USC women's golf coach, stresses that prospective student-athletes (PSAs) need to register with the NCAA clearinghouse no later than the start of the fall semester of their senior year. "I often suggest sooner," she says. "It is important for PSAs to realize that the NCAA core course requirements are more demanding for a student-athlete than for someone who is just planning to go to college." The number of core courses continues to change, making those requirements different each year. High school counselors are not always aware that the student-athlete may be required to have 14 core classes, when in the previous year a similar student consulted needed only 13 core classes. It would be awful to think that all the hard work on the golf course would not be rewarded because his class load prevented him from being a NCAA "qualifier." If your child is home-schooled, it is essential that you know if your child has the appropriate academic requirements necessary to be eligible for collegiate athletics. It has not been unusual for a nationally ranked player to discover at the end of his senior year that he isn't on track. If discovered in a timely fashion, the problem can be rectified. Otherwise, your child may have to attend a junior college to take the required courses, delaying his entry into college and his eligibility to play on a team. The last thing your junior wants to do is spend the summer after graduation in summer school meeting necessary requirements.

Preparation is Pivotal

Choosing the right college – especially when the college experience will include an athletic element – isn't exactly like selecting something off a restaurant menu to eat for dinner. The decision obviously has much more riding on it, and thus involves careful planning and consideration.

Because of that, golfers planning on playing in college – and their parents – should really start thinking about the college choice early. This doesn't mean that a high school freshman needs to be writing college essays during his first semester in high school, but he and his parents should at least start considering what types of schools and programs might interest him, and begin investigating how the college admissions process works. That way, you will be on top of everything you need to know and won't be caught unprepared for any part of what is essentially one of the most important decisions, and surely the first big decision, of your child's life.

Parents with more than one child can involve the younger children in the older child's college selection process, so that the younger ones have an idea of how it all works when they are ready to go through it.

The Process

When preparing to make a college plan, parents and young golfers should look at three distinct areas of the process: academics, golf and the application and recruiting process. It is very important for your junior to commit to and consider every aspect of this process in a timely manner.

Academics

Early on during a golfer's time in high school, most of his academic focus should be simply on establishing and maintaining a solid grade-point average. At a minimum, he should make sure to meet the NCAA's minimum qualification standards, but should also keep in mind that the better his grades, the better schools he will likely gain admission to. A student with a 3.9 GPA may have a chance of getting into Harvard, but one with a 2.5 won't even be considered. Specific classes are mandatory for certain college admission and you need to make sure his high school counselors are steering him correctly.

The GPA that college admissions officers see is a cumulative score encompassing every semester or quarter of high school, so students need to keep in mind that a failing grade in chemistry during their sophomore year won't exactly get wiped off their record by their senior year. Also, the earlier a student establishes a solid GPA, the easier it is to maintain. Suddenly trying to turn a 2.5 into a 3.0 or better during the senior year is a nearly impossible task.

As a student-athlete moves into his sophomore, junior and senior years, his academic workload will begin to include the standardized testing required by most colleges. Students normally take the PSAT (essentially a practice for the SAT) during the fall of their junior year and then take the SAT early in their senior year. The test is usually given seven times a year, and students may take it more than once if they wish to improve their score. The ACT is offered six times a year, and can also be taken more than once. The PING Guide lists the dates these tests are offered each year.

While these standardized tests can't be studied for in the traditional sense like a student might study for an algebra test, many high schools do incorporate preparation time to ensure their students are comfortable with the process of taking the exams. Some parents will also sign their children up for preparation courses offered by private companies like Kaplan. The College Board also offers online test preparation on its web site (More info: collegeboard.com). The SAT and ACT can often be overwhelming for a first-time test-taker, and because the scores have such a significant bearing on which colleges a student will or will not get into, many people consider test preparation a critical element in the academic process.

Importance of Ranking

An aspiring college golfer will surely want to join his high school team and participate all four years, but there is much more to earning a college golf scholarship than that. The world of college recruiting has changed significantly in recent years, to the point that in the case of many sports, college coaches are more interested in results from competition outside of high school.

For young golfers, this puts an added importance on participating in local, regional and state tournaments. Probably the best way to do this is to join the American Junior Golfers' Association (AJGA. More info: ajga.org). The ranking serves as a critical recruiting tool for college coaches, so establishing a high regional or national ranking with the AJGA is an excellent first step in getting noticed by college coaches.

The PING Guide also lists several other local, regional and national junior golf organizations that can provide young golfers with opportunities to compete at a higher level than they might be able to at their local high schools.

Scholarship Reality

Fully funded programs have six scholarships available for women and only four and a half scholarships for their male counterparts. Top-ranked girls typically expect earning a full ride because there is more scholarship money available and more programs that are becoming fully funded, hence more opportunities to be had. Top-ranked boys will find it increasingly difficult to secure a full ride since coaches have to be much more creative to divvy up the four and a half scholarships. With limited resources, it takes astounding logistics to build depth in a men's program. Unless the PSA is a highly ranked player, he can expect to sign for less than a full scholarship his first year. Based on improvement and overall performance, a recruit might not see a full ride scholarship until his junior or senior years. It is even not uncommon for a very good golfer to receive "partial" scholarships the entire four years if he is a member of a top-ranked program. Do your homework and evaluate your priorities.

The Application and Recruiting Process

While the foundation of a successful search for a college and its golf program is the academic and athletic preparation, the framing, drywall, shingles and nails of the process are all the details to be taken care of in applying and managing the recruiting schedule. Just like with the other elements in the journey toward college golf, finding the right college, making contact with the coach and applying is a complicated, detailed process, and it helps to be organized and prepared. The AJGA has awesome resources for you and your child to help navigate the road to college golf.

During your child's freshman and sophomore years, you should encourage him to start considering what characteristics he might look for in a college. While these may change as he gets older and closer to making a decision, some factors to consider are: location, size, public or private, courses of study, level of competition and of course cost (While you may be planning on junior receiving a full ride to the school of his choice, it might be wise to establish a contingency plan, just in case). If your son wants to study writing, he'll likely want to eliminate schools that offer only a business curriculum. Or if his early AJGA results put him near the top of the regional or national rankings for his age group, it might be smart to tailor the college search to top-level Division I programs and not waste much time or effort considering schools with Division II or III programs. If he has lived in the desert climate of Phoenix all his life and is used to playing all year round, it may not make sense for him to attend Syracuse University, where at least four months of the year the ground is covered with snow.

During those first two years, you can help your young golfer get a feel for some colleges by making informal visits to campuses. During family vacations, you might spend half a day wandering around a nearby university, or during summer, weekend trips can be arranged to visit a number of colleges close to your home. Arranging campus visits during travel for junior golf competitions can also be a convenient way to work these trips into your busy schedule. And don't forget that a prospective golfer can always stop in and introduce himself to the coaching staff; as long as you or your child do not accept anything – a free lunch or a team hat, for instance – the visit won't count as an official campus visit.

Most coaches strongly suggest making "unofficial visits" because they help clarify things when it is time to take "official visits." Also it is important for your child to start building relationships with the coaches to determine whether there is some chemistry. Your child doesn't have to be best friends with his coach (and probably won't be), but a college coach will play a very important role in your child's life, and it is important to see that there is a good personality fit. As you and your child begin to establish a list of schools that might be a good fit, he can contact the coaches of those programs by sending them letters of interest. You may also contact them, but the coaches really want to hear from junior. Remember college coaches will keenly observe family dynamics. The parent-child relationship is important to the well-being of most maturing adults, and at times a coach will steer away from top players with overly pushy parents. Let your child develop his own personal relationship with the coaches. In addition to simple correspondence, motivated young golfers will also include a resume that lists their accomplishments, both athletic and academic.

The recruiting process usually begins in earnest during the junior year. Beginning in September of that year, college coaches are allowed to send your child letters and other recruiting material. They can contact him by telephone once he has completed his junior academic year. Juniors who have minimal competitive experience or who are not highly ranked should seek out programs that are more likely to fit their experience. College coaches and your child waste a lot of time writing unnecessary letters back and forth if your junior doesn't do his research. He should be familiar with the university, its schools of study and the history of the golf program itself, including current overall record and ranking.

Once the senior year comes around, the entire college process should be in high gear. This is when junior will start sending out applications (usually during the first few months of the school year) and arranging for official visits to the schools he is most interested in. Athletes are allowed official visits (those that are paid for by the school) to five colleges, so it's smart for your kid to narrow down his choices to a select few by early fall. It's rare that an athlete uses all his official visits, but since they are available, it makes sense to use them if he can fit them all into his schedule.

It is during these visits that an athlete often gets a true feel for the school, campus atmosphere, school spirit and the golf program.

Personal one-on-one time with the faculty, administration, coach and team members is very important to helping junior make a quality decision when faced with several great choices. Junior should make a journal of each trip, noting answers to specific questions and concerns, so that he can reflect on specific pros and cons when it is time to make his final decision. There is a trend to make a verbal commitment during a visit – that is, he verbally tells the coach that he plans to attend that school and be a part of the golf program. Since kids and coaches get caught up in the emotion of the experience, it is wiser for your child to consider all of his options and opportunities with counsel from parents and grandparents and his "swing" coach. He should definitely be away from campus when he makes his final decision. It is important to keep in mind that a verbal commitment is not binding in any way. While we would all like to think that giving our word would be enough – surely most coaches feel this way – it is a somewhat ugly truth of the recruiting world that these verbal commitments sometimes don't hold much weight. We've all heard the stories about the star high school quarterback "verballing" to Florida State, only to change his mind before signing day and commit to Miami. If he doesn't get sucked into making a verbal commitment, then chances are he can walk away from the process with his integrity intact.

To keep athletes from backing out on commitments, the NCAA has established a National Letter of Intent program. Basically, the letter of intent is a contract between the athlete and the school that says Jimmy will compete for the Lions and the Lions' coach will have a scholarship waiting for Jimmy when he arrives in the fall. It is a binding agreement between the school and the athletes, with penalties for withdrawing.

Future college golfers have two periods during which they can sign letters of intent. There is an early signing period in November and the regular signing period in April. Coaches like athletes to sign early for many reasons. Signing early allows the student-athlete to enjoy the rest of their senior year without having to worry about where they will go to school. It frees them up and lets them focus on school and preparing for college early. Let's say early decisions are a win-win for the universities and the athletes involved.

Many juniors and their parents tend to panic if they do not have their plans solidified in this early signing period. Only if a golfer is one-hundred-percent certain he wants to play for State U is it best to commit during the early signing period. Once April comes around, the situations at many schools can get pretty hairy. Because it is hard to juggle the allotted scholarships, coaches have started giving players ultimatums. For example a coach may say, "This scholarship offer is only available until the middle of October, but after that I will have to reconsider the offer in order to insure a possibility with other recruits." It is understandable that college coaches need to finalize their recruiting class, but do not let junior be pressured into making a decision on those premises. If he is good enough for a scholarship; the right opportunity will present itself. On the same token, do not let junior string along a coach from a school that he has no real interest in playing for. Honesty goes a long way in the recruiting process, and coaches will have a lot more respect for your child in the long run if he remains honest throughout the process.

Each coach has a limited number of scholarships available, but will be in contact with more golfers than he has scholarships for because he has to cover his back in case a prized recruit chooses another school. In the same vain, most high school seniors have more than one college they are considering. Billy might be dead set on playing for State U, but when another recruit backs out at a better school and Billy decides to go there, then the coach at State U might call Jimmy with a scholarship offer out of the blue. It's a win for Billy and a win for Jimmy. A lot of things can change on a day-to-day basis when the recruiting calendar begins to wind down. The main point: be patient throughout the entire process.

All this can seem quite complicated, so it's best to be as organized as possible in order to ensure you meet all the proper deadlines. Some might think of negotiating the college recruitment process like writing a term paper – instead of simply sitting down and going from start to finish, it makes sense to craft an outline, or plan of attack, and make your way through it piece by piece.

Ted Gleason, a former UCLA golfer, former professional player and former men's golf coach at both Southern Methodist University and the University of Southern California, has founded a consulting business to help juniors and parents wade through this often overwhelming process. His experiences as a recruit himself, a college player and a top college coach are invaluable to junior golfers and their families. His business "Road to College Golf" is double-faceted. He helps students identify the "best fit" colleges for them according to both their playing experience and their academic ability. He then helps a junior navigate his way through the decision process. "The Road to College" services not only include advice and counsel during the recruiting procedures, but they also include opportunities before the junior enters the process. He helps with player development through establishing practice strategies and routines that will help get a solicitous junior to his goals as he enters the recruiting year. Gleason dedicates himself to finding sound preparation methods and an appropriate action plan for his clients so they can confidently head toward a college program that will best meet their needs, goals, and desires. (More info: Ted@roadtocollegegolf.com) As the competition for scholarships and a place on a starting team get more intense, more consulting companies are apt to surface.

   Parents and students can take heart, though, in the thought that junior's athletic prowess will only help him in getting into college. While admissions standards aren't necessarily loosened for standout athletes at some schools, the process is often speeded along by eager coaches.

   James Shuman and William Bowen explored this phenomenon in their 2001 book, "The Game of Life: College Sports and Educational Values." In it, they wrote, "Athletes who are recruited, and who end up on the carefully winnowed lists of desired candidates submitted by coaches to the admissions office now enjoy a very substantial statistical advantage in the admissions process – a much greater advantage than that enjoyed by other targeted groups such as under-represented minority students, alumni children, and other legacies."

Other Options

Much of the above information applies only to golfers seeking scholarships at Division I institutions. Those hoping to play at a Division II school will likely be met with partial scholarship offers, and those targeting Division III schools or Ivy League colleges should know that athletic scholarships are not offered at all.

   Throughout the journey from the first day of high school to the first day of college, parents should keep in mind that the dream of a full-ride scholarship to Stanford may not come to fruition. With a little planning for this scenario, it shouldn't be a major heartache.

   When communicating with admissions officers at different schools, ask about academic scholarships or need-based scholarships. Look into financial aid options offered by the school or the possibility of taking out student loans from private lenders. Remember that there are more positives to playing college golf than simply the financial. Junior can have a fulfilling experience that will serve him for years.

15
Inside Golf Organizations

....

**"People understand contests. You take a bunch of kids
throwing rocks at random and people look askance,
but if you go and hold a rock-throwing contest,
people understand that."**

Don Murray, football coach

....

People, organizations and money, in that order, make the golf world
go round. When we, as parents and coaches, understand their roles
and motivations, we're in a better position to help our kids develop a
roadmap for their future. Knowing how the system works makes our
own contributions to the golf world more effective.

Here, then, is the inside skinny on golf organizations, ordered in
the way a parent and kid may encounter them.

USGA

The USGA is the backbone of golf in the United States. A non-profit
organization founded in 1894, it is run by golfers for the benefit of
golfers. The USGA is best known for putting on the U.S. Open – one of
the sport's four majors – each year, but is also behind 12 other
national championship tournaments every year. It also serves as the
game's governing body in the United States and Mexico, working with
the Royal and Ancient in St. Andrews, Scotland to develop the internationally recognized Rules of Golf.

The USGA and You

So where does an organization with so much influence across the
country get the money to support its various programs? A major percentage of it comes from golf fans who either watch the U.S. Open,
U.S. Women's Open and U.S. Senior Open on television or attend the
tournaments in person. Of the USGA's $126 million in revenues for
2006, more than $93 million came directly from ticket sales and
broadcast rights for its events.

The second-biggest chunk of money comes from its membership
program. The USGA offers golfers who wish to support the organization a number of membership packages with various benefits. The most
attractive of these, to most golf fans, is preferred status in purchasing

tickets to the USGA's championships, including the U.S. Open.

A one-year USGA membership can be purchased for as little as $15, though there also five higher levels of membership, from Champion Club ($50) to Patron Club ($1,000). With each increased level comes more benefits. At the highest level, two complimentary tickets to the U.S. Open, the U.S. Women's Open, the U.S. Senior Open and the U.S. Amateur are included. Most levels of membership also include a copy of the official Rules of Golf, subscriptions to the USGA's publications, a USGA bag tag and member discounts on apparel and gifts.

By becoming members, golfers help the USGA support programs across the country. The organization commits $5 million every year to a grant program that provides golf opportunities to disadvantaged children and disabled people, and also runs a program that allows for professional development opportunities for college graduates. These are just a few of the positive programs the USGA uses to foster the development of the game.

The USGA also boasts more than 130 state and regional associations. Almost anyone in the U.S. is served by one of these associations and can get involved on the local level. Those who wish to volunteer can do so at any of the USGA's championship events – each is supported by hundreds of eager volunteers every year.

Organization

Promoting golf to a nationwide population of some 290 million people and serving the needs of nearly 30 million golfers require the effort of many individuals and organizations.

The USGA is organized into nine regions, each with a director of regional affairs, with one senior director overseeing all of the nine. Each of the regional directors serves as a liaison between the USGA and the many state and regional associations in his or her specific area. There is also an executive committee made up of 15 volunteer members who function as the USGA's board of directors. The members represent all corners of the country, and, just like the board of any major corporation, the USGA's board has a president, vice president, secretary, treasurer and general counsel. A separate Women's Committee, which includes 14 members and three officers, is charged with running each of the seven women's and girls' championships the USGA puts on every year.

Within the USGA, there are several departments focusing on specific elements of the organization: a Rules Department, a Championships Department, a Handicap Department, a Grants and Fellowship department and a Greens Section department. Each department is uniquely critical to the ongoing growth and development of the game. Every four years, in conjunction with The Royal and Ancient in Scotland, the USGA authorizes revisions made to the Rules of Golf. (2008 will be the next possible opportunity for rule changes.)

The USGA Handicap department was founded in 1912 and continues today to make it possible for golfers of differing abilities to enjoy fair competition. The Championships Department is responsible for handling the details and requirements for all 13 of the game's most prestigious events. Established in 1920, the Green Section involves itself in every phase of golf course maintenance and management and is a leading authority in turfgrass management.

The newest department of the USGA may be the strongest arm of the organization yet. Launched in 1997, the USGA Grant and Fellowship Department is dedicated to young people and their dreams. It is aggressively putting millions of dollars back into the game through its devotion to promoting leadership and philanthropy in its unique fellowship and grant programs for college graduates. The USGA supports a variety of introductory and special golf programs through its enthusiastic grant program. The money put back into the golfing community has impacted hundreds of thousands of people, especially children and people with disabilities, and will continue to foster their ideal: "The game is one for all."

Professional Tournaments

The most popular and well-known of its tournaments, the U.S. Open also brings in the majority of the USGA's revenues each year – significantly more than the $6.25 million purse it hands out. It is open to any male player with a handicap index at or below 1.4, and there are regional qualifiers for the tournament, which is held in June every year at a different golf course each time.

The USGA also puts on the U.S. Women's Open in June or July and the U.S. Senior Open in July of each year. The Women's Open requires a handicap index of 4.4 or lower; the Senior Open takes players 50 or older with an index of 3.4 or better.

Amateur Competition

Outsiders may view the organization of the three professional tournaments as the major function of the USGA, but participation in its 10 amateur events make up an even greater portion of its influence. Included in the USGA's offerings each year is an amateur tournament for every level: the U.S. Amateur, the U.S. Women's Amateur, the U.S. Senior Amateur, the U.S. Senior Women's Amateur, the U.S. Amateur Public Links (commonly referred to as the Publinks), the U.S. Women's Amateur Public Links, the U.S. Junior Amateur, the U.S. Girls Junior, the U.S. Mid-Amateur and the U.S. Women's Mid Amateur.

In addition, the USGA has a hand in putting on the USGA Men's State Team Championship, the U.S. Women's State Team Championship, the Walker Cup Matches, the Curtis Cup Matches and the Men's and Women's World Amateur team events. Most players consider it an honor to be picked as a team member for any of these prestigious events.

While the USGA's championships are, as their names imply, open to all golfers who qualify, the reality is that most golfers would be happy to compete for their local club championship. With that in mind, the USGA maintains a directory of amateur tournaments on its website (usga.org). The directory is searchable by state, month and type of tournament.

The USGA, with its section and district offices, interacts with and offers support to thousands of high schools' golf teams. The state athletic associations operate competitions for high schools. Highly competitive junior players will likely focus on playing in the top USGA championships and regional or national tournaments sanctioned by the American Junior Golf Association (More info: ajga.org)

PGA of America

The PGA (More info: PGA.com) of America touts itself as the largest working sports organization in the world, boasting some 28,000 member PGA Professionals whose purpose it is to promote the game of golf and support its growth. It is a not-for-profit organization started in 1916 by a group of New York-area golfers. The PGA of America is the grassroots organization of golf in the United States, but also is the group that runs the annual PGA championship (one of golf's four majors) and a number of other professional tournaments. The general public often confuses the PGA of America as the same organization as the PGA Tour; and while they often compliment one another, they are two distinctly different organizations with completely different goals.

Organization

The PGA of America is headquartered in Palm Beach Gardens, Florida, where it maintains a staff of about 175. The organization also runs a group of three golf courses in Port St. Lucie, Florida that make up PGA Village, which also includes a learning center and a historical center – all are aimed at making the game of golf accessible to the public.

But what really keeps the PGA of America afloat are its 41 regional sections spread out across the country. Most sections have arms dedicated to supporting the game, golf course development and philanthropic efforts.

It is also in charge of the Professional Golf Management program that is used to educate and certify both teaching professionals and other golf industry employees, and runs the PGA Merchandise Show and the PGA Fall Expo, the golf industry's two significant trade shows each year. The PGA of America is most well known for organizing the PGA Championship and its other professional events each year.

Professional Competition

The PGA of America's four professional events include the PGA Championship, the Senior PGA Championship, the PGA Grand Slam of Golf and the Ryder Cup. The first three are annual events, while the Ryder Cup is held every other year and pits a U.S. team against a team made up of European players.

The PGA Championship is the last of golf's four majors held each year and offers one of the largest purses of any event. In 2005, winner Phil Mickelson took home $1.17 million of the total $6.25 million purse. Because the PGA of America is at its roots an organization dedicated to developing the game through its certified teachers, it allows a number of club professionals into the playing field of the PGA Championship each year.

The PGA also puts on the Senior PGA Championship and the PGA Grand Slam of Golf, a late November event that brings together the winners of the previous season's four majors. Every other year, the PGA is responsible for fielding a team of top touring professionals from the United States PGA Tour to compete against the best professionals from the European Tour in the Ryder Cup competition. The Ryder Cup, one of the last great sporting events founded on prestige rather than prize money, spans 34 competitions over 77 years.

Amateur Competition

The PGA of America has many more events than the four annual professional tournaments that receive most of the publicity. It also puts on a minority college golf championship, a junior series, a club professionals championship, a junior championship and a number of other specialty events that cater to various segments of the golfing population.

PGA Professionals

The heartbeat of the PGA of America is its corps of professionals. These include men and women who are dedicated teaching professionals as well as those who manage every aspect of the business side of golf operations and the endeavors associated with the golf industry.

Learning the game of golf is hardly an easy task, and it is not something a beginning player can quickly pick up on her own. But a general mastery of the basic shots can go a long way toward turning a player getting started in the game into one who is hooked for life. That's where professional instruction comes in, whether it is for a junior player or for an older person newly introduced to golf.

Along with the boom in golf over the last decade or so (often referred to as "the Tiger effect"), there has been an increased demand for qualified teachers. The best teachers are usually those certified by either the PGA of America or through the LPGA Teaching and Club Professional Division. The PGA of America requires that teachers learn their craft through completing a degree at one of 14 accredited universities offering Professional Golf Management (PGM) programs, or they can become PGA Professionals by completing a shorter course after attaining a degree in another field. The LPGA Teaching Professional is certified once she has taken and passed testing requirements associated with their National Education Program Series.

LPGA

Like the professionals of the PGA of America, the LPGA (More info: LPGA.com) professionals are often associated with the organization touting its most notable superstars on the LPGA Tour. However, the Ladies Professional Golf Association is much more than just what you may see should you tune into one of its events some Sunday afternoon. It is a nonprofit association founded in 1950 with the primary purpose being to promote worldwide interest in the game of golf. The purpose behind the LPGA is multifaceted and has continued to grow strong throughout its existence. It is dedicated to establishing and maintaining high standards in the promotion, development and conduct of women's professional golf activities and to provide vocational opportunities and continuing education in teaching, tournament play, golf shop operations, and the support of junior programs. The LPGA Tour is the reason the LPGA was founded, but its organizers quickly realized there was much more needed to support a strong foundation for women in golf.

Teaching and Club Professional Division

The LPGA Teaching Division was originally founded in 1959 as an outgrowth of the LPGA Tour membership. The LPGA T & CP supports the golf industry with a strong network of head professionals, assistant professionals, teaching professionals, directors of golf, facility owners and administrators with an expertise in golf shop operations, as well as high school and college coaches. The LPGA T & CP Division boasts a membership of over 1,200 golf professionals and is considerably smaller than its PGA counterpart, but it has earned a reputation as the leader in research-based golf education and as a pioneer in state-of-the art instruction.

Candidates for membership in either organization are required to play the game at a proficient level and take classes and programs that will educate in all aspects of their profession. Once candidates have completed the playing and education requirements providing them with a basic knowledge of the golf profession, they must take a series of evaluations and tests. In order to be a member of high standing and obtain Class A status, members are required to take tests and pass with high marks in all subjects.

The LPGA T & CP Division is divided into five geographical sections, including support for members living in Japan and Canada. Each section has a governing body that consists of a president, vice president, secretary and treasurer. A full-time staff based at LPGA Headquarters in Daytona Beach, Florida runs the daily operations of the LPGA T & CP. There is a six-member, elected executive committee consisting of the national president and the five regional section presidents.

Juniors' Organizations

American Junior Golf Association

The American Junior Golf Association (AJGA. More info: ajga.org) is a non-profit organization whose mission is to develop young golfers and help them earn college scholarships. Having offered its first national tournament in 1978, the AJGA now has more than 160 former players participating on the PGA Tour and the LPGA Tour. According to its website, the AJGA's influence on college golf is even more substantial – 18 of the last 24 NCAA men's champions and 18 of the last 21 women's champions came through the AJGA system.

The AJGA offers 75 tournaments each year, along with 45 qualifiers. The organization offers three levels of membership – a future player membership ($90) for those 12 and under who are not yet old enough to participate in AJGA tournaments, a junior membership ($195), that is recommended for players who are freshmen in high school or younger, and a college-bound student membership ($245) for sophomores and juniors hoping to play golf in college.

The junior membership allows players access to AJGA tournaments as well as other benefits, while the college-bound student membership offers those players resources valuable to helping attain a golf scholarship: the PING American Golf Guide, a player profile, a video swing analysis and a guide to the process of becoming a college golfer.

Many of the AJGA alumni cherish their tournament days on the AJGA circuit. Putting junior golf into perspective, Phil Mickelson has said more than once that he wanted to stay in the AJGA until they kicked him out, because it's fun. He said, "You're going to be a junior only so long, and then it's over. I'll have the rest of my life to beat my head against the wall."

Future Collegians World Tour

As the name suggests, this junior golf tour is geared to helping young golfers turn their attention to top-level competition and the opportunity to earn the attention of a college golf program. Although it was founded almost two decades after the AJGA, the Future Collegians World Tour (FCWT. More info: fcwtgolf.com) junior golf tour is similar in that it is also a not-for-profit organization committed to the development of junior golfers. It is based in Clearwater, Florida and offers 50 tournaments across the U.S. Membership costs $199 for one year and is available to any player under the age of 19 who has not yet entered college.

International Junior Golf Tour

Founded in 1995, the International Junior Golf Tour (IJGT. More info: IJGT.com) is one of few organizations that helps golfers 19 and under develop and showcase their skills. The IJGT is based in Hilton Head Island, South Carolina and has characteristics similar to both the AJGA and the FCWT.

Players can become members by paying an annual fee of $225, which entitles them to entry in any of the tour's 45 tournaments each year. At least 30 of those are Golfweeek/Titleist ranked events, which ensures that the players are participating in high-profile events. Members can also access the IJGT's player profile service, which allows them to create a profile of themselves and their accomplishments. College coaches can gain access to the site through their own login and password, and many start their recruiting process by scanning these and other player-profile databases.

The tour offers tournaments from September through May (including a tour championship) at distinguished courses across the country. For instance, in Southern California, the tour makes stops at Torrey Pines Golf Course – the site of the Buick Invitational every year and the U.S. Open in 2008 – and La Costa Resort & Spa, where much golf history has been made over the years since both The Tournament of Champions and The World Golf Championships Accenture Match Play Championships have called La Costa home.

California Junior Tour

The California Junior Tour bills itself as the state's premier fall-winter junior golf tour. Started in 2002, it offers competitive golf for boys and girls in two different age ranges (12-14 and 15-18) from September through mid-April. The tour puts on twenty 36-hole events throughout the state, stretching from San Francisco to San Diego, and players can participate in either the fall or winter session.

Tournaments are played at top-flight golf courses: La Costa was on the schedule in 2005-06, as was Empire Lakes Golf Club in Rancho Cucamonga, which has hosted a Nationwide Tour tournament in recent years. The tour's annual registration fee is $165, and it costs an average of $225 to play in each tournament.

The California Junior Tour (More info: californiajuniortour.com) was founded by PGA member Johnny Gonzales and executive director Bernie O'Brien. Its mission is to help junior players develop their games while also assisting them in getting exposure to college coaches. A lot of good players come out of California's junior ranks – this is yet another great venue for the kids to test their skills.

NFHS

The principals, superintendents and school boards of most high schools and junior high schools in the United States are members of their state's school athletic association. The association, also called a federation, sets rules for high school athletics in individual states, controls athlete recruitment and holds championships, among its other duties. The New York State Public High School Athletic Association (NYSPHSAA. More info: nysphsaa.org) and the California Interscholastic Federation (CIF. More info: cifstate.org) are two examples.

State school athletic associations in turn are members of a national organization called the National Federation of State High School Associations (NFHS. More info: nfhs.org). The NFHS provides leadership and national coordination for state school athletic associations. The NFHS publishes reports on sports safety issues and a survey that tracks participation levels in various school sports.

Golf Academies

It didn't use to be that you sent your 12-year-old golfer off to a specialized academy to train like an Olympic athlete. Think again, because times are changing. Golf Academies are becoming more commonplace thanks to the demand for top-level instruction, their successes and, of course, the prize money on the professional tours. There are three junior golf academies in the United States – golf academies dedicated to fueling the dreams of golf kids and their parents from around the world. Each is a sort of pro tour boarding school where youngsters take college-preparatory classes in the morning and hit balls in the afternoon.

While these academies have long since graduated from being specialized college-preparatory schools for golf kids to legendary institutions that seem to control the destiny of golf, the jury is still out on whether these will be the breeding ground for future golf champions on the professional level. It may take many years to analyze their impact on the game, but it is obvious the intense golf training they provide is here to stay. The golf academies are following suit of the tennis academies. While most academies hope to attract the best and brightest young golfers, it is also fair to say that acceptance to a worthwhile program also is dependent on talent and high finances. With the stakes so high, many families are willing to give it all they have to see that junior is well prepared for the highest levels of competition. The focus of most academies is pretty straightforward: to prepare promising junior golfers for possible collegiate golf careers and to eventually prepare them for life as golf professionals.

All the academies have had huge success in placing juniors in promising golf programs at colleges around the country, yet admittedly there are but a few alumni making a great impact in the world of professional golf. Ted Meekma, director of the IMG Academies, which also run schools for tennis, baseball, basketball and soccer, speaks honestly when he says, "Most of the kids here are moving more on the college-scholarship track than the PGA Tour or LPGA Tour track. We're going to help you reach your full potential. Now, that doesn't mean you're going to turn professional. A pretty decent percentage here has a good chance to play on the Tour, but what's that percentage? Might be 10 to 15 percent of the full-time kids."

The David Leadbetter Golf Academy in Bradenton, Florida is proud of its success and hangs a big sign on property that reads, "The Home of Junior Golf," but it isn't the only "school" in town. The Saddlebrook Preparatory School up the road in Wesley Chapel, near Tampa, and the International Junior Golf Academy at Hilton Head Island, South Carolina, are every bit as intensive and arguably as talent-laden.

The Arnold Palmer Golf Academy's home is at Saddlebrook Preparatory, and since 1993 golf legend Arnold Palmer has supported efforts to breed excellence in this academy-style environment. According to saddlebrook.com, Palmer says, "I have personally approved this program and its techniques, and am confident that students will benefit from the training and continue to grow in the healthy learning environment at Saddlebrook Preparatory."

The Director of Junior Golf Programs at the IJGA in South Carolina is Gary Gilchrist. Gilchrist was wooed from The Leadbetter Academy while being its top junior instructor. He has a long history of coaching talented junior golfers who have won virtually every major junior championship in the United States. Some of his former students include Michelle Wie, David Gossett, Aree and Naree Song, Casey Wittenberg, Ty Tryon and Virada Nirapathpongporn, to name just a few. Teamed up with Nike, the IJGA is quickly becoming one of the premier golf academies. Like the other two main golf academies, the IJGA is committed to working with juniors, helping them become the champions of the future.

These academies are not cheap. A full-time course at the Leadbetter school, which includes a full academic program, golf training and boarding, runs $40,000 or more a year, giving it a higher price tag than all but only the most expensive colleges. The school also offers junior camps and sessions for post-graduate players preparing for a professional career, as well as instruction for adult professionals and amateurs.

Just as Palmer continually pushed himself to the next level of competition, these institutions have also resisted the urge to rest on their laurels. Instead, they look forward by bringing in new management, introducing cutting-edge techniques and state-of-the-art equipment and expanding programs. The academies continue to do well, producing young champions as well as good college graduates. Although everything they do is directed to being the best, becoming great and being top dog, Leadbetter himself expresses some caution for such a mindset. "You just hope you're not breeding a false sense of greatness," Leadbetter says. "Not everyone can be a great player. Golf is a great entry to a lot of other areas in life. One has to be realistic, but hey, if you've got goals and dreams and aspirations, why not chase them for a while?"

Mediocrity is not a word you would associate with "Academy Kids." At their best, instructors agree that these kids seem so self-directed and so purposeful that it's almost embarrassing to be around them. A typical day for Leadbetter Academy kids starts with a 7 a.m. breakfast; then a 7:30 bus ride to school (two private schools have specially developed academic programs for Academy kids; a third is on the site of the main campus). Junior then has four hours of classes, which include nothing but college-preparatory-level curriculum (no free periods, no shop class). She then takes the bus back to campus, has a quick lunch, hops on another bus ride out to the range for four or more hours of golf, mental training with the psychologist and physical training. Then it's back to the dorm for a supervised study hall with more studying until 10 or 11 p.m. (unofficial lights out). The only sign of "normal" teenager behavior might be an iPod strapped to junior or maybe a visit from the Domino's Pizza delivery guy somewhere between study hall and lights out.

Students at all three academies come from different backgrounds and from all around the world. The one bond all of these students share is their passion for golf and their commitment to becoming better junior golfers. "There are lots of very talented people here," says Jonathan Yarwood, a David Leadbetter instructor. "If I gave them every option in the world to do anything on any given day, every single one of them would say, 'I'd like to practice golf.'"

Don't expect to have golf great Arnold Palmer or teaching guru David Leadbetter greet your kid personally when she arrives at the academy. These institutions are great examples of American enterprise. Palmer and Leadbetter have spent years developing the programs used at these institutions, handing down systems, techniques and guidelines. Academy instructors use those systems and techniques and follow those guidelines to reflect the master's way. David Leadbetter himself is rarely at Bradenton. That is not unusual. Though the facility bears his name and the instructors are trained in his method, David Leadbetter does not teach your child the finer points of bunker technique, just as Conrad Hilton won't be checking you in at the Hilton.

For example, at the Leadbetter Academy, each coach participates in a cutting-edge, one-year coaching certification program and is then re-certified every 12 months as part of a continuing education program. These highly trained instructors will be doing all of the hard teaching and guiding. Gary Gilchrist, a former Leadbetter disciple and director of instruction at the IJGA says, "You're developing a kid. You know as a parent the energy you need to have. Well, these coaches have eight to 10 kids in their group, and they're there every day being that role model for them, providing that parental guidance." Without a doubt, you must trust the influences that your child will be exposed to.

Paula Creamer, Aree Song and David Gossett are all graduates of the Leadbetter Academy. There are other players who have gone the academy route and look to have a bright future and a promising career in professional golf. Maria Sharapova may be the most famous alumnus of IMG's Nick Bollettieri Tennis Academy, and successful athletes like Nomar Garciaparra, Kevin Garnett and Demarcus Beasley have studied at other IMG Academies. But what about the hundreds of other students who have paid their thousands of dollars and have dedicated themselves to a brutal regimen in the prime of their youth? What happens to their dreams of being the next Tiger Woods, Andre Agassi, Michael Jordan or Garciaparra?

Critics attack the junior sports academy model as being one-dimensional and limiting a student's typical high school experience. There is no question that "Academy Kids" won't be in the school play, in a marching band or on the cheerleading squad. They won't be on the debate team, and they will not participate in any other sports. "Academy Kids" don't spend a lot of time socializing with non-golfers. Organizers at the top academies will point proudly to weekend trips to the beach or the shopping mall among a few other random activities provided for full-time academy students, but mostly it seems an afterthought at best.

Stephen Hamblin, executive director of the AJGA says, "I don't think it's the only model. At our level, I see a lot of kids with the same focus and dedication seen in the Academy Kid. They don't stick out to me." In defense of the academy lifestyle he adds, "Those kids are talented, well mannered, and well-rounded. Every sport is demanding more time these days, and I think at least the academies provide a viable option for serious golfers."

Sport psychologist Dr. Bob Rotella isn't completely against academies. He says that "This is a fine model for some, but I don't see any examples of a kid who was really crummy going to an academy and becoming a great player. If the goal is to get good at a quicker age, then perhaps the academies are a good model. It is more a model of 'put all of your eggs in one basket and hope it works.'"

Success in golf used to be considered accidental or happenstance; now with the academy approach taking hold, it seems more orchestrated and calculated. Meekma says, "I think this is a very healthy option, but I wouldn't say this is the future of professional golf." Experts agree that the academy approach isn't going away any time soon. Most see it improving. Even if golfers are not at an academy, the new generation of golfers is going to train much like those kids strutting around an academy facility. If nothing else, academy lifestyle has raised the bar and demands a much more disciplined approach toward golf training. The continued success of promising prodigies will only fuel the fire and the debate.

As your kid develops her competitive ability, you will often have to make a choice between tournament preparation and the rigors of a school schedule. Golf academies are a good but expensive alternative to traditional options. Most of the serious golf kids, whether they experienced high levels of competitive success or not, enjoyed having their school schedules woven around golf training. Paula Creamer loved her days spent at the David Leadbetter Academy and says, "The place just kind of breeds excellence. There are a lot of people there who understand just what it takes to live a dream." While reality for Creamer is a fairy tale and a dream come true; of course, dreams have a downside, too. Unfortunately others painfully realize that sometimes the dream doesn't come true. Sometimes, a lot of times, it doesn't come true. This is when one must lean on the old adage that the journey is much more worthwhile than the destination.

For more information on golf academies, go to leadbetter.com, ijga.com, or saddlebrook.com.

There are truly thousands of options available for golf schools these days. Type in golf schools on google and within seconds you will have millions of choices. Your choices are wide-ranging and definitely not limited to the all or nothing mentality. All golf academies and golf schools are not of the Leadbetter variety, but how are you to know which one to choose? Research and word of mouth are your best bets. A little knowledge can go a long way in helping you choose the right golf school for you or your child. Big-name instructors are a great place to start, but they are not the only game in town, nor or they always the best value for your dollar. Custom academies are a great option to help meet the needs of your child. For students of the game who want a short-term academy experience to help improve their game, there are plenty of academies across the country that offers four-day or weeklong academies.

At the Sycuan Resort (formerly Singing Hills Country Club) near San Diego, for example, golfers can register in a premier academy or a school of golf for women, or they can personalize their golf package in one of the resort's custom academies. Each of the academy options includes range instruction as well as on-course instruction and many other perks, and the courses are taught by certified PGA and LPGA instructors. Prices range from $1,790 for a three-day academy to $2,790 for the five-day academy, and include lodging at the resort's luxury hotel. This is quite typical of many golf resorts in the U.S.

NCAA

The National Collegiate Athletic Association (NCAA. More info: ncaa. org) is an organization comprised of more than 1,250 institutions as well as the conferences, organizations and individuals committed to the best interests, education and athletic participation of student-athletes. It is responsible for setting rules for academic eligibility and scholarships for college-bound athletes. The NCAA also enforces regulations regarding amateur status and drug testing at championship events. The organization celebrated 100 years of dedication to the student-athlete in 2006. The purpose of the NCAA is to govern competition in a fair, safe, equitable and sportsmanlike manner, and to integrate intercollegiate athletics into higher education so that the educational experience of the student-athlete is paramount.

Divisions

Schools are classified into three divisions based on how many sports they offer and the availability of athletic scholarships. Division I schools must offer seven sports for both men and women and meet minimum financial-aid award requirements for their athletic programs. Division II schools offer four sports for each gender, and student-athletes generally pay for college through a combination of scholarship money, grants, student loans and employment earnings. A Division III school does not provide athletic scholarships but runs five or more sports. Division I has about 320 schools, Division II has 280, and Division III has grown to over 400.

Given the size of athletic budgets, the very best coaches and college players participate in Division I. Consequently, the best college teams are also in Division I. The best teams in Divisions II and III hold their own, though, when they compete against Division I schools at the NCAA Championships. A school's academic reputation has no bearing on divisional classification. Harvard is in Division I, whereas MIT is a Division III school.

The number of schools offering golf programs is higher than those offering football and about equal to those that offer basketball and soccer. Men's golf is available at nearly 780 of the 1,000-plus NCAA schools, allowing some 7,500 student-athletes to participate in collegiate athletics. Title IX has allowed women's collegiate golf programs to grow immensely since its inception in 1982. Women's golf is now offered at about 500 schools, giving 3,600 female student-athletes an opportunity to hone their skills.

Operations

The NCAA holds 87 championships in 22 sports, including golf. Television rights to these championships are a very big deal, generating 80 percent of the NCAA's $340 million in annual revenues. Seventy percent of the championship money is put back into Division I grants-in-aid, coaching salaries and administration.

The 14-member executive committee, comprising school heads, is the driving force behind NCAA operations. Then there are the inescapable sports and rules committees. Men's and women's golf have separate golf committees for each division: I, II and III. The "national office" represents the 350 employees in Indianapolis, Indiana who make up the infrastructure of the Association. The entire organization is comprised of members and staff. Many believe the Association rules college athletics; however, it is actually a bottom-up organization in which the members rule the Association.

NAIA

The National Association of Intercollegiate Athletics (NAIA. More info: naia.org) is the second-largest association, after the NCAA, of fully accredited four-year colleges. Like the NCAA, the NAIA sets eligibility rules for athletes attending one of the 400 member colleges. There are 172 men's golf programs and 128 for women, with five scholarships in each program. Unlike the NCAA, recruitment to NAIA colleges has fewer restrictions and there is no clearinghouse.

NJCAA

Junior colleges offer opportunities for players who are not sure whether they want to attend a four-year school. Many student-athletes want to experience professional golf as soon as possible; other college players eventually transfer to four-year schools.

The National Junior College Athletic Association (NJCAA. More info: njcaa.org) boasts a membership of 530 two-year institutions participating in 15 sports, including men's and women's golf.

PGA Tour

Understanding the difference between the PGA of America and the PGA Tour (More info: pgatour.com) is often difficult for those new to golf, and often the two are used in speech as interchangeable entities. The relationship is quite simple, though, if thought of in terms of a college or university. The members of the PGA of America are the professors in the business school, while the PGA Tour members are the graduates of the institution who have moved on to become successful accountants or financial planners. Put more directly, PGA Professionals teach the game of golf, while players on the PGA Tour play golf each week for prize money.

The PGA Tour has 48 official events each year, plus another 11 unofficial events, for a total of 59. It gives out approximately $250 million in purses each year, and holds tournaments in 22 states plus Scotland, Portugal and Canada. Players can earn a Tour card for each season in a number of different ways, and once they have a card, players are free to participate or not participate in any event they choose.

The Tour is not just about making money for its member players, though. Its tournaments pump money into the communities in which they are held each year, and its charitable donations since 1938 are expected to surpass the $1-billion mark in the coming years. The PGA Tour also has a program set up that provides financial assistance to players and caddies in need.

Other Tours

Under the umbrella of the PGA Tour, there are also two other men's tours: the Champions Tour and the Nationwide Tour.

The Champions Tour (formerly the Senior Tour) is for players 50 and older, and features events every week from late January through late October. Prize money is not as high as on the PGA Tour, but purses can exceed $2.5 million for certain tournaments throughout the season.

The Nationwide Tour is essentially the developmental arm of the PGA Tour. The top players (as many as the top 20) each year from the Nationwide Tour earn exemptions to play on the PGA Tour the following season. Nationwide Tour events are played at lesser golf courses and usually in front of smaller galleries than PGA Tour events or even Champions Tour events. Consequently, the purses average in the $400,000-$600,000 range.

LPGA Tour

The Ladies Professional Golf Association (LPGA. More info: LPGA.com) is the women's version of the PGA Tour, however its organization also encompasses the LPGA Teaching and Club Professionals.

The LPGA is the longest-running women's sporting organization in the world, having surpassed the 50-year mark in 2000. Compare that to the run of the Women's United Soccer Association (five years) or the Women's National Basketball Association (10 years), and its longevity and success is impressive. It has its roots in the Women's Professional Golf Association, which was founded in 1944 and received important financial support from Wilson sporting goods in 1948.

The LPGA Tour consists of 34 tournaments each year and hands out prizes of over $45 million. Average purses are in the range of $1 million.

The LPGA Teaching and Club Professionals has a membership of about 1,300, and like the PGA Tour, the LPGA is involved in various charitable ventures. These include supporting junior golf programs, awarding scholarships to college-bound golfers and raising money for the Susan G. Komen Breast Cancer Foundation, its official charity.

Other Tours

Like the PGA Tour, the LPGA also has other tours under its influence: the Women's Senior Golf Tour (WSGT) and the Futures Tour.

The Futures Tour is intended to develop players for the LPGA and give them competitive opportunities to get there. It includes 18 tournaments each year, with a total purse of $1.25 million. Five Futures Tour players each year are guaranteed LPGA cards. In 2004, 36 additional players from the Futures Tour earned their way through qualifying school onto the LPGA Tour the following year.

The WSGT is for former LPGA golfers who have reached the age of 45, though female club professionals may play on the tour by playing in a national or local qualifying tournament. It is not nearly as large as the Champions Tour – there are just three tournaments on its schedule each year, and it has only 100 members.

For both men and women, there are plenty of other international tours, including the European Tour, the Japanese Tour and the Asian Tour. Some of these have shorter seasons that run concurrently with the off-season for the PGA Tour and the LPGA Tour.

World Golf Foundation

Representing golf organizations all over the world, the World Golf Foundation is a non-profit with the mission of preserving the history and tradition of the game while also helping it grow and introducing it to more and more players. Its four divisions include the World Golf Hall of Fame and three community efforts: The First Tee, the National Minority Golf Foundation and Golf 20/20.

World Golf Hall of Fame

Visitors to the northeast corner of Florida can stop in at the World Golf Hall of Fame, located between Jacksonville and St. Augustine on the Atlantic coast. Admission is reasonable at $15 for adults, $13 for students and $10 for children under 12. The hall of fame features interactive exhibits and areas honoring the game's great players, and there are two challenging courses on site at the World Golf Village.

Of course, it would be just a museum without its elected members. The World Golf Hall of Fame was started in 1974 and now has more than 100 members. There are varying criteria for players from the PGA Tour and the LPGA, as well as other tours, but all the players in the hall have made tremendous impact on the game in one form or another. In 2004, the inductees were Isao Aoki, Tom Kite, Charlie Sifford and Marlene Stewart Streit.

The First Tee

The First Tee is a charitable organization started in 1997 that aims to develop golf facilities and provide access to the game for children who might not otherwise become involved in golf. The organization believes that by involving youngsters in golf, they will learn essential values like honesty, integrity and sportsmanship.

National Minority Golf Foundation

This group's goal is to develop and foster opportunities for minority golfers, specifically through junior college and college golf programs. Founded in the late 1990s, it is a young organization, but it has presented over 600 golfers with the chance to play in national junior programs and has placed many of its members in college golf programs as well as in jobs in the golf industry.

Golf 20/20

Golf 20/20's slogan is "Vision for the Future." Its goal is to enhance the growth of the game through cooperation between the major organizations involved in golf: the PGA Tour, the PGA of America, the LPGA, the National Golf Course Owners Association, the Golf Course Superintendents Association and many others.

National Golf Foundation

The National Golf Foundation (NGF) is a research organization that provides information useful to those in the business of golf. Founded in 1936, the NGF is considered the industry leader in its field, providing information to managers of golf courses and driving ranges as well as retail stores to help them do business more effectively. Their information is available by membership and includes numbers on golf participation, financial profiles of golf courses and new facilities, among many others.

Golf Publications

The two most influential golf publications in the United States are Golf Magazine and Golf Digest. Both monthly magazines, they cater to the recreational player by offering plenty of golf tips (usually broken down to different levels by handicap or average score). They also regularly include information on golf equipment and travel as well as news and feature stories for those players who also like to keep up on what's going on with professionals on the major tours.

Golf Magazine sells more than 1.4 million copies each month, though its readership is far greater than that number because each month most copies are read by more than one person. It also attracts millions of readers to its website (golfonline.com) and publishes magazines for the U.S. Open and the Pebble Beach Pro-Am.

Golf Digest promotes itself as the No. 1 golf magazine, and with its circulation of 1.57 million, does so rightfully. Golf Digest also publishes Golf for Women, Golf World and Golf World Business, as well as a number of international publications.

Both magazines were formerly owned by the New York Times Company and have recently been sold – Golf Magazine to Time Warner and Golf Digest to Advance Publications, which publishes a number of other popular national magazines.

16
Movers and Shakers

....

**"I'm tired of hearing about money, money, money, money, money.
I just want to play the game, drink Pepsi, wear Reebok."**

Shaquille O'Neal, professional basketball player

....

Two or three decades ago you could have counted on the fingers of
one hand the number of companies in the business of marketing and
managing sports. Today there are hundreds of medium to large-sized
corporations and thousands of one-person armies in this line of
work, all making up a multi-billion dollar industry. At the center of
the sports business are three functions: athlete representation, the
marketing of specific sports, and marketing companies that utilize
sports and sports personalities. A quote derived from 18th century
English critic, poet and essayist Samuel Johnson rings all too true in
the 21st century: "Golf is a game in which you claim the privileges of
age and retain the playthings of childhood." This universal truth
attracts many to cash in on the serendipitous benefits the game
offers.

Sports Marketing Companies

Mark McCormack invented sports marketing. If you think you're not
acquainted with his work, then you've never watched television coverage of the Masters, never attended a PGA Tour event, and have never
heard of Tiger Woods or Jack Nicklaus. Let's just say this: McCormack
made it his life's work to connect these dots and more, growing one
of the largest sports marketing organizations in the world.

IMG

After graduating from Yale, Mark McCormack spent several years
with a Cleveland law firm and then hung out his own shingle in 1959.
About that time, a young professional golfer walked through his door.
His name was Arnold Palmer. McCormack was soon getting his new
client lucrative exhibition and endorsement deals. Before long more
young golfers stopped by. Within a few years of his handshake with
Palmer, McCormack had also signed Gary Player and Jack Nicklaus,
who would become golf's "Big Three" of that era.

Business was lucrative and McCormick decided to devote himself full-time to managing the careers of his clients, increasing their earnings through exhibitions, endorsements, advertising gigs, and tournament appearance fees. Along the way he set up the International Management Group (IMG. More info: imgworld.com), and sports marketing was born.

This eventually led to the opening of the now-famous Bolletieri Tennis Academy in Florida, which has since grown to include full-time and part-time academies for aspiring athletes in baseball, basketball, soccer and golf. Its enrollment now includes 550 full-time students and 10,000 part-time students.

Over the years, IMG has become a major player in all aspects of sports. Aside from its roles developing and representing athletes, IMG also has a financial stake in a number of sporting events and has a television arm – Trans World International – that broadcasts events internationally. McCormack has been named the most powerful man in golf by Golf Magazine, and in 1990 was dubbed by Sports Illustrated as the most powerful man in sports, period.

IMG represents many top-ranked golfers, including Tiger Woods, Sergio Garcia, Colin Montgomerie and Morgan Pressel, to name a few. In an open letter, McCormack wrote, "The core foundation of IMG's success has always been and will always be the representation of individual athletes, because it is they who have the power to advance sport to a new level."

Octagon

With sports marketing companies collecting percentages of endorsement earnings and prize money, a top-flight athlete can clearly become a golden goose when it comes to representation. Octagon (More info: octagon.com) is the other leading sports marketing firm, representing both future hopefuls and top-ranked players. Among Octagon's 40 professional golf clients are Davis Love III, Tom Kite, Gary Koch and Meg Mallon.

Octagon is owned by the Interpublic Group, the largest advertising and marketing communications firm in the world. Like IMG, Octagon produces and distributes sports programming for television. It owns nearly 1,500 events, many of them not related to golf, and has a hand in business on all continents.

SFX Sports Group

You can market just about anyone or anything when you own over 1,200 radio stations, 20-odd television stations, and 770,000 outdoor billboards, let alone over 500 of the world's elite sports professionals including Michael Jordan, Andre Agassi, and Jerry Rice. The SFX Sports Group (More info: clearchannel.com) is an independently operated talent agency owned by broadcasting conglomerate Clear Channel Communications.

William Morris Agency

When Michelle Wie decided to turn pro at the age of 16 in the fall of 2005, she chose William Morris Agency (More info: wma.com) to represent her. The company calls itself a talent and literary agency, and professes on its web site that its strength lies in its recognition of the blurred lines between sports, entertainment and business. Perhaps nothing drives this point home better than Wie's decision to sign with the firm. She follows in the footsteps of tennis star Serena Williams, who through her tennis fame has landed a number of acting roles. William Morris began as a talent agency for Hollywood's movie industry, but has since moved into television, music, books and sports.

A Letter to Santa

Dear Santa:

My name is Baylee. I am six years old. I am in first grade at Sunshine Elementary. I have a big brother Alex and a little sister Alycia. I like Christmas because: It brings me joy!

I love golf. I started playing when I was four. My parents drove me to practice and my coach, Mr. Ader, always made the practice so much fun.

I like reading life stories of golf stars. I have read about Annika Sorenstam, Nancy Lopez, Vijay Singh, Fred Couples and Phil Mickelson. Reading about these great players makes kids like me want to learn how to play. But us kids couldn't do anything without our parents and coaches.

There needs to be a lot of help for parents and coaches so they can do a good job teaching us to play and how to be good sports. And we need to be able to get better and better without having to worry so much about winning all the time. Sometimes it's hard to find a course, Santa, so we need lots of places to play, too. Will you see what you can do for all us golf kids out there?

What Baylee wants most for Christmas is a puppy. I also want two polo shirts – one for my Dad and the other for my favorite coach, Mr. Ader. We will have cookies for you. Mom will have a nice mixed salad for the reindeer.

Merry Christmas,

Baylee

Promoters

They're quite a motley bunch, these promoters who bring tournaments and events to a community. Promoters can range from corporations like Silicon Valley Sports & Entertainment, which promotes a variety of sporting events, to players-turned-entrepreneurs like Peter Jacobsen, who has accumulated seven PGA Tour victories and two on the Champions Tour and in 1988 formed a golf promotions company called Peter Jacobsen Productions that has put on more than 250 events.

Sports marketing companies like IMG promote 20 different golf tournaments each year and plenty of other sports events, in addition to the company's million other golf-related business interests.

Indeed, promoters come in all shapes and sizes, but it's the entrepreneurial individuals with strong community roots and a head for numbers who run this segment of the golf industry, either working independently or within corporations. Becoming a golf promoter is more straightforward than you might think.

Facility

Identify a facility to stage the event. Depending upon the profile of the tournament, a public or private golf course are both possibilities, and either a well-known "name" course or a lesser known, but still attractive course can be used.

Some golf tournaments, like the Bob Hope Chrysler Classic in Palm Springs, California, and the AT&T Pebble Beach Pro-Am in Pebble Beach, California, are held at a number of different courses in the same general area. Professional events have specific capacity and attendance standards that must be met.

Players

Set a date and find players. If your event is a PGA Tour, Champions Tour or LPGA tournament, most of this will be done for you because each of the tours has a group of players whose tour cards allow them to play in any tournament. Most events, though, allow a handful of sponsor's exemptions, and some allow for a small number of local amateurs to qualify. If the event is an amateur event or something like a state open, you will likely work with a committee of people who set a date and then use their contacts within the golf industry to recruit players.

Number Crunches

Crunch your expense numbers. Prize money, facilities rental, and accommodations are some obvious expenses. You can find tournaments with prize money as low as $450,000 on the Nationwide Tour and as high as $8 million on the PGA Tour. Network and Cable Television rights are a major factor in coming out ahead. Also, most

PGA and LPGA events have charitable organizations that they support and that will profit from revenues.

Bring on the Stars

You want Vijay Singh for your tournament in Shanghai, where the winner plays 72 holes over four days. Plus practice rounds, to make $22,000. Fat chance? Not necessarily. Appearance fees, my friend, can make all the difference. **Red Alert:** Appearance fees are prohibited for PGA Tour tournaments. Though some sponsoring corporations have tried to work their way around this by offering paydays in the hundreds of thousands of dollars for Tour players to participate in corporate outing preceding Tour events, this practice is also frowned upon by PGA Tour officials.

However, male and female players are not restricted from agreeing to play in international tournaments for appearance fees, and American players will often pad their back accounts in the fall and winter months by playing overseas. For instance, Tiger Woods reportedly accepted an appearance fee of $1-2.25 million for playing in an offseason event in China one winter, a tournament in which the organizers also gave out $5 million in prize money. Because of the dependence on stars to draw large galleries, promoters of events like these willingly pay appearance fees. When stars commit, sponsors open their wallets and fans follow.

During golf's "Silly Season," from the season-ending Tour Championship in early November through January's Mercedes Championship, which officially kicks off the PGA Tour season, there are plenty of events that bring in touring pros by waving money in front of them. Most of these events vary from the traditional stroke play format most tournaments employ, and some are basically made-for-television programming.

The "S" Word

Sponsors – selling your event to them is the true test of a promoter's mettle. Always keep in mind the reasons why companies sponsor events:

- **Advertising**: Corporate identification, target marketing, awareness.
- **Promotion:** Gains attention from trade or consumers.
- **Sales:** Client entertainment, sampling opportunities.
- **Public Relations:** The catchall phrase.

It's not uncommon for a professional golf event to have 50 sponsors, including the all-important title sponsor and a television deal. The Buick Invitational, held at Torrey Pines Golf Course outside San Diego each winter, is part of the Allianz West Coast Swing and includes pro-am events sponsored by telecommunications giant SBC and Sycuan, a large local Indian casino and resort. The ground surrounding the seat-ing areas near the 18th hole are covered with tents inhabited by local and national companies touting their products, and the electronic scoreboards placed throughout the golf course are peppered with advertising. All bring in money that is used to produce the tournament and attract the best players with a large purse.

Now, as the promoter, all you have to do is publicize the event, sell tickets, and hold the tournament. Sounds simple, right? It can be, with good organization and planning and an experienced team. Hopefully, your tournament will make money, even when a star golfer calls in sick and another flies overseas to play a more lucrative exhibition. Welcome to the world of the big-time golf promoter.

Player Agents

A player agent is a business representative who works for the player, negotiating contracts, sponsorships, endorsement deals, and other financial agreements. How well the agent manages often determines how well the player lives after his or her career is over, though few can emulate the staying power of golf legends Arnold Palmer and Jack Nicklaus. Palmer continues to make tens of millions of dollars in endorsements and such, more than 25 years after winning his last PGA tournament. Players are becoming more and more business savvy and 20 years after his exciting 1986 Masters victory, Nicklaus, is a not only a golf legend, he is a business conglomerate.

A growing number of agents are lawyers, while some, like hockey legend Bobby Orr, use their athletic experience and background as a springboard for success in representing athletes. Instead of an independent agent, many players elect to be represented by sports marketing companies such as IMG. In this case, the player is assigned an agent, also called an athlete representative.

Players with interests outside of sports often choose more than one agency. Serena Williams uses IMG for athletic representation and William Morris for her Hollywood interests. For managing a player's career, agents earn a negotiated commission that's a percentage of endorsement earnings, prize money, and appearance fees.

It takes little background or training to get into the agent business as an independent. States like California have a perfunctory law that simply requires agents to file a public disclosure form with the Secretary of State and pay a fee before engaging in business. With the emergence of teenage golf sensations, like tennis, baseball, and basketball, it will be just a matter of time before junior players with good rankings will be courted by scores of agents. Courtship can happen in a hurry too – say, immediately after winning a major tournament. It makes sense to plan ahead.

Michelle Wie is probably among the best and most recent examples of a young player who was courted by agents hoping to represent her when she turned pro. Speculation was that Wie had also considered IMG and Octagon – two of the sports world's biggest players in athlete representation – but Golf World reported that Wie had had an established relationship with the William Morris Agency for seven or eight years before signing. The scary part is that it was just days after her 16th birthday when she signed on with William Morris. That means she and her parents could have been in contact with the agency since Wie was eight years old!

Corporate Sponsorships

While businesses pay famous players to endorse their products, they also sponsor those not yet famous in the hope that one day they'll reach celebrity status. Look at it this way: endorsement budgets are like stock investments, whereas sponsorships are investing in futures. Wie was such a commodity that on the day she announced she was turning pro, she also announced endorsement deals with three different companies worth a reported $10 million. Her management company signed her betting that she will be a success in the future, hoping she'll repeat her previous success: Wie was the youngest player to enter the U.S. Women's Amateur (at 10) and the youngest to win the U.S. women's Amateur Publinx (at 13). At the age of 13, she also became the youngest player to play in an LPGA major, when she played the 2003 Kraft Nabisco Championship.

Sponsorship implies that the company pays a portion of training expenses, while endorsement suggests that the player is a company spokesperson or business representative. A company might sponsor many promising athletes, but hire only one or two more famous players as spokespersons.

It is not common for a Nike or any other club manufacturers to offer mega sponsorship to promising juniors as is customary with young up and coming tennis juniors. Promising tennis juniors could receive $100,000 to $200,000 in annual sponsorship deals. Before accepting any sponsorship monies, juniors are advised to check how the deal will affect amateur status, should the junior choose to continue playing amateur tournaments or want to apply for college scholarships.

Ultimately, players earn sponsorships to help businesses get their brands in front of as many consumer eyeballs as possible, on golf courses and on television. New touring professionals may receive sporadic financial help. In rare cases, a sponsor may make a one-tournament deal with a lower ranked player who would wear a visor or embroidered clothing bearing the sponsors' logos to help out a struggling rookie. Depending on the sponsorship, the deal may or may not require a split of earnings.

Endorsements

A company pays a famous player a fee for making a public endorsement of its products. Beyond wearing the company's shoes, apparel, and logos, the player may be contracted to attend corporate functions, appear in photo shoots and commercials, support related corporate ventures, and lend his name to a new product. Players that endorse products in such a fashion are usually paid well for their product promotions! Makes you wonder if the player "really" likes the product or he is simply getting paid to say that he does.

Shoe Economics 101		
Ever wonder why a shoe with $11 worth of materials costs you $80? Here's the scoop from Nike		
STEP 1:		
Material	$11	
Factory cost	$6	
Factory profit	$1	
Nike pays factory		$18
STEP 2:		
Shoe cost	$18	
Nike cost: R&D to develop new shoes, endorsements, and television commercials	$17	
Nike taxes	$1.50	
Nike net profits		$2.50
STEP 3:		
Product cost	$39	
Retailer cost: Sales people, rent	$38	
Taxes	$1	
Retailer net profit	$2	
COST TO CONSUMER		$80
* Source: Nike		

Golf's first recognized king of endorsements was Arnold Palmer. Largely aided by his alignment with IMG, Palmer still rakes in cash from endorsing products as he moves well into his 70s. "Arnie," as he is affectionately known, has deals with Pennzoil-Quaker State oil, Rolex watches, Ketel One vodka, Callaway, E-Z Go golf carts and the San Diego-based advertising firm Lampkin Corporation. These are in addition to all the other business enterprises his tremendous successes in the world of golf have afforded him.

Endorsement contracts vary. Corporations are interested in phenoms who can move products by virtue of a fickle mix of on-course performance, off-course antics (ex: John Daly is more marketable than an equally talented peer) and, for the younger crowd, aura.

Tiger Woods can probably justify every cent of the estimated $70 million he earns each year from endorsements (for comparison's sake, he averages just $6 million in earnings per year from prize money). Go to any PGA Tour event and you won't have to look at the leaderboard to tell which hole Tiger is on – the swarm of spectators following him like bees on honey will give it away. Television ratings still drop dramatically when Tiger isn't in contention on the final day of a tournament, and tournament organizers may as well write off their tournament if for some reason Woods doesn't appear. His endorsement of Buick has breathed new life into what was once a dying brand overshadowed by Japanese and German automobile makers.

Nike reportedly gave Woods a $100 million endorsement contract in 2002 to represent the company for five years. It has been a worthwhile investment. According to Golf World Business, Nike's golf-related sales hit $500 million in 2003.

After top endorsers like Woods and Wie come the next tier of players, a group that includes Phil Mickelson and Sergio Garcia on the men's side and Annika Sorenstam in the women's game. Mickelson made $14 million in endorsements in 2004, and Garcia averages about $8 million. The women are clearly still battling for equality and a larger share of the public interest, as evidenced by Sorenstam's $1-2 million averaged yearly take from endorsement deals. A handful of other top players will get smaller endorsement deals, while others who have achieved less success mostly are provided with free equipments, gear and clothing.

Interestingly, a variety of organizations and individuals make up the inside world of endorsements. You have the player and his immediate entourage, including coach and family members. Then there's the player agent or athlete representative from the player's sports marketing company. And finally, you have to have lawyers and accountants – Price Waterhouse Coopers, for example – to pore over the fine print.

Then you have a business like Burns Sports, which maintains a database of agents and their sports celebrity clients. Corporations call Burns when they need a sports celebrity for their ad campaigns. The folks at Burns find an appropriate match for these corporate clients. PGA Tour and LPGA management are also on the bandwagon, playing a larger role in marketing their respective tours to corporations and thus expanding the endorsement base for all professional players.

Endorsements are a big-time business because we gladly part with a few dollars more to pick up a Tiger Woods Nike striped polo shirt that will make junior look and feel good on the golf course. Who knows, one day it might be *your* golf kid that is high on the endorsement list, motivating millions of buyers.

••

"A kid grows up a lot faster on the golf course. Golf teaches you how to behave."

Jack Nicklaus

••

Select References

Bob Rotella, Ph.D., *Golf is Not a Game of Perfect*, Simon & Schuster, 1995

Dean W. Frischknecht, *PING American College Golf Guide*, Dean Frischknecht, 2007

Earl Woods, *Training a Tiger*, Collins, 1997

Jack Nicklaus, John Tickell, *Golf & Life*, St. Martin's Press, 2003

Jack Nicklaus, *My Story*, Simon & Schuster, 1997

John Feinstein, *Caddy for Life : The Bruce Edwards Story* , Little, Brown & Company, 2004

Pia Nilsson, Lynn Marriott, Ron Sirak, *Every Shot Must Have a Purpose*, Gotham Books, 2005

Pia Nilsson and Lynn Marriott, *Golf Parent for the Future,* Booklet by Golf 54

Steven Ungerleider, Ph.D., *Mental Training for Peak Performance*, Rodale Press, 1996

Tiger Woods, *How I Play Golf*, Warner Books, 2001

Timothy Gallwey, *The Inner Game of Golf*, Random House, 1998

Credits

- Jeff Troesch attributions by permission of Jeff Troesch, Mental Golf Expert.
- Jim Flick quote by permission of Jim Flick.
- Attributions to Shane Murphy from the book 'The Cheers and Tears' are reprinted by permission of author Shane Murphy, Ph.D., Associate Professor of Psychology, Western Connecticut State University.
- Tables 6.1 and 6.2 references page 7 of the booklet 'Golf Parent for the Future' by Pia Nilsson and Lynn Marriott, Golf 54.
- Golf Fitness Tests references tests developed by Kent Brizendine, Nexus Physical Therapy, San Diego.
- Shoe Economics 101 from media release by Nike.

Index

Get More!

Sizzle Up Your Next Golf Event

Contact Jacqui and Johnny, and discover new ways how they can support your golf team, fund-raiser, club and community.

Email or Call Today
**Jacqui McSorley: jngolf@san.rr.com
Johnny Gonzales: jgonzales@sycuanresort.com / 619-442-3425**

Consumer Copies

Go to MansionGroveHouse.com for a current list of retailers and special offers for copies of *Golf Guide for Parents and Players*. Also available through leading chain and independent bookstores, online retailers, golf pro shops, sporting goods stores, and catalogs.

Visit Today
MansionGroveHouse.com

Reseller Copies

Distributor, Retailer & Golf Group Inquiries to:
Email: sales@mansiongrovehouse.com
Phone: 408.404.7277
Fax: 408.404.7277
Website: mansiongrovehouse.com

Big Smiling Series

ISBN 1932421114
2006 Second Edition

RAISING BIG SMILING TENNIS KIDS

Whether you are a tennis playing parent or a parent curious about tennis, this book will empower you to raise kids who swing the tennis racket with as much aplomb as their happy smiles.

The best age to get your kid started in tennis. How to motivate kids to go back, practice after practice. When to focus exclusively on tennis. Save on lessons, find scholarships and sponsors. How to pursue a career in professional tennis. Gain insight into tennis organizations and agents. Have fun along the way at the best tennis camps and resorts.

RAISING BIG SMILING SQUASH KIDS

Stanford University recently added Squash to its athletics, joining Yale and Cornell. Forbes magazine rates Squash as the number one sport for fitness. With courts and college programs springing up across the country.

Richard Millman, world-class coach and Georgetta Morque, a prolific sportswriter, offer a complete roadmap for parents, professionals and kids. The best age to get started in squash; how to motivate kids; the road to top colleges; and attractive career options. Plus: cultivating friendships, character building and achieving a lifetime of fitness.

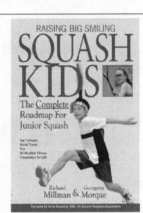

ISBN 1932421432
2006 First Edition

ISBN 1932421076
2006 First Edition

LACROSSE: A GUIDE FOR PARENTS AND PLAYERS

Lacrosse is America's fastest growing team sport. Action-packed and fun, lacrosse is a game anyone can play — the big and small, boys and girls. Lacrosse offers a positive outlet, a place to fit in at school, motivation to excel, and opportunities for team travel.

Whether your kid is 8 or 18, experienced or just starting, this book is the complete guide to all that lacrosse has to offer. Empower yourself with practical answers and unique ideas, whether you are new to lacrosse or once were a player. Make lacrosse an exhilarating part of your family life.

AVAILABLE WORLDWIDE

Made in the USA